Basketball is in My Blood

Basketball is in My Blood

A Basketball Addict's Autobiography

Martin Groveman

Copyright © 2017 by Martin Groveman.

Library of Congress Control Number:		2017918427
ISBN:	Hardcover	978-1-5434-7006-2
	Softcover	978-1-5434-7005-5
	eBook	978-1-5434-7004-8

All rights reserved. No part of this book may be reproduced or transmitted in any form or by any means, electronic or mechanical, including photocopying, recording, or by any information storage and retrieval system, without permission in writing from the copyright owner.

Any people depicted in stock imagery provided by Thinkstock are models, and such images are being used for illustrative purposes only.
Certain stock imagery © Thinkstock.

Print information available on the last page.

Rev. date: 01/10/2019

To order additional copies of this book, contact:
Xlibris
1-888-795-4274
www.Xlibris.com
Orders@Xlibris.com
766495

Contents

Chapter 1 Basketball Beginnings 1

Chapter 2 Basketball Awakenings 6

Chapter 3 High School Days 16

Chapter 4 My College Years 44

Chapter 5 In the Army 87

Chapter 6 Back to the Real World 93

Chapter 7 Marriage, a Few Career Decisions, and
Parenthood 108

Chapter 8 Settling in Suburbia 115

Chapter 9 Growing Up and Getting Older 134

Chapter 10 Lots of Changes and Adjustments 169

Chapter 11 Blessings and Heartaches 207

Chapter 12 Nostalgia and Tying It All Together 220

THIS BOOK IS dedicated to two groups of very special people. The first are those who were so instrumental in the attainment of my basketball dreams and accomplishments. Their contributions were both instructional and inspirational. Included in this select category are Venty Leib, Les Yellin, Abe Kleinman, Nat Holman, Dave Polansky, and Syd Levy. My mother and brother are among the honorees as their sacrifices and encouragement provided me with the opportunity to realize my goals. Lastly, my terrific sons, Jon and Seth, richly deserve inclusion. They have always proudly cheered me on even when believing it was time for me to hang up my sneakers.

The second group are teammates, friends, and acquaintances with a love for basketball that have kept my round ball fires burning. I've arrived at the following names through a ninety-second free association. With apologies to so many others who deserve mention, these are the guys that flashed into consciousness:

Don "Red" Goldstein
Irwin "Red" Blumenreich
George Bruns
Alan Seiden
Herb Wein
Norm Nebel
Jack Langbart
Jerry Fleishman
Sid Tanenbaum
Jerry Domershick
Norm "Feeny" Fields
Jerry Stuckelman
Joel Tendler
Lenny Sherman
Jerry Houston

Benny Bessan
Lou Roethel
Larry Kaufer
Gary Wood
Solly Walker
Mel Davis
Lou Carnesecca
Hy Gotkin
Dave Gotkin
Ivan Kovac
Gus Alfieri
Tony Jackson
Herb Turetsky
Stacey Arcenaux
John Pitts
Steve Nisenson
Mark Reiner
Mark Rich
Bob Sack
Jim Signorili
Tim Cluess
Steve Scheinblum
Jack Ryan
Troy Murphy
Archie Sinuk
Danny Culley
Hank Whitney
Al Schreiber
Nick Gaetani
Peter Ruh
Hank Lam
Julie Levine
Joe Benardo
Bob Silver
Jerry Jackson
Bill Schaefer

Walt Szczerbiak
Wally Szczerbiak
Floyd Layne
Ed Roman
Cal Ramsey
Carl Green
Eddie Gard
Marv Kessler
Mel Kessler
Charlie Hoffman

CHAPTER 1

Basketball Beginnings

I'M CLOSER TO eighty than seventy, and basketball is still in my blood. I have had two major reconstructive surgeries, one to each knee, both after age fifty, primarily caused by jumping, pounding, and cutting on too many surfaces of hundreds of gyms, parks, and schoolyards. And basketball is still not out of my system. Shooting around, playing horse, and dribbling up and down the court as my primary form of cardio exercise are all part of my regular activities.

When and how did this addiction begin? I think back, trying to pinpoint its inception, and can now more clearly than ever tie it to one man's arrival at my kindergarten through eighth grade elementary school. The school was PS 233 located in the East Flatbush section of Brooklyn. The man who had this profound influence upon my life was Aaron "Venty" Lieb.

I have no idea why he was called Venty, but everyone who knew him used the nickname. He was a teacher who transferred from Abraham Lincoln High School to PS 233 in 1949 when I was a seventh grader. He was bigger than life–athletic, articulate, and humorous. To me and my schoolmates, he defined the term charismatic (even though this was not a word in our vocabulary). For many years, he was one of the premier high school basketball coaches in New York City. His Lincoln teams had won city championships and made playoffs just about all the time. It was indeed a mystery as to why he would leave such a prestigious position, having accomplished so much in a distinguished career, to teach in a community school.

Speculation has always been that he left under some high-school-related political cloud which forced him out, but none of us ever really learned the actual story. More importantly, it didn't matter because Venty became our coach and also our hero.

Prior to Venty's coming on the scene, baseball and its derivations–softball, stickball, punchball–were our main athletic involvements. We played some basketball, but measured in interest, time, or intensity, it was far down the list of favorite sports. Baseball was the glamour activity, especially when we progressed to the point of forming teams, entering leagues, and of course, wearing uniforms. Within the neighborhood, we played at "Mosquito Field," a barren lot ladened with every insect and vermin known to the northeastern USA and the Linden Boulevard trolley car barn, which was a dirt field on the grounds of the Church Avenue Trolley Depot. Later on, when the trolley became extinct, the field was paved over to make room for the more modern buses. Our league games were held at the famed Parade Grounds and Marine Park. Much to our credit, even at ages twelve and thirteen, we organized and coached the teams with minimal adult assistance or interference.

I can't speak for all my friends, but my conversion to the religion of basketball, inspired by Venty Lieb, was swift. Venty made it clear from the start that although not every boy at PS 233 would make the basketball team, all who were interested would develop the basic skills and learn how to play. Basketball instantly became a major focus in our gym classes and was a feature in the school's intramural athletic program. Venty did more than coach basketball. He taught it–and with such a fervor. He stressed that it was essential to master the layup before we could ever think about playing a game. I remember so vividly the layup drills and extraordinary patience he demonstrated in teaching us how to go up on the correct foot. He taped a square above each basket to serve as a visual guide for us to utilize when shooting off the backboard. In whispered tones, he stated that the ball was like an egg that must be shot softly lest the egg would break (and the shot missed). We practiced dribbling in lines and contests and threw chest passes, pitchouts, and bounce passes until we were arm weary. Through it all, he joked, charmed, and mockingly threatened to do bodily harm to those who screwed up. He would playfully grab the offender by the T-shirt, pulling and shaking like a malt machine. I loved every moment of it. I couldn't wait for school practice and followed up by playing in the schoolyard, often after dark.

I cannot imagine the potential depths of my depression had I not made the PS 233 basketball team. Not that I ever felt that I was in danger of being cut. I sensed that Venty liked me, probably more as a wide-eyed, spunky left-handed kid than a real player. He told me that I was a "student of the game," an expression that I had never before heard and most likely translated to my displaying enthusiasm and good listening skills, balanced against a lack of height, average speed, and no discernible talent. At age thirteen, I was four feet, eleven inches tall, skinny as a rail, and barely strong enough to reach the basket from the foul line. The betting odds, at that time, would have been prohibitively in favor of my growing up to be a short frail adult. Although by no means a physical specimen, the long shot paid off as I grew to about six feet and 165 pounds by the time I was nineteen. Unfortunately, my weight has steadily increased by five-pound increments every ten years of my adulthood. Eating had become an addiction somewhat below yet close to basketball.

Well, I made the PS 233 basketball team. I was the sixth man on what turned out to be a terrific squad and was rightfully proud of this accomplishment. Our team featured a six foot, four inch soft-shooting center, Gerry Stuckelman, who later on would become the center on the 1954 Thomas Jefferson High School city championship team, a unit as good as any in the history of New York City. At the forwards were Joel Tendler and Harold "Butch" Siegel. Tendler was an excellent shooter, possessed huge hands, and was strong as an ox. Siegel was even stronger and much meaner. Joel went on to play basketball and baseball at Tilden High school and Long Island University. He had major league baseball potential but gave it up after a few years in the Dodger organization. Butch became an all-city lineman at Stuyvesant High School and then played for The Citadel. The guards were Joel "Snake" Mandel and Harvey "Sleepy" Richer. Joel was lightning quick and could slither his way to the basket like a snake. He became an outstanding player at Tilden, but his interest in girls and making money outstripped his enjoyment of basketball. Harvey was a defensive specialist and a tough competitor but today is better known for his business acumen than basketball prowess. Two prominent reserves on the team, both of whom later played for Tilden, were Jerry Bloomberg and Stan Feldstein. Bloomberg, another eventual business mogul, made the freshman team at Louisville. Feldstein became a prominent writer of history books.

Although we were basketball neophytes, Venty's coaching style and communication skills made us feel like big-time players. He emphasized that everything we do on a basketball court should have a purpose. There should be no wasted movement, nor excess dribbling. He spent much time teaching us the "weave." This taught us offensive spacing, how to properly deliver the ball to another player in stride, and to cut off ground while moving toward the basket. We learned man-to-man defense based upon being properly positioned between the man and the basket and realigning the total body to react to the moves of the player that one is guarding.

By far, the biggest thing to us was the "X play." Within our motion offense, it was the special element that, when properly executed, could not be stopped. It was a play from a half-court set which featured a pick, a cut, and a pass from the wing to the cutter that most often resulted in a layup. The letter X was completed by the crossing of the picker and the cutter. The play is really a simple one, but it was highly effective. Moreover, the repetition of doing it taught and reinforced the concepts of setting screens, changing direction, and moving without the ball. Looking back, we were indeed learning sophisticated aspects of the game.

Our diligent efforts and Venty's persistence were richly rewarded. PS 233 won the 1951 Brooklyn Borough Basketball Championship for schools whose terminal grade was eight. We wanted to go further, and Venty fueled our fire by telling us how we were going to play for the city, state, national, and world championships. Reality and the coming of spring, however, dictated that our quest could not be continued. We remained proud champions of our small realm. For me and perhaps a few others, this wonderful experience had such a powerful impact. It changed me forever and certainly helped to better prepare me, both as an athlete and a person, for the road ahead.

CHAPTER 2

Basketball Awakenings

THE NEXT PHASE of my basketball education was one that actually began during seventh grade, gathered momentum throughout eighth grade, and continued over several years. It was my awakening to the basketball world beyond PS 233. Initially, my basketball horizon expanded at the PS 233 evening community center. Spurred by Venty's influence, the center transformed itself from a dodgeball, tag, shootaround fun thing to a serious gathering place for competitive basketball.

In late 1949, the seventh and eighth graders at the center formed a four-team full court basketball league. The teams used the names of the four major college powers in New York City. Thus, our league was comprised of CCNY (City College of New York), NYU (New York University), LIU (Long Island University), and St. John's. The games were sloppy but spirited. The true value, however, was that by constantly playing, we were getting better.

Calling ourselves St. John's or CCNY increased our awareness and interest in metropolitan area basketball. What a wonderful era it was for New York City college basketball. The four big schools were often nationally ranked, and the "Garden" (Madison Square Garden) was usually packed to the rafters for the college games. Seton Hall, Manhattan, Fordham, and Columbia also fielded competitive teams, and many of the smaller schools, St. Francis to mention one, were no pushovers. I remember listening to the games on radio and, when we got our first television, watching spellbound with my father and brother. I can still hear Marty Glickman's mellifluous "swish" or "good like Needick's" when a basket was made.

So in 1949, I got hooked on college basketball. It drew me like a magnet. I read everything I could get my hands on. Daily, I followed the teams and the star players and even maintained statistics and cut out starting lineups, box scores, and pictures from the newspapers. This obsessive devotion reached a crescendo in early 1950 when my future alma mater, CCNY, shocked the nation by winning both the NIT and NCAA Basketball Championships. At that time, colleges could play in both tournaments, and the Garden-based NIT was easily on an equal par with the NCAA's. The unheralded Beavers whipped up on powerhouses Kentucky and Bradley to attain the unthinkable grand slam. This team coached by the legendary Nat Holman, led by four sophomores– Ed Warner, Ed Roman, Floyd Layne, and Al Roth–and anchored by senior Irwin Dambrot with assistance from fellow seniors Norm Mager and Joe Galiber became instant household names and New York City heroes. "Allegaroo," the opening cry of the CCNY cheer, became the symbol for this Cinderella story. For New York City basketball fans, it was an incredibly uplifting time.

Buoyed by the euphoria of CCNY's double championship, most other local college basketball devotees and I anticipated a glorious 1950–1951 season. Almost tragically, this did not occur, as it all came down with a booming thud in February of 1951. A point shaving basketball scandal of unparalleled dimensions brought college basketball to its knees. Current and former players from CCNY, LIU, Manhattan, Seton Hall, Kentucky, Bradley, etc. were implicated, arrested, and in some instances eventually served prison time for accepting money to "fix" games. The four junior CCNY stars (Warner, Roman, Layne, and Roth) were included in the tarnished group, as were LIU's great forward/center Sherman White, pogo-stick-jumping guard LeRoy Smith, graduated playmaker Eddie Gard, and ex-marine strongman Dolph Bigos.

The scandal devastated local college basketball to the point that the Garden never again quite attained the mecca status that it previously enjoyed. LIU even temporarily suspended its basketball program and deemphasized when the sport resumed. CCNY kept playing but was banned from the Garden.

So much has been written about the basketball scandal that I do not intend to make it a major focus here. As a young kid who loved basketball, it saddened me greatly, although I can't say that it made me cynical. I felt terrible for the players whom I admired and somewhat angry that they short-circuited their athletic careers. It wasn't unjust for them to have been banned from participation in the then fledgling NBA, yet they were all so young, in most instances poor, and after paying for their serious transgressions, deserved to be forgiven in life's greater scheme. I and most of the people in my little circle certainly did.

It is gratifying that most of the affected players have since led productive, successful lives and have long been accepted into the camaraderie of the overall basketball community. I can speak with definitiveness about those individuals that I got to know personally in my adulthood. Ed Roman, who died several years ago from leukemia, was a prince of a guy. He was a respected New York City Clinical school psychologist who worked primarily with emotionally handicapped adolescents. I too became a special educator and enjoyed both a professional and cordial social relationship with this fine man. The ageless, dynamic, and charming Floyd Layne has given as much to the inner city youth of New York as anyone. It is fitting that Floyd was afforded the opportunity to return to CCNY as its basketball coach. The irrepressible "Chief" is still coaching. Now in this mid-eighties, he is at the helm at George Washington High School in upper Manhattan. Ed Warner initially struggled to gain his equilibrium, but he, like Floyd, became a positive influence in Harlem and the South Bronx. As a teacher and drug counselor, Ed's influence helped to straighten and strengthen the lives of countless temporarily lost youths. He overcame great odds to survive a near-fatal automobile accident and carried on his efforts despite being wheelchair bound. Ed led a productive life until his untimely death in 2002. Eddie Gard is a successful businessman, devoted father, and grandfather and for years has been an enthusiastic mentor to aspiring young basketball players.

As a teenager, I was a fan of the dynamic CCNY trio of Ed Warner, Floyd Layne, and Ed Roman. Warner, at 6'3", played much bigger than his height. His great strength and explosive jumping ability enabled him to post up and score effectively, control the boards, and overpower opponents. Layne, a tall guard, led the fast break beautifully, had great court vision, and played outstanding defense. Roman had an incredibly soft touch from both inside and out. At 6'6", he was neither fleet of foot nor a leaper. He made these deficiencies up with great court intelligence, good body positioning, and remarkable passing skills from the pivot.

Although I was transfixed in general by all New York City college basketball, the team that I rooted for was the Blackbirds of LIU. I was awed by little Leroy Smith's high altitude act and his spectacular jump shooting. Dolph Bigos's toughness, strength, and defensive prowess combined to make him a premier "garbage man." He had a great knack for creating turnovers and scoring opportunistic baskets. For me, however, there was but one man, my boyhood idol, the magnificent Sherman White.

A lithe, sinewy 6'8" White blended skills, fierce competitiveness, and power into a dynamic package that earned him All-American recognition and the mouthwatering attention of every pro scout and coach. He was so many years ahead of his time. His ability to run the court and his offensive efficiency, catlike reflexes and rebounding, and defensive dominance constituted the composite picture of the ideal modern NBA power forward. He displayed agility and versatility in marked contrast to the typical awkward and ponderous big men of that era. It is truly a shame that his poor judgment deprived him of fulfilling the promise of a glorious NBA career.

Having no other professional basketball alternative, he, as did most of the other scandal-involved guys, played in the Eastern Basketball League, a weekend conference that was the predecessor to today's CBA (Continental Basketball Association). In the Eastern League, his legend did not diminish as he was a perennial all-star. It is fitting and touching that several years ago, this great talent finally received official plaudits by the basketball establishment. Madison Square Garden honored Sherman White by selecting him to the ten-man all decade basketball team for the period 1941–1950. The induction occurred at a formal ceremony and reception held at the Garden.

At about age thirteen when my PS 233 friends and I were old enough to play in non-school-affiliated leagues, we drifted away from our neighborhood cocoon to other area gyms and parks. For me, by far the most fascinating place to play was Brownsville's amazing Betsy Head Park. Located on Hopkinson and Livonia Avenues, in the shadows of the elevated New Lots IRT Seventh Avenue subway line, Betsy Head was a recreational complex consisting of baseball fields, outdoor handball and basketball courts, and a huge outdoor swimming pool. Actually, there were two pools, but the smaller, deeper one was reserved strictly for diving. I deliberately leave the indoor basketball facility for last because it was makeshift at best, usable only after Labor Day when the swim season concluded. It could not have been more unique, for the two gymnasiums, each consisting of a full court, were the vacated boys and girls swimming pool locker rooms. The courts were of adequate dimensions and featured concrete floors. It is unbelievable that given these most modest of resources, Betsy Head spawned such great play and so many outstanding players.

The first time I set foot in Betsy Head, I was cautioned to never go to the bathroom on the far side of the main gym. I was told that gambling and reefer smoking were the principal activities in the bathroom and that it was risky, especially for an outsider, to intrude. Heeding this advice, I never entered that forbidden domain. If I had to go, I used the bathroom on the girls' side. Initially, until I could really play a decent game, the girls' gym (against all male competition) was more suited to my modest skills. The real action, however, took place on the boys' side.

Betsy Head was also my first meaningful contact with black people. Other than attending games or watching on television, I had no firsthand experiences with any Afro-Americans. At Betsy Head, young black and white men (primarily Jewish) played together in a highly competitive yet healthy, friendly environment. I know it may sound trite, but I firmly believe that my time at Betsy Head and the relationships that I developed both on and off the court helped broaden my perspective, significantly enhanced my interpersonal skills, and for better or worse, have contributed to mold the person that I am today. Even with the passing of so many years, I treasure those experiences. And not to forget from a basketball standpoint, the intense, often self-deflating competition made me a much improved basketball player.

One of the best teams at Betsy Head was the Rimsters. Comprised mainly of players from Thomas Jefferson High School, they were an exciting cohesive unit. Through the years, Jefferson consistently produced elite teams and tremendous players. To illustrate, at the time that I discovered Betsy Head, Sid Tanenbaum, Harry Boykoff, Max Zaslofsky and "Dutch" Garfinkel, all Jefferson graduates, were playing in the NBA. The Rimsters were not quite at that level but featured players with pro potential and some with great nicknames. To mention a few, there were "Hebel," "Stiff," "Turtz," and "Hickel." Jerry Domershick, CCNY's finest post-scandal guard, was "Hickel." Smooth as silk with a deadly outside shot, he was selected to play in the annual East/West College All-Star Game at the Garden. The Rimsters center was Boris Nachamkin. Graceful and versatile Boris played a few years in the NBA after an outstanding career at NYU.

The Rimster that dazzled me was Davey Gotkin. He was an all-city guard at Jefferson who effortlessly excelled at every aspect of the game. He also came from a great gene pool as the Gotkins were easily one of Brownsville's most prominent basketball families. His older brother, Hy, and his cousin, Java, were both outstanding players at St. John's. Another relative, Davey's uncle Harry, referred to in the neighborhood as "Harry Baskets," was a kind of freelance scout who knew everyone and helped scores of young players get college scholarships. In the case of Sidney Green, UNLV All-American and longtime NBA player, Harry took him in and provided him with a home when his personal life was in crisis. As for Davey, upon graduating from Jefferson, he received a scholarship to North Carolina State. Injuries and perhaps immaturity impeded Davey's basketball growth. He returned to New York, where he completed his education and became a teacher and recreational director.

Three high school stars who I saw play for the first time at Betsy Head and immediately admired their respective games were Tommy Hemans, Solly Walker, and Sihugo Green. Hemans, a string bean 6'8" was a prolific rebounder and scorer. He was outstanding at Jefferson High School, Niagara University, and in the Eastern League. Walker and Green, both great players at Boys High School, possessed fantastic athleticism and could play just about any position on the court. Solly, at 6'4", was fluid, strong, and strikingly handsome. He became St. John's first black basketball player and holds an historic place in US college basketball. Solly was the first Afro-American man to play in an integrated college basketball game in the South. This occurred at the University of Kentucky. Like Tommy, Solly–who is my friend and professional colleague–chose a career in education. For many years, he served with distinction as the principal of the Manhattan High School, a special education school for emotionally handicapped adolescents. Sihugo was truly an unbelievable performer. His name alone was intriguing, but there was so much more. What a physical specimen! He was the first person that I saw with a sculptured body. At 6'3" and two hundred pounds, although still a teenager, he was a man among boys against high school competition. He drove to the basket at will, used his wondrous leaping ability to control both backboards, and was an awesome defender. He was almost as dominant at Duquesne University, where he was named

All-American. Professionally, he was a solid player with the St. Louis Hawks, only lacking the shooting ability to reach an all-star level. Sihugo, who was a terrific human being, unfortunately died far too young, succumbing to cancer.

I've already described my devotion as a college basketball fan to LIU. At Betsy Head, I had an equally passionate commitment to one specific group of players. This team was the Viceroys. Young black men, for the most part in their twenties, they were the epitome of style and cool. They carried themselves proudly with a regal bearing. Basketball-wise, their game was distinctly up-tempo, characterized by sparkling fast breaks, wonderful passing, and the most spirited team chemistry. Perhaps the years have dulled my memory, but I cannot recall them ever losing.

I remember the lightning quick hands of the little dynamo, Danny Culley. In years to come, whenever playing against Danny, I was smart enough to know to never put the ball on the floor if guarded by him face to face. Gerry Harper, who became a respected referee, was a sweet shooter with one of the all-time intimidating game faces. Roy Chapman was a marvelous athlete whose excellent play on the hardwoods was secondary to his major league–caliber baseball talent. Deservedly, Roy was a legend for his exploits on Brooklyn's baseball fields.

I've been told that during his prime, about the time that Jackie Robinson crashed the color barrier, Roy was right in step with the very best. He just never got the chance. The Viceroys' most spectacular player was James "Dutch" Sparrow, a magician with the basketball. He was to Brooklyn playground basketball in the forties and fifties, as were storied players like Rabbit Walthour and Earl Manigault to the uptown scene. The word is that devastating substance abuse eventually dimmed "Dutch" Sparrow's star and led to his early untimely demise.

Not just confined to the Viceroys, but there were so many outstanding players at Betsy Head who never received neither the guidance nor assistance to enable them to complete their education and elevate their economic status. It was the rule rather than the exception for minority youths to quit school and go to work to help support their families. Few programs existed then to, at least, facilitate high school graduation and to provide meaningful career counseling. Some made it on their own, but so many more never got out of the neighborhood.

Over the years, the Viceroys evolved beyond Betsy Head and played in numerous leagues and tournaments throughout the metropolitan area. As I got older and also better, I had the pleasure of competing against original and newer Viceroys.

One thing remained constant. The team always retained its Brooklyn and primarily Brownsville flavor. They added Jefferson's dynamic duo of Bernie Tiebout and Nurlin Tarrant, who will be written about in greater detail in the pages to come, and another Brownsville guy, Bob Keller, who started as a stiff and developed into a tremendous forward. Other excellent pickups, all former college stars, were Jake Jordan, Gil Williams, Arnold Branch, and Al Vann (respected state assemblyman). The Viceroy heritage is a fabulous one and occupies a significant place in New York City sports lore.

A highlight at Betsy Head was the annual visit by the Knicks. Every year, three or four players would give a basketball clinic and participate in some assorted shtick with our resident heroes. A regular feature of those sessions was the midcourt shooting contest against the fabulous "Blitz." Although not a top-level player, Blitz's long-range set shots were equaled in Brownsville only by former LIU bomber Jackie Goldsmith. Short (5'7") and slight of build, Goldsmith never achieved star status at LIU but was a deadly shooting specialist. In perhaps his finest game at the Garden, Jackie's missiles led to an upset victory over top-ranked Oklahoma A&M and All-American Bob Kurland, one of the first seven footers. As for "Blitz," he usually succeeded in embarrassing the Knicks by winning the contest. It also amazed me that in a brief three-man game, the Betsy Head guys more than held their own. I remember one particular close and spirited game against Carl Braun, Harry Gallatin, and Ernie Vanderweghe. In that one, a young and highly poised Bernie Tiebout, just a high school underclassman, drove around and scored easily on Carl Braun.

Sitting in the stands, I felt pride in Bernie's performance and its reflection upon the caliber of basketball at Betsy Head. It was similarly evident that the Knicks too were impressed.

Our neighborhood team, the Hoopsters, wore the red and white uniform of St. John's. We were competitive and improving but were no match for Brownsville's Rimsmen, naming themselves after the older vaunted Rimsters they were our insurmountable barrier. Their coach was Irv Blitzinsky "Blitz," the set shot artist. He was several years older than his players, a vocational high school graduate, and already a wage earner. His trustworthy assistant was Shelly "Red" Schneider, a fastidious dresser who was the best-groomed teenager I ever knew. Coaching was Shelly's passion as evidenced by his later success in this role at Brooklyn Technical High School. As an opponent, I respected the dedication and tenacity that they both exhibited. They operated the Rimsmen in a serious corporate-like manner. Much like the Yankees, the players displayed an arrogant professionalism and were obviously proud to be a Rimsmen.

The Rimsmen provided a substantial talent pool, mainly for Jefferson and for other local high schools. Blitz would call for an open tryout at Betsy Head and attract more than a hundred aspiring players. Mistakes were sometimes made as many future high school and college players did not survive the final cut. Among the future greats who did make the roster were all-city selections Harvey Salz (Jefferson), Don "Red" Goldstein (Tilden) and Marty Berkowsky (Brooklyn Tech). Don, who I first met at Betsy Head when he was a gangly all-bones fourteen-year-old, would become my high school teammate and good friend. Unbelievable, but we were to play basketball together for almost fifty years.

CHAPTER 3

High School Days

IN SEPTEMBER 1951, I entered the ninth grade at Samuel J. Tilden High School. It was a tough time for me and my family. In late August, my father, at age forty-three, died of leukemia. He suffered for about eight months, going faster than the doctors predicted. It is an understatement that we were not in good financial shape. Following a brief period of official mourning, my mother, who had not worked for almost twenty years, obtained a full-time job. Sadly, my brother, who had just begun college and was an excellent student, was forced to join mom as an income earner. He didn't drop out of school, however, transferring from Brooklyn College to CCNY to be closer to his workplace. Admirably, he attended four nights a week, taking twelve credits each semester. As for me, I was just fourteen and had no such burden to carry other than to be generally helpful and not cause trouble. Needing to be distracted from a once blissful world suddenly made complicated, I immersed myself in sports more than ever. Basketball, of course, was my primary diversion.

Tilden is located a few blocks from Kings Highway, in a tree-lined residential community of private homes and small apartment buildings in the East Flatbush section of Brooklyn. Ethnically, its student population in the fifties was mainly Jewish with Italian Catholics being the group of the second-largest number. Very few blacks or Hispanic students were enrolled, totaling no more than fifty out of a few thousand. The school enjoyed a fine academic reputation and was competitive athletically. Our baseball and swimming teams, however, were consistently excellent, often being among the city's best. Specifically, the baseball program was bolstered by the prowess of the Italian students from Canarsie. They revered baseball and played it year round in the expanse of open fields in their sparsely populated neighborhood.

Tilden's basketball teams were rarely bad, just generally not as good as Erasmus Hall's or James Madison's, the traditional leaders of our conference. Thank God that Jefferson and Boys High, the two great Brooklyn powers which were closest to us geographically, were in another division. Tilden did experience a brief period of basketball superiority in the late thirties and early forties when it featured a trio of future NBA players. The three skilled and exciting players were Irv Torgoff (Washington Capitals), Ossie Schectman (Knicks), and Sidney "Sonny" Hertzberg (Knicks, Celtics). Those glory days were short-lived, for finishing third seemed to be Tilden's yearly destiny. Going up against Erasmus and Madison, the battle was more than player versus player. It meant having to contend with the wizardry of their nationally esteemed coaches, Al Badain (Erasmus) and Jamie Moscowitz (Madison). It had frequently been said that both refused several major college coaching offers to remain at their high school posts.

The quality of coaching at Tilden, which I will comment on extensively in future pages, was unable to maximize the potential abilities of its players, yet the basketball talent was usually plentiful. A sizable portion of this player pool came from boys who lived in Brownsville. Jefferson, a smaller and older school than Tilden, was overpopulated. As a result, parts of Brownsville, in some not fully understandable patchwork pattern, were zoned for Tilden.

This distribution brought good fortune to our sports program, particularly basketball. Elliot Press, who was to become a standout at St. Francis College, and the marvelous Don "Red" Goldstein were two of Brownsville's most generous gifts to Tilden. To name another, a baseball player of some note, Willie Randolph, also came via this route.

My street, East 96th at the intersection of Linden Boulevard and Avenue A, was actually closer to the western edge of the Jefferson zone than the distance to Tilden. It was a fourteen-block walk from my house to the school. And walk I did, as it was ruled that East 96th Street was not far enough away for bus pass eligibility. Where I lived eventually was a significant factor in my search for varied basketball action. My proximity to Brownsville drew me to its parks and gyms. Like my discovery of Betsy Head, I will soon write of other places that evoked fond thoughts and feelings and figured so prominently in my basketball development.

I didn't dare to go out for the Tilden basketball team in my freshman and sophomore years. I was still tiny and only in the beginning stages of puberty. My game was advancing in terms of court smarts and ball-handling skills, but the absence of minimally acceptable size and strength made playing against physically mature teenagers highly impractical. This delay though never dampened my aspirations. I believed that I would grow, get stronger, and then have an equal footing to compete with my peers. My mother would jokingly plead with me to settle for 5'7". I adamantly rejected this suggestion, holding out for six feet. Whether attributable to fate, luck, or the answering of my prayers, my prediction eventually came to fruition. It's just that it took so darn long to happen.

The PS 233 schoolyard was always a busy one. Males from preadolescence to adulthood engaged in a variety of athletic activities. In season, softball and touch football were more popular than basketball. In fact, on weekend mornings, neighborhood guys in their twenties and thirties played fast pitch softball for relatively big dollars. The basketball courts which were situated in the outfield were off limits until the conclusion of the softball games. When we did have the opportunity our basketball was comprised entirely of three-man half-court play. A refreshing change to full court choose-up games occurred during those early high school years. The best part of this was the intermingling of younger boys like myself with some of Tilden's better present and recently graduated players. These valuable games also enabled me to go directly against classmates closer to my own size like Stan Feldstein or Harvey Richer, while at the same time learning from the more experienced, accomplished players.

The three Tilden products and fellow combatants in the PS 233 schoolyard who had the greatest impact on me were Jack Langbart, Norm Nebel, and Les Yellin. I looked up to all of them for their kindness and interest as much as their substantial basketball abilities. Jack Langbart, the oldest of the three, was four years my senior, lived directly across from the schoolyard, and was playing for Brooklyn College by the time I was a tenth grader. At 6'1", he was the picture of grace and fluidity. He seemed to do everything so effortlessly, giving a false impression that he wasn't hustling or trying his best. His steady coolness on the court mirrored his Gary Cooper–like personality.

Norm Nebel was even more taciturn than Langbart. A good guy but one who was difficult to know, his aloofness held an air of mystery. He was one heck of a two-sport athlete. A grade ahead of me at Tilden, he starred in basketball and baseball. All arms and legs, this lanky 6'4" string bean dazzled with deception, motion, and surprising strength. In basketball, he possessed a unique and deadly jump shot. Effective from long and short range, he excelled at getting his shot off in traffic. He would leap high, arch his back, and then release the ball from far above his head with uncanny accuracy. Norm was also our baseball team's best pitcher. The guys in the neighborhood believed he was going to make it to the majors. Well, he didn't but was skilled enough to be granted an athletic scholarship to the University of Miami, where he continued to shine in basketball and baseball. Keeping relationships in the Tilden family, Norm married Les Yellin's sister Marilyn and settled in the Miami area.

My friend Les Yellin, two years older than me, was an unforgettable character. Regretfully, "was" applies as the appropriate verb because this sweet, warm man suddenly died of a heart attack at age fifty. His irrepressible, upbeat personality was the polar opposite of the demeanor exhibited by Langbart and Nebel. He was eternally exuberant and so loquacious as if he was on speed, but long before the drug became fashionable. His high was a natural one. He loved talk, people, and boy did he love basketball. On the court he possessed a world-class set shot and scintillating passing ability. In college at St. Francis, he paired in the backcourt with Tony D'Elia to help put their small school on the basketball map. Les and Tony–bolstered by the excellence of Al Innis, Danny Mannix, Walt Adamushko (another local guy), and George Fox–led St. Francis in 1956 to one of the nation's longest winning streaks and a surprising top-twenty ranking.

My relationship with Les, even as a fourteen- to fifteen-year-old kid, was special. He was just so helpful and encouraging. He was the first person to tell me that someday I would be a better player than all the guys who swatted me away like a fly or had little respect for my game. He used to say that I was the caterpillar who would soon turn into a butterfly. An interesting side bar to Les and our schoolyard is that he never attended PS 233 and didn't live in the immediate vicinity. Much like the basketball vagabond that I was to become, he simply played everywhere. The distinction may be that once Les arrived, he never left. As it was with me, many in my crowd became his friend for life.

Les never got rid of his basketball bug. Years after graduating from college, he dedicated himself to coaching. Eventually, he coached at Jacksonville University (post Artis Gilmore) and his alma mater, St. Francis. In his last ten or so years, on a voluntary basis, he became the assistant coach emeritus at Princeton University. Several days each week, he would trek great distances from his New York City job to assist his close friend Pete Carril. As a tribute to Les, following his death, Pete dedicated the Princeton basketball season in his memory. The unbelievable outpouring of the basketball community at Les's funeral was another testimony to the special man.

During my Tilden years, our basketball teams never lacked size. Most of the big people plateaued early, failing to live up to expectations. Two that I remember best were Harvey "Bonehead" Berringhaus and Arthur "Satch" Goldstein. I first got to know them at Betsy Head and became friendlier because Les Yellin, who was their age and teammate, brought them around to the neighborhood. They resided in Brownsville, near Betsy Head, where they unwittingly achieved "clown" status.

Intellectually, Harvey Berringhaus was no bonehead. He was a serious, studious fellow who was to become an engineer. At 6'5", his appearance and gait belied his true substance. He was heavy-featured, stoop-shouldered, and walked with his long arms swinging side to side. Given these characteristics, it was easy to see why cruel comparisons were made between Harvey and a Neanderthal. Therefore, the "bonehead" tag was conceived, and it stuck. As a basketball player, Harvey's best asset was his soft touch. He had a classic hook shot from the pivot and could do it with either hand. His liabilities were his lack of speed and fragile level of confidence. At times, it seemed that playing was not really fun for him. Unlike Harvey, Arthur "Satch" Goldstein enjoyed the role of buffoon. His nickname alone was revealing, and it derived from "Satch," so hysterically acted by Huntz Hall in the East Side Kids/Bowery Boys movies. A hulking 6'7", Satch was a gentle giant, in some ways likened to Lenny in John Steinback's classic, *Of Mice and Men*. He was teddy bear warm and affectionate and laughed often and loudly. He wasn't stupid but displayed social simplicity and, to a degree, immaturity. "Satch" certainly made you smile and was fun to be around yet he would not be a first choice to go with on a double date.

He should have been a good basketball player. He was agile for his size and ran and jumped well. Although an inconsistent shooter, he had a decent variety of shots, favoring the jumper. Correlated closely with his off-court behavior, he frequently lost concentration and lacked the seriousness that the task demanded.

Conditioning was an afterthought for Satch. He was never in top shape, and even as a teenager, he had a substantial gut. Despite a spotty career at Tilden, he attained a scholarship to Southern Illinois University, the school that a decade later won the NIT under the leadership of Walt Frazier. Satch instantly became the darling of the campus, not for his basketball exploits, but because of his clowning and carousing. Needless to say, he soon returned to Brooklyn.

As an adult, Satch was unable to find his bearing. He had no specific occupation nor skill and drifted from one job to another. Things went from bad to worse until finally shocking disaster struck. Many years ago, Satch was arrested, indicted, and subsequently convicted of being an accomplice to two murders. Specifically, his crimes were aiding in disposing of the bodies. The murderer was a guy from Brownsville, always a troubled individual who, supposedly out of kindness, took Satch in as a rent-free border at his East Side Manhattan apartment. From the start, we were suspicious of this peculiar arrangement but still never dreamed of such horrible consequences. Elliot Press, former Tilden and St. Francis standout, was his attorney and could do no better than reduce his eligibility for parole to twenty years. Tragically and predictably, Satch never made it out of prison. He died of a heart attack at Ellenville, an upstate New York penitentiary.

While several of my PS 233 buddies and fellow sophomores were already participating in the Tilden basketball program, I was out seeking new places to practice my game. Stuckelman, Mandel, and Tendler were starting to realize the promise originally begun under the tutelage of "Venty" Lieb. I was happy for them yet envious that I was not on their level. My meandering took me to Lincoln Terrace Park, a diverse recreational area at the south end of Eastern Parkway. The park, hilly and tree-lined, was situated on the common border of Brownsville and Ocean Hill and not too distant from Crown Heights. It was the first place that I ever saw tennis being played. It was also a hub for the nation's best blackball handball contests. Outdoor basketball courts were in two areas of the park, the more popular one unusable during the summer months. The Lincoln Terrace main courts were off limits in the summer because they were in the two-foot-deep kiddy wading pool. The baskets were regulation height but were embedded in a recessed, below-ground-level surface. It certainly was a very different and interesting place to play.

At Lincoln Terrace, I both played and watched. I competed in games against the park's lesser players, most of whom were older and more experienced. I spent at least as much time viewing the hard-fought contests on the main court. The participants were a mixture of young rising talents and established players, ranging in age from late teens to fortyish. Most came from the three sections cited above that were in closest proximity to the park. The best of the grizzled veterans was Jerry Fleishman, a man who in later years would become my teammate and sometime opponent in countless hours of joyful basketball. When I first saw Jerry, he had just retired from a productive professional career. For several years, he played guard for the Philadelphia Warriors, a team that won an NBA championship, and ended his pro days with the New York Knicks. He was an indefatigable fierce competitor and was equally proficient on offense and defense. A lefty, he possessed an excellent hook shot off the drive and an accurate open set shot, which he uniquely released from slightly above his waist. He was warm and considerate away from the court, always going out of his way to spend some helpful time with kids like myself.

Another of Lincoln Terrace's outstanding players and a very likeable guy was the enigmatic Connie Schaff. At 6'3", with Hollywood-like good looks and an array of offensive skills to envy, it would seem to the outsider that Connie held the world in his hands. In reality, the opposite was true. Just a few years prior to meeting him, Connie, who played for NYU, was among the local college stars named in the basketball scandal. Connie was the only one implicated from NYU. The charge against him was conspiracy to bribe rather than the actual act of attempting to keep the score below the gambling point spreads. Sadly, Connie was one of the few who never rebounded from his fall from grace. More than simply play in the park, he hung around as if it was his refuge. He was also the first Jewish person that I ever saw with a bottle of wine in a brown paper bag sticking out of his jacket pocket. I cannot pinpoint a specific time, but within a few years, Connie disappeared from Lincoln Terrace. Predictable and tragic, he died young and unfulfilled–a wasted life.

Occasionally, I continued to play at Lincoln Terrace into my twenties. It pleased me that as I matured and sharpened my skills, I progressed to the main court down the hole. Generally, I would hook up with my good friends, Syd Levy (CCNY) and Lenny Sherman (LIU), whom I will write about later in-depth. We were difficult to beat at Lincoln Terrace as was the case in so many places we were to play together.

At about age fifteen, another Brownsville basketball facility stirred my thirst to become a real player. One of my father's sisters lived on Sackman Street, less than a block away from Nanny Goat Park. Aside from the unique name, it was a bit more than vest-pocket size and approximately a mile easterly walk from my home. It was strictly an outdoor venue and contained the courts where the Betsy Head crowd played in warm weather (when the gym was converted into the swimming pool locker room). Not only did I again get to see the Viceroys and others whose game I respected, but I met and played with guys who taught me much about basketball and the raw side of New York City.

Just as Langbart, Nebel, and Yellin were my PS 233 schoolyard role models, three others at Nanny Goat affected me in a similar way. They were Benny Bessen, Herbie Weinand, Abie Kleinman.

Benny Bessen was nearly six feet tall, thick-bodied, but certainly not flabby. At that time a recent graduate and former Jefferson player, Benny had no burning desire to continue pursuing formal education. Even at a young age, he had a propensity to make a buck, so his first priority was to work and then play ball in his leisure hours. As a basketball player, he was tremendously deceptive. His style was far from pretty yet extremely effective. Driving to the basket was his thing. He could beat you off the fake or dribble, relying upon bull-like strength rather than speed. He was equally adept at dishing to a teammate when defenders converged on him, thereby creating an opening. Off the court, he was the supreme street corner philosopher, dispensing humor-laden wisdom in a Damon Runyan-like manner. His perceptions and insights were always entertaining and often quite poignant.

Classify this next bit of information in the strange and ironic category. Through their ball-playing, Benny and Les Yellin knew each other but were acquaintances rather than friends. Les got married and looked for an apartment in the general vicinity where he was raised. He found one in a four-family building owned by Benny's parents. The Bessens had recently moved from Brownsville to the slightly upscale tip of East Flatbush. They became the Yellin's landlord, and in the process, Benny and Les started a lasting close friendship.

Every neighborhood had guys who were actually better players than some with big names and reputations. Herbie Wein was a prime example of the star without a portfolio. At 6'2" and reed-thin, Herbie was a big guard with superior skills. With the ball, he had a wondrous jab step, which he utilized going either left or right. If the defensive player got too close, he would blow by him sailing in for the easy layup or shooting a picturesque running one-hander. One the other hand, when an opponent gave him room, he would launch his deadly outside shot.

Herbie didn't receive the acclaim commensurate to his ability, mainly due to his difficulty sticking with things. He would get distracted and bored, often stopping an involvement to pursue something new. For one short period, however, he went out to Seattle and made the university's fine basketball team. He didn't stay for the full ride but returned with a most prophetic piece of information. Herbie informed us of a player at Seattle from Washington, DC, who was spectacular and would soon become an NBA super star. That player was Elgin Baylor. Finally, always one to do the unpredictable, Herbie chose a career as a fireman and rose through the ranks to attain officer status. The third admired individual at Nanny Goat Park several years older than his friend Herbie and more than ten years my senior was Abie Kleinman. He was a pure Brooklyn gem, a fabulous eccentric character. In his mid-twenties when I met him, Abie was a full-time cabbie. He was extremely bright and articulate and possessed a great fund of knowledge in a wide range of topics. He was a Brownsville version of the man for all seasons, but beyond a doubt, his two greatest passions were basketball and gambling. His work and even athletic activities took a back seat to the schedule at the New York racetracks. It may be apocryphal, but friends of Abie's swear that he dropped out of college at NYU because it interfered with his making the races at Aqueduct and Belmont. Abie, like Benny, was a local Socrates, although his brand of philosophy focused upon his personal agenda. This included advice on how to gain a psychological advantage in basketball, a practical guide and handbook about hookers, and his views on the seedy side of life in New York. By listening to Abie's pontificating, I received a free and valuable streetwise education.

On the basketball floor, playing with him was wonderful. He was a wiry, 5'10", a good dribbler with soft, quick hands and excellent court vision. Reminiscent of Dick McGuire, he was totally unselfish, rarely taking shots (although he was capable) and had a knack for creating movement, especially without the ball. He was one who elevated the game of his teammates to a higher level. Not so much at Nanny Goat Park but a bit later on when I matured physically, playing with Abie and also Herbie Wein was instrumental to my basketball development. Aside from Les Yellin, Abie was the person whose encouragement was most vital to my believing that I could succeed as a player. He too said he saw qualities in my game that one day would blossom.

My grandmother lived in Brownsville on Stone Avenue, a few blocks from Nanny Goat Park. Down the street on Linden Boulevard, in the early 1950s, a spanking new facility, a replacement for the venerable Brownsville Boys Club, had just been completed. The original Brownsville Boys Club was a renowned center for athletic, social, and cultural activities. Comprised of a few storefronts, it enlightened and nurtured Brownsville's youths in its modest quarters. Through many years of sweat, fund-raising, and politicking, the Linden Boulevard structure finally became a reality. Among the plethora of modern resources, the building featured a spacious gymnasium and an indoor swimming pool.

A man as responsible as any for making the dreams of so many come true was Abe Stark. Abe, a major officer of the Boys Club who wore many hats within the community. He was an activist, a successful local merchant, and an emerging politician. He owned a men's clothing store on Pitkin Avenue, Brownsville's main drag that became famous for a most unique reason. His advertisement at Ebbet's Field, the Abe Stark sign at the base of right field scoreboard, became etched in baseball lore. It is long since the Dodgers moved to Los Angeles, but still today old fans remember the theme of the sign: "hit it and win a free suit." Apart from his business, Abe's tireless efforts helped to bring the Boys Club to its new location. One may think of it as a reward, for a few years later, he was elected to the position of Brooklyn borough president. As for the Boys Club, faced with a huge overhead for its upkeep, it could not be sustained as a private organization. It survived by transferring control and responsibility to the New York City Department of Parks. Hence, the Brownsville Boys Club became the Brownsville Recreational Center.

Irrespective of its name, in 1953, from the first moment that I stepped into that gym, the building became my basketball home. Betsy Head was my inspiration, but it was the Brownsville Recreation Center (BRC) that brought about my transformation from basketball enthusiast to basketball player. At this point, I will just begin to scratch the surface concerning my considerable time spent at the BRC. In my description of experiences following graduation from high school, its significant effects will be detailed in-depth. At the beginning, most of my time spent at the BRC was devoted to shooting around and half-court games. I practiced foul shooting extensively and was delighted that I was able to make the transition from a two-hand to one-hand technique. I took it as a definite sign of maturation and growth and became a formidable contender in foul shooting contests. The problem in the total basketball picture was that in actual games, I didn't draw many fouls and, therefore, seldom made it to the line. My priorities were obviously somewhat misguided.

Sunday morning was generally not a time that I would go to the BRC. On one specific Sunday, however, I had to bring something to my grandmother. When I finished my errand, it was still early, probably about 10:30 AM. As I was in no hurry, I decided to see what was happening at the center. The gym was crowded with grownups, men, not boys or even young adults. An intense game was underway with one player clearly dominant, especially on the offensive end. That man, a name that I certainly had heard but never before seen play was Sid Tanenbaum.

It took just a few minutes during that first viewing to realize that Sid was a special player. In college at NYU during the late forties, he was a two-time All-American. He had a brief NBA career (Knicks and Bullets), which he curtailed in favor of entering his father-in-law's business. I was told that he wasn't crazy about the travel or the money that post-World War II professional basketball offered. He loved to play, and Sunday morning at the BRC was just one of several regular workouts in which Sid participated.

Sid was a slender, six-foot guard. As a set shooter, he took a back seat to no one. His driving one-handed/baby hook was equally devastating. The thing that set him apart from the norm was his extraordinary quickness. His change of direction, especially without the ball, was like lightning. Not only could he destroy via the give-and-go, but his lateral movement was incredibly quick. While the defender was "looking for his jock" in embarrassment, Sid was off by himself enjoying an open shot or prancing alone to the basket. Added to his spectacular offensive game, he was a terrific passer and an unselfish team player.

There was a player in those workouts who far and away did the best job of defending the unstoppable Tanenbaum. He was a lean, muscularly toned neighborhood guy nicknamed "Feeny." I found eventually that his real name was Norman Fields, but at the BRC, everyone called him Feeny. He also was another quality player who never attended a big-time school. I thoroughly enjoyed his unique style. He had sharp reflexes, great deft hands, and was fleet of foot. He possessed the uncanny ability to stop on the proverbial dime, going from a full run to a sudden halt without being guilty of traveling. At the conclusion of his dribble, he would fake, most often forcing the defender off balance. He would then finish the play in a flourish by ducking under and shooting with his body leaning toward the basket. That sequence was Feeny's patented specialty.

In all the Sundays that I watched Sid and Feeny play, I never spoke with them. Fate would have it, however, that many years later, when at age thirty, I bought a house and moved to Long Island, I would catch up with them again. This time we shared infinite hours of basketball pleasure at the gym at Hewlett High School and the park at North Woodmere. Best of all, I got to know them well enough to call them friends. As people, they were just as nice and classy as they were skilled on the basketball court.

By the start of my junior year at Tilden, I was encouraged by the clear signs of a growth spurt. I finally surpassed 5'6" (even if it was only 5'7") and for the first time, my ribs appeared to be under, not over my skin. Enthused by these developments, I decided that it was time to try out for the basketball team. I fell just short of making the varsity and was dispatched to the JV. As I was one of the last to be cut, I was invited to practice with the varsity.

Our head coach, Jack Krugman, was a tall, pleasant, soft-spoken man of few words. He was my first adult coach since Venty Leib and seriously paled by comparison. I genuinely liked him as a person but inwardly questioned his competence and commitment. Our practices were loosely run and disorganized and lacked coach-player communication. Basketball teaching was also minimal. It was primarily roll the ball out and play.

Despite having the presence of a star in Norm Nebel and an emerging superstar in Don Goldstein and otherwise deep and fairly talented team, we again finished behind Erasmus and Madison in our league. It was also another year of failure to live up to expectations and to attain a record that would qualify us for the playoffs. Another blow to the team was the transfer of my closest friend, Gerry Stuckelman, the team's 6'6" center, at the start of the school year to Jefferson.

It was truly humorous, but Gerry actually contrived a story in order to transfer to Thomas Jefferson, the school in closest proximity to Tilden. He knew, as did most astute observers of Brooklyn high school basketball, that all that Jefferson lacked to contend for the city championship was just a center, one big man. He definitely wanted to be that player. So he concocted a tale about a stolen jacket with himself as the falsely accused thief who was being threatened by the Amber Kings, Tilden's notorious street gang. Gerry's mother, Sarah, naive and overprotective, bought the story and marched to the school to meet with the principal. She pleaded that Gerry's life would be at risk if he remained at Tilden. The principal brought the situation to the Brooklyn Central High School Office and the transfer was granted.

Gerry Stuckelman's arrival at Jefferson was indeed the final piece to that championship puzzle. He was a sweet hook-shooting bucket man who also was a skilled passer and aggressive rebounder. He was another weapon on a team already loaded with awesome talent. Without specific mention of the individuals, they became unstoppable and a joy to behold. In regular season play, they were undefeated in their powerful conference and lost just one nonleague game, an upset on the road to Alan Seiden's Jamaica High School squad. The growing power was to become the New York City public high school champions in 1954. As for Jefferson, on the way to the championship, they stormed past four easy victims in the playoffs, the margin of victory never falling below twenty points. They were crowned the undisputed 1954 New York City champions.

Many knowledgeable basketball people proclaimed Jefferson to be one of the best teams ever on the high school level. Speaking for myself, even today, they remain the finest that I've seen play. Finally, even though I was a student at Tilden, I took pride in Jefferson's triumph. Stuckelman was my buddy, and I knew all the other guys from the Brownsville parks and schoolyard and from playing against the Rimsmen.

Now, for the personnel on that Jefferson team, it boasted three all-city players. These outstanding talents were Bernie Tiebout, Nurlin Tarrant, and Harvey Salz. Tiebout, the same young man who did so well against the Knicks at Betsy Head, was the epitome of versatility. At 6'4" and sturdily built, he was advanced in every phase of the game. He was coolness personified and, with startling efficiency, did whatever it took to win. After high school, Bernie earned junior college All-American honors at New York Tech. He turned away numerous scholarship offers to four-year colleges in favor of playing AAU ball for the New York Tuck Tapers and, in addition, the opportunity to work for the corporation.

Nurlin Tarrant, a 6'1" superb playmaker and deft dribbler, was a magnificent basketball entertainer. With his vivacious personality and dramatic style, he was a high school Harlem Globetrotter. Nurlin chose to play college basketball at Tennessee State where his backcourt mate was a pretty fair player by the name of Dick Barnett.

Harvey Salz, the junior of the fabulous trio, was as good as any high school jump shooter. A 6'2" guard, he was a gifted athlete who possessed extraordinary jumping ability, speed, and grace. These attributes combined to make him a veritable scoring machine. It was remarkable how easily he could get free for his deadly jump shot or blaze past a defender to score an easy two points. Harvey's scholarship took him to the prestigious University of North Carolina, where he eventually started on some excellent teams.

Gerry Stuckelman and Fleet Clarence Jones completed the starting lineup. Gerry was awarded a scholarship to the University of Houston where he played briefly. In actuality, he was a reluctant student and also didn't like being so far from home. He was eager to earn enough money to buy a car. So he went to work, bought a car, married his neighborhood girlfriend Fran, and retired early from basketball. Clarence took his game to one of the predominately black colleges in the south and relocated there.

A meaningful commentary regarding the depth of talent on that Jefferson team is that its bench would have comprised one of the better teams in the city. Players such as Alan "Red" Miller and Marty "Bot" Botwinick had successful college careers at William and Mary and Adelphi respectively. My good friend Jerry "Cookie" Wolkoff, Brownsville's version of Robert Redford in his role in *The Sting*, had a set shot comparable to that of Les Yellin. Several other substitutes (Normie List, Dave Newmark, and Milty Gold) came up through the Rimsmen, had college level ability, and could hold their own against top competition. The team was easily ten deep.

By the end of my junior year, dissatisfying only from a basketball perspective in the summer of 1954, Brighton Beach became the in place for the hip teenagers to congregate. Situated on the Atlantic Ocean, just to the east of the famous Coney Island, Brighton was a popular Brooklyn resort. Today, it is much better known as the neighborhood that is home to the greatest number of Russian immigrants in America. At that time, the beach, the boardwalk, the boy-girl thing, and the music were its popular features. For me, the whole music scene on the beach itself was the most exciting and special happening. In the fifties, Latin music–the mambo, cha-cha, meringue–were the rage. The "mambo-nicks," as we called them, would converge on the beach, forming a huge circle around bongo and conga drummers and timebales-playing musicians. For hour upon hour in the sun, a festival atmosphere of clapping, singing, and sand dancing prevailed. It was just a wonderful setting and a carefree time.

Among my crowd, very few were old enough to drive a car or, if licensed, owned one. Living far from the beach, most often we had to endure a long Church Avenue bus ride followed by another trek on the Brighton train line to reach our destination. The few occasions that we were able to ride by car evoked joy akin to winning the lottery. Regardless, it was worth the trouble, for again those were great days.

As much as I enjoyed the beach, I still would not be reminiscing about those good times unless there was a basketball connection. Just off the boardwalk, between bays four and five, there was a small playground with two full basketball courts. From the boardwalk view, the games, especially on weekends, looked to be of high quality. After spotting the busy courts, I decided to bring along a basketball and add hoops to the beach agenda. The games were competitive, enjoyable, and helpful to my continued development. The action on the main court, however, was far too advanced for me. To my delight, some of the players were among my favorites. These included the former NYU stars Abe Becker and Jimmy Brasco and the then-current NYU big bruisers Mel Seeman and Mark Soloman. I also fondly remember the rough-and-tumble style of retired Knickerbocker Fredo Frey and a park player of considerable girth known as "Fat Phil."

Phil Albert, about 5'10" and at least 275 pounds was an immovable object. He would post himself down low and use the body to shoot short-distance hooks. He also took an accurate overhead pop shot and moved considerably quicker than one would expect from a man his size. Phil was basically a warm, gentle, and caring person. Unfortunately, his few on-court eruptions ended in his use of fists, where he won the fights but due to the involvement of lawsuits and the police lost the wars. I'm familiar with these bits of trivia about Phil because our paths crossed many times long after the days at Brighton Beach were over. A few years later, I was his waiter when he and his wife vacationed in the Catskills and played ball with him at the hotel.

Still again, about a decade down the road, I found him along with Sid Tanenbaum and Feeny on the courts of Long Island. The interweaving and repeated connectedness of the lives of us basketballs lunatics is like something out of the *Twilight Zone.*

Another local Brighton guy that I met for the first time in that playground and was to eventually become a lifetime friend and teammate in leagues and tournaments was Mark "Whitey" Reiner. In 1954, he had just concluded his freshman year at Lincoln High School where as a guard, he already was a key member of the varsity. A blond, freckle-faced Brooklyn Huckleberry Finn, he was a precocious offensive player with obviously unlimited potential. In his years at Lincoln, Mark realized his promise, earning all-city recognition. A scholarship to North Carolina State University ensued. He didn't remain there long, transferring to NYU where he became an important contributor on some high-profile teams. His career highlight as a "Violet" was a fantastic thirty-seven-point long range shooting barrage against Temple University. With no exaggeration, had that game occurred in the current era of the three-point field goal, Mark would have been credited with a mind-boggling minimum of thirteen three-point shots. Now deceased, Mark Reiner was a whirlwind both off and on the court. He was irrepressible, articulate, and supremely confident. He is at the top of my list of unforgettable people. I will have much more to write about Mark–the player, the coach, and the person. There are many reasons to account for my admiration of him, but none (as it will be revealed) is greater than his courage.

The summer of 1954 was exciting and eventful. I discovered that I liked girls, Latin music, and the beach. Approaching my seventeenth birthday (September 14), I had my first real date during August. Before that, social contact with the opposite sex took place at theme parties, social dances, or just hanging out together at the popular neighborhood spots.

As summer dwindled down toward Labor Day, it was evident that my favorite baseball team, the Yankees, winners of five consecutive pennants and World Series, would yield the American League crown to the Cleveland Indians. It took guts to live in Brooklyn and root for the Yankees, especially when the Dodgers were their World Series victims. For weeks after the seemingly annual Dodger disappointment, I and a few other Yankee rooters in the area would have to be at our nimblest to avoid the penalty for traitorous behavior. The punishment was to be the removal of one's pants, which would then be hung high on the PS 233 schoolyard fence. My record for escaping the Dodger fans wrath was good and was bolstered by the precaution of always wearing gym shorts under my trousers.

These other interests, whether new or old, did not in the least diminish my basketball fervor. My senior year and final basketball season at Tilden was at hand. More than optimism concerning the prospects for personal success, I knew that we were a talented group and had a chance to become an outstanding team. We had experience, skill, good size, and best of all Don "Red" Goldstein. Don, 6'5½" all everything, was clearly among the top three of four high school players in New York City.

Slender and square-shouldered with huge hands and long spidery fingers, he glided over the court with the grace of a swan. He literally could and, at times, did play every position on the floor. There were no weak aspects to his game. He was a superb ball handler, passer, defensive player, rebounder, and scorer. As a shooter, his arsenal consisted of three deadly weapons. He shot jumpers, hooks, and set shots with equally deadly proficiency. His shooting form was so exquisite that he even looked good when he missed. His ability to hit hook shots from the baseline was uncanny and a definite crowd-pleaser. Topping off this wonderful and complete basketball package was Don's unselfishness and team-oriented play.

Our second big man on the twelve-man squad was Stu "Ichy" Berlin. His Ichy moniker, which he didn't like and was a jab at his long and hawkish nose, was a shortening for Ichobod Crane, the large-beaked schoolteacher in Washington Irving's "The Headless Horseman." Stu, the boniest 6'5" imaginable, was a versatile offensive player with above-average speed and jumping ability. He demonstrated a soft touch, particularly from long range. Ichy overcame the constant ribbing regarding his substantial nose through basketball success at Tilden and in college at Gonzaga University.

Considering that PS 233 was but one of ten feeder schools which contributed to Tilden's student population, it is noteworthy that five of twelve varsity players were from PS 233. In addition to myself, the others were starters, Joel Tendler and Joel "Snake" Mandel, and reserves Jerry Blomberg and Stan Feldstein. Had Gerry Stuckelman remained at Tilden, our guys would have comprised 50 percent of the team. I guess it spoke well for us as athletes, but clearly the greater credit belonged to Venty Lieb and his coaching excellence.

By the time basketball practice began, my height, moving further upward, was 5'9" and my body still in the filling-out process. I thought that a slim possibility existed to capture a starting position at guard alongside Mandel. To my chagrin, this didn't happen as I was beaten out by Marty Bell, a brash Brownsville street guy. Initially, I felt that Coach Krugman didn't give me a fair chance, but Bell really was the right choice. He was more aggressive, particularly on defense, and was better at penetrating and driving to the basket. He had an air of confidence and a swagger that I lacked. I was basically a smart mistake-free player whose presence wouldn't hurt the team but exhibited no specific standout quality. Although I was attempting to get rid of my mediocre set shot in exchange for the more pragmatic jump shot, I had not yet mastered its mechanics. As was the case with many lefthanders, I had a decent running hook shot, which of course, I took moving to my left only. In games, however, I was reluctant to use it or challenge the big people when they picked me up on switches. The bottom line was that I was an adequate backup and role player on that Tilden team. I came in briefly to give a tired player time to catch his breath or in instances of foul trouble or injury to a starter. Frankly, I understood the situation, accepted it, and was happy to be part of a very good and exciting team.

The skeptical opinion that I formed the previous year regarding the quality of the basketball coaching at Tilden was unfortunately solidly reinforced during my senior season. Jack Krugman, as before, was the same decent man but hardly a leader or teacher as our coach. Practices would consist of mainly scrimmages, designating the sides, and simply playing until a predetermined number of points was reached. Oh, pardon me, we did have two out-of-bounds plays, one each for under the basket and the side. On defense, we played straight man to man and, when necessary, pressed in a similar manner. Traps or zone presses were concepts that were never mentioned. Reserves rarely practiced on the same teams with the starters, and the fundamentals of the game were not taught. Mistakes committed in practice went uncorrected, and some capable players were completely ignored. Jerry Schwartz, a tall talented junior member of our team who became an excellent player at Brandeis University, never left the bench.

In reality, we coached ourselves. Our team performed well because the guys knew how to play and was a compatible group. If the opposition deployed a zone, "Red" or Tendler would simply organize and set up the offense, the way we had previously been taught to attack the defensive scheme. It's funny, but none of us ever disrespected Mr. Krugman. Despite the coaching cluelessness, he carried himself with dignity that we recognized and even admired. On the court, the team just worked around him.

The season itself was Tilden's best since the days of Torgoff, Schectman, and Hertzberg. For once, we were able to surpass our main rivals, Erasmus and Madison, on the road to winning the division championship. In a nonleague game, we surprisingly rolled over formidable Jefferson, a team that we seldom beat. Don had the monster season that everyone expected, averaging better than twenty-five points per game and led the team in rebounding and assists. He also announced that he accepted a scholarship offer to attend the University of Louisville.

Erasmus and Madison were no pushovers. Erasmus featured an all-city forward in Alex Mantell and a blur at guard in the person of Olin Barton. Waiting in the wings and luckily a few years too young were three decent prospects by the names of Julie Cohen, Doug Moe, and Billy Cunningham. Madison had the strongest front line and probably the deepest team in the city. Their trio of horses were Mel Kessler (6'5"), Charlie Hoffman (6'4"), and Rudy LaRusso (6'7"). The guard who fed them the ball was Steve "Peewee" Matell, an exciting playmaker and scorer (whose nose I would accidentally break about twenty years later in a game on Long Island). Interestingly, Matell, Kessler, and Hoffman were recruited by Muhlenberg College, which fielded excellent teams in those days. They enrolled there as a package and continued playing together throughout their college days. As for LaRusso, any basketball fans of the sixties would know that he enjoyed an outstanding lengthy career in the NBA, playing primarily for the

Los Angeles Lakers. Before that he starred at Dartmouth, the Ivy League champs.

As division champions, we drew a bye in the first round of the playoffs, which were held entirely at Madison Square Garden. Practicing on that court and in that famed building was the greatest thrill of my life. Firsthand, I experienced dribbling over the dead spots on that glistening floor and shot at those soft rims. Just standing at center court and looking up at the vast expanse of seats in the arena was awe-inspiring to this seventeen-year-old basketball dreamer.

We drew New Utrecht as our first round opponent and dispensed of them easily. They had no answers for Don Goldstein, who totally dominated the game. In the quarterfinals, which coincidentally would determine the Brooklyn champions, we once again had to face Madison. It's awfully difficult to repeatedly beat the same team, especially when the rivals are so evenly matched. The hurdle was made considerably higher for us because of an incapacitating leg injury suffered by our outstanding guard, Joel Mandel. In Joel's absence, Coach Krugman chose to match size against size and started Alan Lipton, our top reserve forward. The strategy didn't hurt as the game was a classic marked by numerous lead changes. It went down to the wire with Madison prevailing in the last minute of play. It was one final great performance by Don Goldstein in the kind of game where the cliché "there were no losers" applies. Sadly, the fine effort was no consolation as we were down and out of the playoffs.

As for Madison, they were favorites to win it all and made it to the finals against Jamaica High School. They fell short as they could not contend with the prolific Alan Seiden (St. John's), who destroyed Madison with his unstoppable drives and near-perfect foul shooting. In retrospect, Madison might have fared better playing a zone, thereby forcing Jamaica to shoot from deep. At that point in his basketball development, outside shooting was not Alan's forte.

A few weeks after the conclusion of the high school basketball season, a special all-star game was arranged. The theme of this contest had New York high school stars matched against the best of Philadelphia. The exhibition played before a standing room–only crowd, took place at Long Island City's Sunnyside Gardens, an antiquated arena known primarily for staging boxing and wrestling events. The main attraction for this one-time-only basketball promotion was Philadelphia's phenomenal Wilt Chamberlain. The 7'2" high school wonder more than lived up to his publicity on that chilly Friday evening. Single-handedly, he overwhelmed the otherwise more talented New York team. He dominated both backboards, ran the court like a gazelle, and scored at will. On defense, he was the ultimate intimidator. Taking advantage of the highly lax rules of that era pertaining to goal tending, he blocked a minimum of a dozen shots. His performance was totally awesome and discouraging to his excellent yet mortal opponents.

That game was the first time that I ever felt sympathy for Don "Red" Goldstein on the basketball court. He had the unenviable assignment of guarding Wilt. Eight inches shorter and yielding considerable poundage and strength to Wilt, Don's disadvantage was monumental. In a losing cause, he battled valiantly, earning the respect of Wilt and the informed spectators. During halftime of the game, while taking a bathroom break, I overheard two men discussing Don Goldstein's basketball future and his choice of Louisville. One expressed the opinion that Don would be the ideal Ivy League player because he lacked the toughness essential for success at Louisville's level and their very arduous schedule. The other didn't quite agree but pointed out that Don might be happy at an Ivy school for reasons other than basketball. These considerations he said were Don's excellence as a student and his "silver spoon in his mouth" upbringing. When I heard these words, I exploded. I began yelling at them to shut their mouths because they were talking nonsense and bullshit. They knew nothing about Don Goldstein, neither the player nor the person. I stormed away without even getting to the urinal.

In truth, I've never known a person who had less of a silver spoon upbringing than Don Goldstein. His story about overcoming adversity to achieve great success is drama worthy of the old Bill Stern radio portraits. For those under fifty, Bill Stern was a sportscaster best known for his overly emotional and exaggerated style. In addition to sports announcing, he had a radio show in which he would weave tales about individuals who triumphed over severe difficulties and eventually attained a degree of fame. At the end of each story, playing the role of thespian to the extreme, Stern would pause and then reveal the hero's name. Don Goldstein's early life fits the Bill Stern profile.

Donald "Red" Goldstein grew up on Amboy Street directly across from Betsy Head Park. He lived in a cramped apartment in a rundown tenement with his father, grandmother, and younger brother "Heshy." Amboy Street, although far from picturesque, rose to glamour status because it was the setting in Irving Shulman's blockbuster novel about a Brownsville youth gang entitled *The Amboy Dukes*. Years later, boxer Mike Tyson would speak often of his first criminal activities when he lived on Amboy Street.

Don's father, "Big Red," was deaf and mute. His mother, who I never knew, suffered a debilitating illness that irreversibly affected her mental capabilities. This condition tragically resulted in permanent institutionalization. His grandmother was a lovely elderly woman who spoke only Yiddish and carried the primary burden for maintaining the stability of the household. Money was scarce. Don's dad, a strapping tall redhead, worked as a laborer. He was a warm, affable man with a winning smile, always proud of his children. Don and "Heshy" communicated with him via sign language and conversed in Yiddish with their grandmother.

Even the modest luxuries that most of us enjoyed were out of the Goldstein's reach. Don seldom had an extra nickel in his pocket. Going to the Ambassador or People's Cinema to see a movie was a rare treat. When pizza finally came to the neighborhood, he never indulged. He never went with us to the beach or to sporting events. Mainly, he remained close to home, doing the things that didn't cost money and which he loved best. That, of course, was playing basketball.

In those days, I remember him hanging out and shooting baskets with his good friend and Rimsmen teammate Shelly "Schneck" Kastner. "Schneck," a bright, humorous fellow, was about a foot shorter than Don. The two of them together were quite a sight. As Don's game significantly improved, he began to get around a bit more. Guys like Danny Culley and Bernie Tiebout would pick him up and take him to places such as Kingston Park in Bedford-Stuyvesant to play against the Boys High crowd. Through it all, his major concern was his family. He was a good and dutiful son and grandson.

Some in our group saw Don as aloof and a loner. Initially, as a teenager, he was uncomfortable in large social settings. His hesitancy should have been completely understandable to anyone with a modicum of intelligence. In actuality, his adjustment was excellent. None of us experienced growing up with his worries and responsibilities. Our lives were hedonistic when compared to his reality, which compelled him to become a man before he was finished with childhood. Given these circumstance, Don's accomplishments as a student and an athlete at Tilden were admirable and extraordinary. And that was just the beginning.

A high percentage of Tildenites, myself included, wondered how someone who had never been away from home and lived a restrictive existence would function in a distant and strange environment like Louisville. Happily, the doubts and pessimism were unfounded. He took splendid advantage of the fully funded scholarship, which was the only way possible that he could attend college. Don flourished athletically and academically and enjoyed a rich campus life at the southern university.

Don's basketball career at Louisville was outstanding. He capped it off by attaining All-American recognition in his senior year, leading Louisville to a berth in the NCAA tournament final four. At season's end, he was selected to the East All-Star Team and played on the same squad with all-time greats Oscar Robertson and Jerry West. In a non-Olympic year, he represented the US in the Pan American Games. His teammates on that gold winning squad again were Robertson and West, along with such stars as Bob Boozer (Kansas State) and Adrian Smith (Kentucky).

He also was not ignored in the NBA draft. In those days, the NBA was an eight-team league with fewer than one hundred players. He was selected in the second round by the Pistons, whose first choice was Bailey Howell, a man who became a terrific pro. Don thought long and hard and made a decision not to play professional basketball. Instead he opted for a career in dentistry. Louisville provided him with the opportunity to extend his scholarship through dental school, an offer too good to refuse. At that time, he was also seriously dating Roberta, his future wife, whom he met at Louisville. It's my conjecture that Roberta's father, a successful businessman, was in a position to ease Don's initial financial burden in attempting to establish a practice. These factors and the stability of an esteemed profession and settled home life as opposed to a tenuous basketball future helped to solidify Don's decision. He followed his plan and for five decades has been a respected and skilled dentist.

I hold the strong opinion that had Don chosen the NBA path, he would have been an excellent small forward. He had all the playing tools as well as the intangibles. Still, today Louisville honors Don Goldstein. His name is mentioned in the company of so many of their great players—a list that features Darryl Griffith, Wes Unseld, Butch Beard, Purvis Ellison, Charlie Tyra, the McCray brothers, etc. As a promotion for the 1994–1995, Louisville basketball season, the university printed an illustrated basketball calendar depicting its all-time players. Brooklyn's Don Goldstein was one of that very select group. Best of all, in January 2000, Don's number was retired at a ceremony held at the University of Louisville.

My high school days were drawing to a close. While most of my friends were celebrating the passage from adolescence to the emerging independence that college signifies, I was not the least bit gleeful. Despite being an excellent student and gaining acceptance to every school to which I applied, my options, in reality, were quite limited. I could not even allow myself to delight in the fantasy of attending and playing basketball for Colgate, Lafayette, or Idaho State (yes, Idaho State)–the three schools from which I received recruitment letters. Actually, it was amazing that someone who was a nonentity as a high school player could receive such positive and complimentary letters signed by the head coaches. I decided that CCNY, a school that I long admired for its basketball tradition, would be the most practical choice. The decision, however, had nothing to do with basketball. The overriding consideration was my family's situation. There I was, a fully matriculated student, headed for CCNY's night school and full-time employment. Following graduation, by July of 1955, I obtained a job as a shipping clerk/messenger at *Newsweek* magazine's Manhattan headquarters. That summer was an unhappy blur. Officially, I was no longer a kid and, for the first time in my life, felt lost.

CHAPTER 4

My College Years

IN SEPTEMBER OF 1955, my brother Howie got married and soon after was drafted into the army. My mother, a most determined woman, had made considerable advancements in her garment center job but still needed additional monetary assistance to get to a firm financial footing. With my brother no longer able to be the magnanimous contributor that he had been in the four years since my father died, the supplemental role fell to me. During that period, Howie completely subordinated his personal needs and pleasures to the betterment of our family. He never complained nor did he ever falter in his ambitious and demanding evening college studies. In June of 1955, he was rewarded by graduating from CCNY with a BBA (Bachelor of Business Administration) degree in accounting. He set such an example that I could not protest mom's request to duplicate his efforts. She also was fixated on the principle that fairness to my brother necessitated that I endure similar sacrifices. As already stated, I was totally miserable. Nevertheless, I registered at CCNY's Baruch Evening School and began attending three nights a week. Following in Howie's footsteps, my major was going to be accounting. I hated it from the start.

My unhappy plight put my basketball dreams on indefinite hold. Yet I never considered giving up playing, even if it was to be just for fun. I sought solace at the BRC (Brownsville Recreation Center), spending most of my time away from work and school playing basketball there. I rededicated myself to becoming the player that Les Yellin and Abie Kleinman thought I could be. From a physical standpoint, this was a possibility, as over the summer I had grown another two inches and put on about fifteen pounds. In terms of size and strength, I no longer felt overmatched by most backcourt men. I was also so proud of my newfound jumping ability. I was now able to touch the rim, leaping from a running start.

By far, the one thing that impacted best upon my game was perfecting the jump shot. At every opportunity, I took hundreds of left-handed jump shots from distant and close points on the court. I would begin at one baseline, move up to the top of the circle, and end at the other baseline, making a minimum of three in a row from each spot. I'd run scores of one-man fast breaks, pulling up at the foul line to shoot the jumper. This drill could not be completed unless I hit at least nine out of the last ten shots. When shooting around with a partner, I would concentrate on practicing running to a spot, receiving his pass, and releasing instantly. I became equally proficient at shooting from a standing position, behind a screen, or taking it off the dribble. A natural lefty, I developed the ability to move to the left in full stride and then square up, jump, and shoot in rapid and rhythmic cadence. A running "shake and bake" jumper accompanied by a head fake completed this new repertoire. In a few months' time, my jump shooting accuracy increased dramatically. I realized that practice was far different than shooting under pressure in game conditions. However, I attained a critical first step in believing that swishing an open shot was automatic.

Although primarily self-motivated, I gained additional jump shot inspiration from a younger Jefferson High School player. His name was Tony Jackson, and he was one of the greatest jump shooters to ever play the game of basketball. A bold statement, but I'm talking about any level and against the recognized finest shooters. When I first got to know Tony, he was a junior at Jefferson and was already acknowledged as one of the best high school players in New York City. Our shooting styles were not very much alike. Rather, his disciplined practice habits and commitment to excellence were qualities that I found worthy of emulation. By observing Tony's technique, I also learned the importance of setting the body and shooting the ball the same way every time.

Tony's ability to shoot the deep jump shot was incredible. For him, a twenty-five-foot jumper was as comfortable and makeable as a foul shot. When played defensively, he used his superior jumping ability to soar over his opponent and release his feathery shot. His most uncanny shooting skill was spotlighted by his jumper from the deep corner. With his back to the basket, he would leap, spin, and shoot, simultaneously facing and sighting the hoop only at the very point of release. For most players, just getting that shot off would be a major accomplishment. In Tony's case, it was a surprise when he missed it.

By the time his high school days were over, Tony joined the ranks of legendary stars. In his junior and senior years, he averaged better than thirty points per game and led Jefferson to the brink of another city championship. His reputation was on par with two slightly younger players who are considered to be among the best ever produced by New York City. I refer to Wingate's Roger Brown and Boys High's Connie Hawkins. The highlight of Tony's high school career was a spectacular fifty-four point performance in the playoffs at Madison Square Garden against New Utrecht.

The 6'4" forward, wanting to remain close to home, accepted an athletic scholarship to formidable St. John's University. He did not debut until his sophomore year because in that era, freshmen were not permitted to play on the varsity. His eventual arrival on the varsity scene in 1958–1959 propelled the Redmen to one of their finest seasons in the school's storied basketball history. Teamed with the stellar backcourt tandem of Alan Seiden and Gus

Alfieri, Tony helped lead St. John's to championships in Madison Square Garden's Holiday Festival and the NIT. That was the first time that one team won both tournaments in the same year. Tony was named co-MVP for his excellent performance in the NIT. Throughout, he devastated opponents with his patented classic jump shot. Clearly, his greatest accomplishment occurred in the championship game against favored Bradley University. Added to his prolific scoring, Tony pulled down an amazing twenty-seven rebounds. When postseason honors were announced, both Tony and Alan Seiden, each averaging better than twenty points per game (unprecedented at St. John's), earned All-American recognition.

Tony's star shone brightly in his junior and senior seasons at St. John's. He was selected the winner of the Haggerty Award presented to the outstanding college basketball player in the New York Metropolitan Area. His reputation as a premier jump shooter also continued to grow, and it was anticipated that he would be a first-round NBA draft choice. A cloud, however, appeared, which dramatically dimmed and forever altered his basketball future. In 1960, another basketball scandal, far less extensive than the one a decade before, reared its ugly head. At the center of the storm was Jack Molinas, a former Columbia University standout and promising professional player. Molinas was expelled from the NBA when it was discovered that he was gambling on games, some in which his team participated. A subsequent investigation revealed that he also had his hand in attempts to fix college games by obtaining the cooperation of players to keep the scores below the betting point spread. It was alleged that Tony associated with Molinas, accepted some favors from him, and most importantly, failed to report a bribe. Although Tony was never accused of dumping games, he did admit to his silence concerning Molinas. The outcome was a legal slap on the wrists but far more significantly resulted in an unofficial blackballing from the NBA.

It is ironic that a similar fate befell Roger Brown and Connie Hawkins, Tony's high school superstar contemporaries. They were just freshmen at Dayton and Iowa Universities respectively when the taint of scandal permanently detoured their college careers. As they were not eligible to play varsity ball, their peccadilloes were entirely of the nature of accepting favors from Molinas. Both would never play a day of college basketball but still rebounded from the severe setback to become excellent pros. When the ABA (American Basketball Association) was established, Roger joined the Indiana Pacers and developed into a perennial all-star. Connie similarly starred in the ABA but for years pressed a suit against the NBA, protesting his being banned and attempted to gain compensation for monetary damages. In a much-celebrated case, Connie prevailed. He was awarded a substantial sum of money and granted the right to pursue playing in the NBA. Although his wonderful skills had somewhat diminished from his true prime days, he was good enough to attain immediate all-star status as a member of the Phoenix Suns. At a rubbery 6'8" and possessing huge hands, his deft ball handling and swooping hawklike drives to the basket made Connie a crowd favorite and a forerunner to the eye-popping exploits exhibited by Julius Erving "Dr. J."

As for Tony, I never fully understood why he took such a passive stance against the overly punitive treatment. He just seemed to accept his fate. Tony was a good guy but never one to display much emotion. His reaction to that very harsh blow was probably an extension of his noncombative personality.

Years later, Tony too received overdue redemption. The ABA, in its first season, welcomed Tony into the league. He was selected by the New Jersey Americans, the team that would soon become the New York Nets. Nearly thirty years of age and a shadow of the scoring machine that he was a few years back, Tony was still a productive player. The marvelous shooting touch never abandoned him. For a few seasons, Tony was one of the ABA's leading three-point shooters and co-held the single game record for quite some time. The passing of years had not eroded my affection and admiration for Tony Jackson. On occasion, I saw him at basketball-related functions. It was always a pleasure to spend a few minutes with him, getting caught up with the latest changes in our lives and reminiscing a bit about the past. Invariably, I always would walk away convinced that he was the best shooter that I ever have seen. Unfortunately, lung cancer took Tony's life in 2007.

I did much more than simply shoot around at the BRC. Whatever the game of the moment, be it full or half court, I was there. My preference was full court, but there were occasions when it was necessary to settle for three- or four-man ball because another group wanted to play half court at the other end of the gym. I began to get some definite external signals that told me that my game was improving. Suddenly, guys would ask me if I wanted to play on their side. It also was refreshing to be one of the first selected in choose-up games. The major personal evidence of my rapid advancement was that friends who were better just a few months back were now having trouble guarding me. For the first time in my basketball life, I felt that I had the upper hand against the old Hoopster crowd and could, at worst, hold my own with the respected Rimsmen. With the exception of Don Goldstein, I was easily on a par with all my former Tilden teammates. I even visited Tilden and took part in a scrimmage against the then-current varsity, mainly to show Coach Krugman that I could really play. To my delight, he did notice and further astonished me by saying that he believed I could successfully play on a college level.

In 1955–56, I played on the BRC house team. Night school prevented me from playing most of the weekday games, but I eagerly was present for all of the Saturday and Sunday contests. It was wonderful to play in formal games on the same team with Abie Kleinman and Herbie Wein. I continued to learn so much from them, particularly Abie. He forced me to move without the ball, relying upon hard stops and changes of direction to free myself. No doubt, Abie was a major factor in the eventual deterioration of my knees.

In that season, we had great fun, scored a lot of points, and won much more than we lost. The BRC atmosphere contributed to the good feeling. It was warm and so homelike. Men whom I looked up to and enjoyed conversing with were working on the BRC recreational staff. The two who most came to mind were the Gotkin brothers, Hy and Dave, the local basketball legends. They were very good people, the kind that steered you to see the bright side of otherwise bleak circumstances. All of that, the ball playing and the guiding hands, helped to take me out of the doldrums. From late fall of 1955 through the early spring of 1956, it made my job and night school bearable. However, as the months rolled toward June, I decided that I could no longer tolerate my dreary grind.

I determined that I wouldn't spend another year working full time and attending night school. Since work appeared to be the priority, it was logical to make it the focus of my time and energy. School, unfortunately had to be the loser. I therefore planned to drop out at the conclusion of the spring semester. Putting it mildly, my mother did not react gently to the presentation of my plan. Leaving school was both unthinkable and unacceptable. Yet she perceived and empathically felt my anguish. As the loving and understanding parent that she had always been, Mom reassessed her position concerning the work/school dilemma. She conferred about the situation with my brother, who was married and in the army. He compassionately and without hesitation agreed with our mother's tentative ruling. It was resolved that I would be permitted to attend day school at CCNY but still had to assume some financial responsibility by working part-time. When Mom informed me of this decision, my joy was indescribable. I guess it was comparable to receiving a pardon from a jail sentence. I thanked them both and pledged that I would not disappoint them.

I'd be lying if I said that the goal of playing basketball at CCNY was not a persistent thought. It wasn't, however, a pursuit for the immediate future. Having attended evening college for a year, I lacked the thirty-course credits to qualify in fall 1956 as a sophomore and therefore was ineligible to participate in varsity athletics. In my mind, I already eliminated the possibility of trying out for the junior varsity. I believed it would be best to concentrate on getting a good start academically and obtain a decent part-time job. My basketball game plan was to intensify activities at the BRC, taking advantage of the open evenings since night school was out of the picture. Summer employment became my most pressing concern. While I was pondering what to do about the *Newsweek* job and when to give notice of termination, an intriguing opportunity suddenly surfaced. A PS 233 schoolyard friend, Howie Cohen, also known as Hymie Mambo, worked summers as a waiter at a Catskill Mountain hotel. He was looking for a reliable bus boy to assist him and approached me with his offer after learning that I was transitioning from evening to day college attendance. I was lured by his promises of earning more money in a ten-week period than I could ever make in the city, with time to play plenty of basketball, perhaps against top competition, and entry into a new and exciting world that I had not previously experienced. I instantly bought into Howie's sales pitch. I brought him home to have him repeat only the part about the money to Mom. She reacted favorably to the proposal and gave it her blessing. So by the fourth week in June, I was off to Waxman's Overlook Hotel in Loch Sheldrake, New York.

Mambo was correct on all counts. I spent four wonderful summers working and frolicking in the mountains. I worked all of them at the Overlook, serving one season as a busboy and the other three in the capacity of waiter. The hotel was small, accommodating about two hundred guests, and certainly not very lavish. We used to joke that it got its name because everyone "overlooked" the place. Yet it did a brisk family business, with much of the clientele returning there to vacation every summer.

Prior to the breaking of the scandal in 1951, Catskill basketball was huge. Most of the major hotels were represented by stars who also happened to be the outstanding college players from major eastern and southern schools. My fallen heroes–Sherman White, Ed Roman, Ed Warner, etc.–were part of this group of employee/athletes. The games were great entertainment for the guests and a healthy business attraction for the general resort area. Betting pools, generally entailing the final scores and the total number of points in the games, were a feature of these events. Looking back, scandal analysts were in agreement that the Catskill-type gambling environment played a role in the creation of a climate which encouraged and gave rise to the fixing of games.

By 1956, when I arrived in the mountains, hotel basketball was deemphasized. Some resorts, however, maintained the tradition, only minus the betting. Kutsher's Country Club clearly became the leading proponent of sports promotion. Red Auerbach, for years, was on the hotel's staff and coached the team. Card-playing seemed to be his primary function, but his name alone drew top players to the hotel. Wilt Chamberlain worked as a bellhop for a few summers. Wake Forest's All-American Len Chappell and Niagara's talented Al Butler, both of whom later played for the Knicks, were at Kutsher's during my Catskill days.

Clair Bee, famed coach at LIU, esteemed for his innovativeness, organized one of the nation's first basketball camps at the Harmony Hotel, down the road from Kutsher's. The entire property was sold to the Kutsher family, and the camp was reestablished as Kutsher's Sports Academy. The indoor arena, the only one of its kind in the Catskills, was named in honor of Clair Bee. A unique feature of the gym is the basketball court floor, which was the original surface at the Boston Garden.

Over the span of decades, The Clair Bee Arena has been the scene of countless memorable games. It is best known, however, as the site for the annual Maurice Stokes Game. Maurice Stokes, "Big Mo," was a marvelous college and professional basketball player at St. Francis of Pennsylvania and the Cincinnati Royals. A seemingly indestructible 6'7" strong man, Maurice fell victim to encephalitis, a paralyzing brain infirmity, during the very prime of his life and playing career. He never recovered, unable to speak or significantly move his limbs. His condition required full-time medical care and continuous physical rehabilitation. Naturally, the cost of such treatment was staggering. Two compassionate and dedicated forces, the Kutsher family and Maurice's Royals' teammate Jack Twyman, combined their efforts to raise funds by creating a foundation on his behalf. One vehicle in this worthy cause was the annual game. Played at Kutsher's each July, it attracted many of the best present and former NBA stars and was a culmination of the year's activities to assist Maurice. Today, sadly Maurice is gone, but the game and the cause continued until the late 1990s.

The Overlook was never one of the hotels that had a basketball team. It did have a fairly decent court which I, of course, utilized extensively. Mambo and some others from the kitchen staff were good athletes and, in response to my urging, would often play following the lunch cleanup. We also added to our group, guys who worked across the road at the Lakeside Hotel. They were smart and tough players out of Brooklyn's Lafayette High School and the Bensonhurst Jewish Community House (JCH), a place with a solid basketball reputation.

Playing at the Overlook was the best that I could do basketball-wise in my rookie Catskill summer. There were a few nonhotel affiliated teams that made the rounds against the likes of Kutsher's, Brickman's, Klein's Hillside, etc. Outside of the BRC, I had no status and little access to those who might be able to hook me up with such a team. As the summer moved along, I did make some good contacts at games that I attended as a spectator. It provided me with optimism concerning mountain basketball involvement for the future.

One thing that I didn't do much of in the Catskills was sleep. To begin with, the dining room working day was a long one. At the Overlook, reporting time for breakfast was 7:00 AM, and dinner cleanup usually wasn't completed until approximately 8:00 PM. It was possible to catch some shut-eye between meals, but I've never been much of a napper. In the mornings, once fully awakened by the brisk pace of breakfast, I never felt the need to rest. Following lunch, when I was capable of nodding off, I chose to play basketball and bask in the sun. And what about getting a good night's sleep after all the work was done? We now come to the crux of the problem. There was just too much to do and endless fun to be had.

Clearly, the most eye-opening aspect of my summer's practical education was the male-female action going on at the big hotels. The singles-oriented resorts such as Tamarack Lodge, Laurel's Country Club, and Shawanga Lodge were wilder than anything that I had ever seen or experienced. Young men and women, on hiatus from their regular routines, turned into Catskill party animals. Nightly, the drinks flowed, the music and dancing were continuous, and inhibitions melted. Basketball may have been my priority, but I wasn't that stupid to pass up the opportunity of a lifetime.

A unique phenomenon of Catskill nightlife was the transformation of loving and devoted wives, vacationing at bungalow colonies or as long-term hotel guests, into slinky fun-seeking vamps. The husbands would generally spend Friday to Sunday in the mountains with their families. The wives would greet them warmly upon arrival and tearfully bid adieu upon departure. Between those times, many would proceed to have a blast. Their haunts would be the upscale hotels like the Concord, Grossinger's, Raleigh, and The Pines. I was far too shy and lacked the line to approach older women. Surprisingly, on a few occasions, I was recruited by them. I was told that I was the sensitive type who women enjoyed nurturing.

Of all the unbelievable mountain leisure activities, the one that kept me up the latest were the nights of "Mambo Madness." Several of the hotels, once weekly, beginning at midnight, held a Latin festival of music and dance. The very best Latin musicians–Tito Puente, Charlie Palmieri, Randy Carlos, Machito, Monchito and my favorites, The LaPlaya Sextet–would convene at the designated hotel and put on a spectacular show into the wee hours of the morning. I, who loved the Latin beat when I first heard its sounds at Brighton Beach, was rendered spellbound by the frenzy. I never before was into dancing but could not resist the mambo, cha-cha, and merengue. Within a brief period of time, I developed better moves on the dance floor that I had on the basketball court.

I returned home after Labor Day from my summer of enlightenment eager to begin college in earnest. The imminent objectives were to get rid of accounting as my major and to obtain a part-time job. At registration, I switched to advertising, which also would be short-lived. As for employment, the neighborhood's Don Rickles, Freddy "Pimple Back" Katz came through for me.

The future prominent obstetrician, (a surprise to our guys), was leaving his part-time position as a runner for a midtown Manhattan jewelry store. I jumped at the chance as the afternoon hours were flexible, the pay was a bit above minimum wage, and the location was close to CCNY's Baruch Business School.

My new schedule afforded me with considerably more time to play basketball. Following the path begun the previous year, I spent most of it at the BRC. My enthusiasm was further fueled by the decision of the BRC administration to field house teams at several different age levels that would play against established recreational organizations throughout the city. Our squad, which competed in the center's league, was basically kept intact and formed the core of the BRC's open team. We were to proudly wear the New York City Parks Department traditional green and white colors on our green-trimmed with white BRC uniforms.

Before the official start of the BRC's season, I was approached by a bunch of CCNY acquaintances, primarily Jefferson graduates, and asked to play with them in the college's intramural tournament. They believed the Turrets, the name of their team, lacked only a scorer to put them over the top. The word around Brownsville and East New York was that I had improved dramatically and could provide that missing element. I felt flattered by their invitation and certainly agreed to play. We were able to arrange a little practice time at the Baruch gym and, after scrimmaging, was impressed with the athleticism and basketball intelligence of the guys. One or two sat on the bench at Jefferson and/or were ex-Rimsmen. Moreover, they were a terrific and fun-loving group with whom I would soon socialize. The mischief makers were little Solly Lomito, Jason Berman, Shelly "Shneck" Kasner, and Harvey "Brom" Sklar, the most comical guy I've ever known. War cries and defensive gymnastics were two of their in-game shenanigans. The straight men, all skilled players, were Leon Altman, Normie Becker, and our center, Charlie Foreman. Charlie played previously at Ft. Hamilton High School and was the only one on the team not from Brownsville or East New York.

The intramural tournament was double elimination. When it was done, we were the last team standing–the CCNY intramural champions. Winning for me was made even sweeter as I was selected as the MVP. At the awards ceremony, "Doc" Henderson, a physical education professor and faculty advisor for intramural sports, asked to speak with me privately. He informed me that he took the liberty of speaking with Dave Polansky, CCNY's interim varsity basketball coach about me. Legendary coach Nat Holman was on a leave of absence and his return to coaching was uncertain. I thanked Doc and informed him of my family situation. I told him that playing for CCNY would be the fulfillment of my dream but obtaining permission from my mother was an obstacle. He offered to talk to her, which I declined. I stated that if I could resolve the conflict, I'd go out for the team in fall 1957. He smiled and in mock anger growled, "If you don't play next year, I'll find you and break your legs."

Back at the BRC, the basketball was plentiful, intense, and pleasurable. We strengthened the house team through the addition of two high-quality players who were temporarily home from college due to personal reasons. One of these was Harvey Salz, the former Jefferson great who was simply the epitome of smoothness and imperturbable implacability on the basketball court. As much as I respected his ability prior to playing on the same team, I became a truer believer in his talent after the BRC experience. It always surprised me that Harvey didn't blossom into a star performer at the University of North Carolina. The second acquisition was Len "Fuzzy" Kaplan, a marvelous all-around athlete whose basketball style was that of a smaller Anthony Mason. Not that Fuzzy was little, for at 6'2" and about 215 pounds, he possessed bull-like strength and determination to match. Although he excelled in baseball and basketball, he eventually made his mark in football. He was an outstanding fullback at Memphis State University, where he displayed both his superior, bone-jarring strength and breakaway moves. The kid from Brooklyn was a fan favorite and became the toast of Memphis, the city in which he settled following his football days.

Our very able team was difficult to beat. The most formidable competition came from the St. John's Recreation Center, another parks department facility located in Bedford Stuyvesant. St. John's drew most of its athletes from Boys High and Franklin K. Lane High School and was situated in an area well-known as a perpetual hotbed of basketball. Its team was coached by Zeke Clement and Sparky Smith, both tremendous playmakers who attained prominence in the forties at Boys High and Erasmus. They were equally respected for their powerful influence and positive role within the Afro-American community. Lenny Wilkens, Tommy Davis of Dodger baseball fame, and Sihugo Green are some of the notables who played at St. John's Center. The team that we competed against, however, consisted of players not necessarily well-known outside of Brooklyn nor were students at the publicized schools. Yet ability-wise they were top grade. I refer to guys like Ed "The Eel" Willis, John Gibson, "Beany" Jones, and Lester Roberts who honed their skills at St. John's. Our games with them were wars, with neither side enjoying a decided advantage. The competition was fierce but wholesome and in the best tradition of sportsmanship.

Our choose-up games at the BRC were often as much fun as the formal contests. They also had a wonderful mix of older and youthful players. One of the more interesting and better veterans was Al Schreiber. Al, a nightmare to defend, was a speedy guard with deceptive herky-jerky moves. He had recently returned from a unique basketball and educational experience. A few years earlier, a player named Bevo Francis was the sensation of the sports world. Playing at tiny Rio Grande College, Bevo scored an incredible one hundred points in one game and averaged approximately sixty points. Al, wanting to participate directly in the excitement, joined Bevo at Rio Grande and became the team's point guard. Bevo, although a great shooter, at 6'9", was too slow and weak to make it in the NBA. We, of course, received an early Bevo evaluation from Al, who predicted his failure at the professional level.

Clearly, the best of the younger group at the BRC were Tony Jackson and his Jefferson teammates Bobby Johnston, Walt Hendy, and Lenny Sherman. There was a 6'10" string bean, however, who was not in great demand to be included in the workouts. We rooted for him because he was a wonderful friendly kid but shook our heads over his poor hands and unsteady coordination. The one hope for his basketball future, other than his height and coachable attitude, was his deer-like running ability. One day, Cookie tested that speed by giving the young man a head start and then drove behind him in his red MG sports convertible on the sidewalk outside of the BRC. That gangly frenzied Linden Boulevard runner was LeRoy Ellis. LeRoy exceeded our most optimistic hopes. He just kept getting better. His outstanding college career at St. John's was surpassed by long and distinguished play in the NBA. I can't think of anyone who worked harder or deserved success more than LeRoy Ellis.

Driving on the sidewalk for Cookie was something quite routine. In those days, he was completely untamed and unpredictable. Hands down, he also was the favorite of the BRC cheerleading and twirling squads. It was not uncharacteristic for Cookie to stir up trouble on the court. In one memorable incident, an irate opponent jumped on Cookie during a game. A few baton swinging twirlers suddenly emerged from the stands to defend their imperiled hero. A near riot ensued, which had to be quelled by police intervention. At another game, "Red" Blumenreich, Yeshiva University's all-time best player, was giving us fits. Cookie deliberately provoked the usually mild mannered "Red" into throwing a punch. Cookie retaliated and both were thrown out. We then proceeded to win easily.

Not everyone associated with the basketball aspect of the BRC strove for athletic stardom. Lenny Zeplin was one who participated enthusiastically in the basketball program but displayed an even greater fervor in regard to the betterment of the center. I had never before met a teenager with a greater sense of civic commitment and unselfish devotion to the common good. Throughout his adulthood, Lenny has remained the same special and caring person. An educator, he rose to the position of principal where his dedication to school and community earned him the admiration of all who crossed his path.

Herb Turetsky was another benevolent youngster refreshingly different from the unusual BRC jock. He supplemented his playing by volunteering to maintain the official score book at games. He learned that job so well that he has been doing it professionally for the Nets since the team's inception in the now-defunct ABA. Herb, much like Lenny Zeplin, has given considerable time, effort, and resources to a variety of worthy causes. Herb's ultimate dream came true when the Nets moved to Brooklyn in 2015. He is still the scorekeeper, making it all the way up from the days of the New Jersey Americans to his hometown Brooklyn Nets.

The most unique and oddest character at the BRC was Sam "Frenchy" Resnick. About ten years older than me, Frenchy was round-faced, heftily built, and of medium height. He dressed somewhat formally, always wearing trousers and a rumpled shirt with a collar that usually turned up toward the neck. He spoke slowly as though every word was being measured. He was definitely not an athlete, yet he lived for basketball. His weekdays were spent loading and pushing clothing racks through the streets of Manhattan's Garment Center. His evenings and weekends, however, were spent at the BRC watching, commenting upon and announcing the action on the court. He attempted to imitate Marty Glickman, although his voice was gruff and his inflection was monotoned.

What stood out the most about Frenchy was that he was a true savant. He would recall and recreate actual college and pro games play by play from start to finish. The details were remarkably accurate. Impaired in his social acumen, his self-esteem was greatly enhanced by the attention he received for his astonishing sports-related memory. He also was fixated on bad calls made by referees and heckled them relentlessly and unforgiving. For some reason, his prime target was respected referee Lou Eisenstein. When he worked at the BRC after the college season, Frenchy would seek him out to say, "You blew that call. You are a bum."

A final interesting thing pertained to Frenchy's sibling. Sam had an older brother, Marcel. He was better known by his nickname, Big Frenchy, and was a mobster affiliated with Murder Incorporated. He made certain that no one would mess with his little brother. His warnings were heeded by all.

In the spring of 1957, the BRC hosted the third annual Brownsville Boys Club Athletic Association Invitation Tournament. Although a newcomer to this genre, it had already achieved status equal to the region's most prestigious single elimination competition. The schedule was carefully crafted to avoid conflicts with the established tournaments: St. Francis of Xavier, St. Anthony's of Padua, and Don Bosco of Portchester, to name a few of the best. The players were a Who's Who of New York metropolitan area basketball. Former college stars, a smattering of Eastern League pros, and top graduating high school seniors highlighted the rosters of the invited teams. Current college underclassmen did not participate in the tournament for fear of jeopardizing their eligibility. The NCAA rules of that time permitted college players to participate, solely in AAU (Amateur Athletic Union) sanctioned competition. Competing with professionals in a formal contest was another serious violation and a reason to lose eligibility.

I had never before played in the BBC Invitational, primarily because I wasn't up to that level of competition. In 1957, however, I believed I was ready and, more importantly, was on a team that was entered in the tournament. Our BRC squad was to be the center's entry. Although eager, against that field we were decided underdogs, particularly in terms of size and big game experience. We were also weakened by the departure of Harvey Salz and Fuzzy Kaplan. Harvey was previously committed to play for the stacked HES club (Hebrew Education Society), and Fuzzy returned to school for the spring semester. We were fortunate to pick up Walter Hendy and Bobby Sobers. Hendy, a Jefferson senior, at 6'5" and with arms down to the floor, was a terrific rebounder and defensive player. Sobers, LIU's high scorer, was tough as nails and displayed outstanding moves to the basket.

Surprisingly, we breezed through our first two games, easily defeating the Flatbush Jewish Center and Mt. Carmel of the Bronx. Our team shot extremely well, exceeding a hundred points in both contests. I was pleased with my performances, scoring about twenty points in each game, and exhibited confidence and poise. The quarterfinal, however, was an entirely different story. Unfortunately, we were pitted against the great HES team, who overmatched us physically and talent-wise. Despite our valiant efforts and just a four-point deficit at half time, we eventually faltered, suffering a double digit loss.

If that HES team competed as a unit on a collegiate level they, no doubt, would have been contenders for a national title. Three of its best players, all of whom I have already admiringly written about at length, were Tony Jackson, Bernie Tiebout and Harvey Salz. To make matters worse, they added "Chink", a 6'8" refugee from Philadelphia who was living temporarily with Tiebout. He was the second black person that I knew with the nickname of Chink. The other was Dick Gaines, a marvelous Mack Truck-built guard who starred for Seton Hall and in the Eastern League. Most puzzling he never was given an opportunity to play in the NBA, although he was better than many of its veteran backcourt players. This was not the case with the second "Chink," who, as Ray Scott, became a quality NBA forward and later a coach. Ray was a versatile and resourceful player with small man agility and shot his hooks and jumpers with a feathery touch.

The team's fifth man, a position that was rotated, and its bench, were as good as any of the other teams in the tournament. The key role players were ex-St. Francis stalwart Elliot Press, CCNY's fine center Syd Levy, Brandeis' captain, the aggressive Mel Sokolow, and two former Jefferson players of unfulfilled major college potential, Ronnie Mazzilli and Vicky Guralnick. Mazzilli, a relative of Lee, the baseball star, was an exciting offensive player. The chunky Guralnick was the prototypical point guard with superior court vision and instinctive precision in his ball distribution.

The squad was coached by the unassuming and gentle Julie Bender, a late 1930s LIU All-American, who served as the HES's athletic director. Julie's coaching skills were barely tested, as his great patchwork team functioned with frightening, self-directed efficiency. It was also evident that being of the Jewish faith was not a requisite for representing the HES.

The HES decisively stormed to the Brownsville championship. In the finals, they soundly defeated Xavier, a team featuring Manhattan College's great scorer Angelo Lombardo and Gerry Paulson, University of North Carolina's outstanding forward, Pete Brennan, and St. John's skilled center, Mike Parenti. They went on to capture the crown in every tournament in which they competed that spring. The unparalleled string of HES victories and the untarnished record would remain unchallenged. After the season, the team disbanded. Tony was off to St. John's. Harvey returned to North Carolina. Bernie's business future became his major focus, and "Chink" was readying himself for the pro game. It was a short ride, but a dazzling, unforgettable one.

"The Search for Better Basketball" was the theme of my second Catskill season. I was determined to expand last summer's activities beyond the Overlook's tepid basketball competition. My promotion to waiter, where the tips were substantially greater than that earned by a busboy, propelled me to a state of optimism. This good feeling quickly extended to the basketball arena. My friend Joel Tendler obtained a job at Brown's Hotel, which was situated about a mile away from the Overlook. Brown's incidentally was the resort made famous by comedian Jerry Lewis, a former employee who returned there often to perform. As for Joel, he immediately informed me of the spirited afternoon basketball games that took place at Brown's. The main participants included the hotel's athletic director, Sam Tolkoff, an irrepressible extravert and a tough grab-and-push competitor who once played for LIU, and Mark Hassen, an all-city guard from Taft High School in the Bronx. Mark was outstanding defensively and would soon shine in that capacity at Utah State University. Most afternoons, after serving the lunch meal, I'd get a ride over to Brown's and join in the frenetic satisfying action.

The only drawback to the otherwise thoroughly enjoyable games at Brown's was the hotel's disinterest in sponsoring a team to participate in Catskill evening basketball. Fortunately, I would soon have the opportunity to finally play in that elusive summer competition.

One afternoon, I was obligated to join the Overlook staff in a softball game against the Evan's Hotel, which was one of Loch Sheldrake's fines resorts. While there, I ran into Lew Daniels, a New York city principal whom I knew from Brooklyn, where he supervised a community center athletic program. Lew worked summers at Tamarack Lodge but that day was at Evan's visiting a friend. A former player himself, he gave me the phone number of someone connected to a team representing Schwartz's Delicatessen in Monticello, New York. I rushed to call the guy, who informed me that his team's roster was complete but put me touch with another basketball nut who was in the process of organizing an itinerant squad. This time my persistence hit pay dirt, as I became the newest member of the Monticello All-Stars.

Our team wasn't bad but played a thankless role comparable to that of the Washington Generals. The Generals, a group comprised of former college players, were the foils to the Harlem Globetrotters. They traveled with the Trotters, played the part of straight men, and probably lost five hundred games in succession. Our club wasn't exactly in that category, although none of the big hotels relished the prospect of losing to a team without a "main lobby." It was nevertheless fun to play against the likes of Kutsher's, Laurel's, or Brickman's. The Brickman game had special significance to me because my friend, Don Goldstein, and some of his Louisville teammates played for the hosts. Overall, we griped about the perceived unfair "homer" officiating but were more than soothed by the postgame buffet and free drinks. The atmosphere was one of excitement, and contributed to a growing sense of importance. I also established friendships with Charlie Hoffman and Mel Kessler, two of my all-star teammates. Interestingly, they were previously bitter adversaries as members of the Madison team that defeated Tilden in the high school playoffs.

Despite the paucity of victories, the summer basketball experience was a valuable one. For one thing, it helped to keep me away from the racetrack. More significantly, however, I came to the realization that I would not be embarrassed at any level of basketball competition. I finally considered myself a player and was itching to prove it.

During the latter part of the summer of 1957, my burning desire to play basketball at CCNY became an obsession. I firmly believed that I was capable of making the team. The big problem was to make the case to my mother, anticipating that she would view the request as both frivolous and selfish. Yet I could not allow my consuming dream to go unspoken and unfulfilled. College ball was something that I had to attempt or carry regrets and bitterness for the rest of my life.

I planned to support my plea with a statement of my financial condition. The reality was that I earned at least as much in ten weeks at the Overlook as I would working part-time from September through May. I could easily cover my expenses over the course of the basketball season by drawing from my Catskill savings. I even was prepared to speak about an offer that my friend "Shopper" made to me regarding waiting tables on weekends at a resort in Lakewood, New Jersey. I would begin working there after basketball concluded.

I remember so vividly that Saturday morning when I summoned the courage to present my plan to Mom. I got it all out, expressing everything, exactly as it had been rehearsed. The funny and wonderful thing is that it wasn't necessary to go to such lengths. Knowing me like the proverbial book, mom was expecting my CCNY basketball proposal. Without an eye blink, she gave it her blessing. She had already spoken to my brother who was all for it. After exchanging kisses, Mom emphatically stated, "I don't want you sitting on the bench. You better be a starting player." At last I had the green light. My goal was now within reach.

On the afternoon of October 15, 1957, I took that journey uptown from 23rd Street to 138th street and Convent Avenue, a trek that would instantly become part of my weekday routine. The CCNY gymnasium located in Wingate Hall was an old, cramped but well-maintained facility. A circular track looked down upon the court, which served as a balcony and seated spectators at crowded games. At the east end of the gym, away from the principal court, were two rims at regulation height, attached to a long metal arm that was perpendicular to the floor. The backboardless rims were installed by Nat Holman as a means to improve foul shooting proficiency and, in general, to reinforce concentration upon the front of the rim when getting ready to shoot. From the first moment that I walked into the building, I felt its history and the school's rich basketball tradition. Playing on that court, I was always conscious and appreciative of the past great CCNY basketball stars who ran the floor and shot at those same baskets.

Until that first day of tryouts, I had never before met Coach Dave Polansky. In his thirties, he was handsome, fit, and compactly built. Dave, a CCNY alumnus, was a two-sport athlete, playing some basketball but excelling in track. A near Olympian, he had been a premier half-miler and was still able to outrun his basketball players. Dave was erudite and articulate and enjoyed challenging the intellect of those he coached by applying advanced vocabulary to practice and game situations. It was not uncommon for Dave's players to bring dictionaries to the gym.

If "Doc" Henderson in fact spoke with Dave about me, he never acknowledged it. From the start, however, I liked and respected Dave as a man. I was at home with his style, particularly his manner of communicating with the players. I immediately noticed that the veterans called him by his first name, not a sign of disrespect, but because that was his preference. It took me a while to relate to him that informally but soon was comfortable enough to refer to him as Dave.

On the court, I was shocked by the ease and suddenness in which I became part of the team. I was the only nonvarsity holdover nor former freshman player to make the squad. Frankly, in scrimmages, I shot consistently well and exhibited poise and skill in my ball handling. Dave was both encouraging and complimentary, sparing me any anxiety over the possibility of being cut. After just a few weeks of practice, I began to get the crazy notion that making the starting five was not implausible.

Three starting positions on the team were sure things. Bob Silver and Joe Bernardo were regulars on last season's successful squad. Silver, a 6'5" forward, was solid defensively and a horse off the boards. Bernardo, a 5'10" guard, was clever, rarely made mistakes, and possessed an accurate set shot. The third starter was Hector Lewis, a 6'6" free-spirited Jamaican who ran and jumped as well as anyone his size in metropolitan area college basketball. Hector received significant playing time the previous year and had the potential for stardom. He literally could sky over the rim up to his elbow and enjoyed displaying his assortment of spectacular dunks. Lack of basic basketball experience and difficulty sustaining concentration were Hector's demons.

Vying for the remaining frontcourt slot were burly 6'3" penetrator Len Wallitt and even stronger immoveable 6'5" Joel Ascher, a prolific rebounder. Anytime Joel got his hands on the ball, it was his. The battle for the final guard position was among myself, Stan "Bugs" Friedman, and Julio Delatorre. Bugs, a 5'10" senior, was a slick ball handler and a deft passer. Julio, a sophomore at 6'1", was swift and resourceful although an unorthodox offensive player with a tendency to get out of control.

As the first game of the season drew near, I became ever more convinced that the position was mine to win. My offense was stronger than Bugs on a team with few pure shooters. I also took better care of the ball than the wild and inconsistent Julio. My optimism soared in light of Dave's words which appeared in the *New York Post*'s college basketball preview, "Groveman, a newcomer, is an excellent shooter and is coming on so fast that he may start for us." Aside from the praise, I was just thrilled to have my name in the newspaper.

I knew that my stock was rising when I was welcomed to the trainer's room. The facility was situated in the bowels of Lewisohn Stadium, CCNY's outdoor replica of the Roman Coliseum. In addition to being the site for our fresh air sports programs, it was renowned as the home for quality summer concerts and musical presentations. Another piece of trivia relates to Lewisohn as the place where the school's ROTC (Reserve Officers Training Corps) drilled. Athletes, on the way to the trainer's room, would pass through that area used by the ROTC's crack drill team, The Pershing Rifles. I, for one, would often joke with them about joining the ROTC. In actuality, it was at the bottom of my list of things that I wished to attempt. A member of the student soldiers was a tall, slender, pleasant young man who looked like he had modeled for the army dress uniform. I made no predictions about his future, but that person, Colin Powell, didn't exactly make a poor career choice.

"Max", Albert Maxtutis, was the CCNY trainer. He was a strange little man who vacillated between warmth and snobbery. If he liked you, he would issue an open invitation to visit his office, well known as a center for stimulating and humorous conversation. On the other hand, if you lacked status or Max perceived you to be inappropriately pushy, he would treat you with disdain. If Max's buttons were pushed beyond the brink, he could be fully capable of delivering a painful message by taping ankles without using underwrap. In my case, when Dave insisted that I tape my ankles before each practice, Max was not resistive. Our relationship became quite cordial and resulted in my receiving Max's approval to shoot the breeze in his room.

I accepted his invitation and became a regular at the prebasketball practice bull sessions. Wonderful nostalgic storytelling occurred daily in Max's room. Dave spoke often of his track experiences, the most interesting yarns being the ones he spun about his navy days. Max fascinated me with tales about the double championship team and that unbelievable season. By far, however, no one matched the stories or the delivery of lacrosse coach, Leon "Chief" Miller. Chief, a full-blooded Native American, was a great all-around athlete and a teammate at Carlisle College, as well as a close personal friend of the legendary Jim Thorpe. Chief was funny, wise, and a bit of a forgivable braggart. At that time, he was at least in his sixties and could still give high jumping and hurdling demonstrations. He was tall, stood and walked straight as an arrow, and overall carried himself with a majestic bearing. When he told us about the past, I, like most others, was held spellbound. Leon Chief Miller was the personification of the strong and independent Native American and made a meaningful and enduring mark in our country's history.

About a week before the season's inaugural, we scrimmaged the New York Athletic Club, an upscale place represented by a team comprised of former college players. Dave started me, and I came through with a good showing, particularly on offense. Following that informal game, he gave me the great news that I would start the opener against Columbia. I rushed home to tell my mother and to call some friends. Among the first to be contacted was Les Yellin, one of few people who had faith in my ability when my potential was not very evident. I realized that I had attained a most significant accomplishment and felt grateful that the years of persistent hard work were finally rewarded. Yet I also knew that making the team and earning a starting position was just an important first step. I still had much to prove.

All signs pointed to a difficult game against Columbia. During the fifties, aside from being an Ivy League power, Columbia's teams received considerable national attention. The main reason for the spotlight was the presence of its magnificent high scoring 5'7" guard, Chet Forte. Chet's outstanding basketball career culminated with the honor of his selection as the 1956–1957 College Player of the Year. Although we were fortunate to avoid facing the recently departed star, Columbia was still a talented and deep team. It featured four former New York City high school all stars. These were John Adams's Rudy Milky, Brooklyn Tech's Ted Harvin, and two promising sophomores in Jamaica's Rich Rodin and Forest Hills's Stan Needleman. Rodin and Needleman were a year behind me in high school but caught up due to my time spent in night school purgatory.

The Wingate gymnasium was jam-packed for the opener. Columbia was a solid favorite despite our home court advantage. In the warm-up, I was both excited and very nervous. However, I calmed down quietly once the game started when I successfully made my first attempted jump shot. From that point, the game flowed with a rhythm better than I had imagined. We played a terrific game, pulling away in the closing minutes, and won by a 76–70 margin. I scored fourteen points, shooting six for twelve from the field (all jump shots), and was two for two from the foul line. My performance was not headline-worthy but pretty darn respectable for a rookie's first game. I relished the congratulations and pats on the back, enjoying best those which came from fellow students. That night, the long subway ride from 137th Street to my Saratoga Avenue stop on the New Lots line didn't bother me at all. I actually believe that I floated home.

The rest of the season was not as memorable or as successful as that first game. We had a fairly good team, garnered a winning record, and, in fact, almost received a bid to the NCAA "small" college tournament. In terms of student population, CCNY was not a small school; however, our post-scandal de-emphasis resulted in a schedule where more than half of our opponents awarded no athletic scholarships and were not in the major college basketball category. Still, we continued to play all of the local powers (e.g. St. John's, NYU, Fordham, and Manhattan) and also scheduled schools with ambitious programs such as Rutgers, Farleigh Dickinson, Wagner, and St. Francis. As for that near NCAA bid, to qualify, we had to win one of our last two games. Unfortunately, we were up against St. John's and NYU, two of the better teams in the country. We fought hard, played well, but lost to the two superior squads.

Considering our modest talent level and the still imposing schedule, I developed considerable respect for Dave Polansky's coaching ability. In the years that he served as interim varsity coach, Dave's teams were consistently above five hundred. His style was not very exciting nor flashy but was usually effective, giving us the best chance to win. It kept us close in games against the big-time schools, which caused their coaches much anxiety. We didn't beat ourselves, rarely committing turnovers, and took few low percentage shots. Dave, in some ways, was similar to the coach played by Gene Hackman in the wonderful basketball movie, *Hoosiers*. When we appeared in games to be disorganized or unfocused, Dave would call out "on six," which instructed us to make a minimum of six passes before attempting a shot. We didn't always like it, but it most often helped to get us back on track.

Our offense against man-to-man defenses started with a pass to either the high or low post from a point as distant as the top of the circle but extended midway toward the sideline. Once the pivot man received the ball, a succession of cuts and picks ensued. If an opportunity for a shot failed to materialize, the guards and forwards, who were rotating, had the responsibility to begin the process again. Usually, the restarted play would commence from the side opposite the pass of original entry. Upon evaluating his personnel, Dave would introduce some options into the system. Mine featured me as a decoy as a cutter, circling the baseline and ending up moving across the foul line area as the trailer, where I was often free to shoot the jumper. Playing for Dave and within his system, I became a disciplined player and, for the first time, understood the concept of team defense. Offensively, I learned the importance of spacing and how to make optimal use of screens and picks.

On balance, I was pleased with the results of my first season: I averaged about twelve points per game, was satisfactory in all the critical basketball aspects, and retained my starting position. The positives greatly overshadowed the negatives, although I had one major setback. In practice, midway through the season and the day before our game against formidable Manhattan College, I dislocated the middle finger on my shooting hand, the left one. Dave pulled it into place and sent me for an X-ray when the nagging pain did not abate. I sustained a hairline fracture and was fitted for a metal splint, which easily slipped over the injured finger. The next evening, I played with the splint in the Manhattan game. Needless to say, I shot miserably, hitting but two of seventeen attempts. Dave gave me considerable playing time because he felt my overall performance was strong. We lost, and I was totally embarrassed. Even worse, it shook my confidence though there was a valid reason for my pitiful display. I immediately removed the contraption and played the remainder of the season simply taping two fingers together for support. My fragile psyche was bruised. Honestly, I was subpar and tentative for several games. Eventually, I regained confidence and my shooting touch. In time I was even able to laugh about that nightmare game. At the team's end-of-the-season banquet, Julio Delatorre, our poet laureate, put the episode in perfect perspective. He recited the following:

> Ah but mingled with all the work and sweat
> Are some memories which I will never forget.
> I'll remember how, after the Manhattan fling,
> Groveman showed up with his arm in a sling.

Some of the year's sweeter high points included our upset victories over Rutgers and Rider (a road game) and capturing the Metropolitan Municipal Championship, a conference consisting of all the colleges under the aegis of New York City. Although I was delighted by my frequent high-scoring games, personally I was proudest of what Dave said about me to *New York Post* sportswriter Leonard Cohen. It occurred in a postgame interview after a decisive victory over Queens College in which I hit five consecutive first half jump shots to establish a lead that was never threatened. The article quoted Dave, "Groveman right now is the smoothest player on our squad. I don't care who guards him, Marty will score his share. He's got a fine one-handed jump shot and can also drive for layups."

Not exactly a highlight but a compliment of sorts took place in our game with St. Francis. It was a thrill to compete against my good friend and mentor, Les Yellin. I was not, however, prepared for the trap that he set. Les convinced his coach, Danny Lynch, to make me the focus of a "box and one" defense. St. Francis's speedy guard, Tony D'Elia, pressed me from end to end for the entire game. I had very few shooting opportunities and was held to a paltry six points. Again, we dropped a close contest to a better team. Over the years, I chided Les for his deceitful ambush.

In the spring of 1958, I kept my commitment to my mother and went to work on weekends in Lakewood, New Jersey. I did it, but I didn't have to like it. The hotel lacked the familiar, cozy Catskill flavor and, worse, didn't have a basketball court. Basketball was something I played all year-round. Despite recently completing a rigorous season, I never felt the need for a break from the sport. Therefore, I continued playing at the BRC and the neighborhood's outdoor schoolyards and parks and also in the mountains during the summer. The difference from the usual pattern, however, was the exclusion from participating in formal games or established leagues. Dave lectured the team about the increasing stringency concerning violations of athletic eligibility. It pained me to sit on the sidelines watching the BRC invitational or to take a rain check on the big hotel games, but it simply wasn't worth the risk. Actually, I played in some minor Catskill games under a pseudonym.

Financially, my third Catskill summer was substantially more rewarding than the previous two seasons. I inherited the Overlook's prime waiter's station as a result of Mambo and a few other staff veterans' decision to end their dining room careers. They all graduated from college in June and were busy pursuing their "real" job future. I did remarkably well with the generous racetrack crowd and returning vacationers who requested to be seated at my tables. A delightful monetary and social bonus was an outgrowth of the surrogate son status I attained from a table of attractive and affectionate long-term guests. By Labor Day, I knew that my savings were sufficient to carry me through the school year and spare me the agony of having to again work in Lakewood. As for school, I finally was sticking with my major. I loved the psychology classes, achieving As in all four courses that I took during the prior fall and spring semesters.

As October drew near, I impatiently began counting the days until the start of college basketball practice. I thought about the changes on our team, particularly the loss, through graduation, of Bob Silver and Joe Bernardo. They both were steady, dependable, players and stabilizing forces as mature young adults. I felt back then that they had qualities which surely should lead to success in their chosen fields. It turned out to be a safe prediction as Silver rose to the position of director of personnel for the prestigious

Bloomingdale's department store, and Bernardo demonstrated excellence as a mechanical engineer.

Stan "Bugs" Friedman was another departing player who I was to miss. Although a competent reserve guard, his witty personality and street-smart sophistication were his greatest contributions to the team. He was unusually quick with his quips and similarly shrewd in outlining money-making schemes. His sharp thinking, however, did extend to the basketball court. In the closing seconds of a close game in which we were ahead by just a couple of points, Bugs was trapped in the backcourt with no clear passing lane. He took the ball and threw it as high as possible without hitting the ceiling. While the ball was in the air, Stan calmly strolled off the court, and the final buzzer sounded.

Following his graduation from CCNY and law school, Stan became a prominent lawyer and effective politician. Politically, he rose through the Democratic Party ranks and ascended to the post of Bronx county leader. He continued his climb and was appointed deputy mayor in Ed Koch's administration. With shocking abruptness, he then suffered a crippling blow. He was implicated in a widespread scandal from which he could not escape. He was tried, convicted, and served time in prison. Since his release, Stan has shown typical determination and resiliency in rebuilding his life. He entered the business world and did very well. He has also been active in several humanitarian causes.

A far more significant change than losing three graduating seniors was about to happen to CCNY basketball. After a three-year leave of absence, the legendary Nat Holman was returning to coaching. Dave, who filled in so admirably in Holman's extended absence, would again be at the helm of the freshman/junior varsity. I felt bad for Dave and perhaps a little sorry for myself.

Coach Holman called a meeting of the returning players about a week before the NCAA-approved beginning of practice for the 1958–1959 season. He said that he wanted to greet us and share his practice format and his expectations concerning preparedness. For me, that brief conference was the first time that I ever saw Holman in person, although he claimed that he had been to a few of last season's games. Regardless, I was impressed with his dignified manner and distinguished appearance. More specifically, I was definitely intimidated by him.

It was plain to see that looking presentable was important to Nat Holman. Beyond being a handsome man, which he was, he was always impeccably dressed with never a hair out of place. His silvery mane was stylishly combed back and carefully cut each week. Although almost sixty years old, Coach Holman was slim, well-toned, and youthfully energetic.

His posture and gait exemplified grace, and his body language oozed with confidence. As for his speech, he sounded like someone educated at Cambridge or Oxford. It was hard to believe, and quite funny that he was raised on New York's Lower East Side and received his schooling within the city. There definitely was an arrogance about him, but to me, the trait wasn't distasteful. Nat Holman liked himself and enjoyed his status as a revered coach, an elder sports statesman, and one of basketball's all-time great players.

I never saw Nat Holman play, but from all accounts, he was one of the best. His name consistently appeared on the Ten Best Lists of outstanding players for the first fifty years of the twentieth century. Nearly six feet tall, he was a good-sized guard for that era. He was versatile, displaying superior skills on offense and defense. I have been told that his mental toughness and ability to outthink opponents was equal to his physical gifts. Holman played professionally for a number of clubs but was best known as a member of the Original Celtics, the finest team of its time. Interestingly, he continued to play professional basketball in his early years as coach of CCNY.

On the whole, playing for Nat Holman was an enriching and pleasant experience. From the very first practice, I knew that it would never be dull. He amplified his voice through a handheld megaphone and was highly animated in the way be moved about and demonstrated the points that he wanted to stress. His reputation attracted a constant stream of visitors to our practices. Included among the guests were his sportswriting friends, other coaches, and young people striving to become coaches and a parade of assorted observers. He always welcomed the visitors and rarely failed to put on a show.

None of us ever called him Nat, at least not to his face. I addressed him as "coach." Some referred to him as "professor," which strangely, he seemed to like. He presided over the team very formally, seldom communicating about anything other than what was happening on the court. Unlike Dave who welcomed lighthearted talk, we'd never attempt to chitchat with Coach Holman.

As a coach, he was a marvelous teacher. In our workouts, he frequently stopped play to correct errors and reinforced positive things that he wanted to emphasize. He was terrific at taking an individual and instructing him on the spot, either in front of the group or off to the side. His approach was flamboyant, articulate, and directly to the point. He wasn't the most patient person, particularly with those lacking talent. I and the majority of my CCNY teammates felt that he had a difficult time dealing with the vastly inferior post-scandal player as compared to his former elite athletes. If he was to inquire about a player's status as a student and infer that he should concentrate upon his studies, you could predict that the poor guy would never get off the bench. Similarly, if he called you an All-American, it was time to pack the bags and get out.

Holman was not a proponent of establishing intricate patterns or deploying a large number of plays. He taught and preached the fundamentals. His system was relatively simple: a basic framework which encouraged intelligence-free lancing and individual creativity. His basketball philosophy and the facets of the game that he constantly drilled comprised much of the foundation utilized by Red Holzman, a former CCNY star, in his successful NBA coaching career. The concepts of perpetual movement, excellent spacing and balance, the importance of seeing the ball at all times, and team unity–all things that made the Knicks of the late sixties and early seventies such a great team were derived from Holman's influence upon Red Holzman.

It's my opinion that Coach Holman's relatively loosely structured style was difficult for his lesser-skilled teams to master. The inability of some of his players to carry out what seemed so basic to Holman contributed to his impatience and further hampered their basketball performance. With regard to myself, however, we got along fine, and on the court he treated me with considerable respect. He told me of his reluctance to accept the jump shot as an effective and practical offensive weapon. He firmly believed that for most players, the two-hand set shot was easier to control. The coach failed to consider the startling difference in the time needed to get off a jump shot as opposed to the set shot, as well as the jumper's distinct advantage off the dribble. When I played, his attitude toward the jump shot softened, but he still contended that it was not for everyone. Yet he never discouraged me from shooting it nor did he ever criticize my technique. Unlike several of my teammates, I always had his support.

As terrific and in command as he was in the gym, he often became too excitable in the actual games. When he coached his great teams, there usually was a highly capable assistant such as Bobby Sands to keep things calm and help with the strategy. Ordinarily, he was very poor at remembering names and far worse during the heat of games. An incident that occurred in a past contest entailing Coach Holman's problem with names is a CCNY favorite. In a critical time, in a close game, he pulled a player off the bench, grabbed him by his shirt, and told him to "go in for that son of a bitch." The player reported to the scorer's table but quickly ran back to the bench, shouting, "Coach, which son of a bitch?"

Holman's locker room speeches were always spirited and sometimes unintentionally hilarious. During a half-time, he was comparing the hapless play of one player to the good performance of another. Staggering like a drunk, he pointed to the player who was the object of his anger. He bellowed, "What were you doing out there? You're not playing basketball. You're walking, talking, and squawking." He then messed the hair of Rudy Rimanich, the one who was playing well. Now Holman began moving like a graceful dancer. "Look at Rudy," he said. "He's helping us. He's out there sliding, gliding, and hiding." Sitting there, I pretended to cough in my towel to mask my laughter.

I was optimistic about the quality of our team and our chances for a successful 1958-59 season. Our two big men, Hector Lewis and Joel Ascher, were excellent rebounders and showed promise of becoming enforcers on defense. We added Guy Marcot, a junior guard, who like myself in the previous year, came out for the team as a walk-on and wound up a starter. Guy, a former Lafayette High School standout, was more the prototypical point guard than myself and was a perfect complement to my game. He was fast, smart, and totally team-oriented. Offensively, his driving ability was his best asset. Coach decided to insert Julio Delatorre, a third guard, into the starting lineup. I thought it was a sound idea as Julio jumped well, was capable of defending tall people, and presented another scoring threat.

Our bench, comprised mainly of green sophomores, was the big question mark. It was Holman's plan to bring the young players along slowly, hoping they would benefit from incremental increases in game experience. We, therefore, could ill afford to sustain injuries to our starters, especially at the beginning of the season.

Unfortunately, what we hoped to avoid hit us like a ton of bricks. Both Ascher and Lewis suffered serious leg injuries and played but sporadically. In addition, Hector was further sidelined due to academic problems. The raw players–Shelly Bender, Marty Egol and Barry Klansky, along with Hal Bauman, a veteran forced to play a big man's role–worked diligently and showed some promise but could not make up for the loss of Lewis and Ascher. The result was frustrating, inconsistent play and a record with losses slightly exceeding victories. Considering the difficult circumstances, I thought that Coach Holman held up admirably. He spent much time working with the sophomores, all of whom made significant individual progress. The fact was that they were outtalented and outsized against St. John's, NYU, Manhattan, Fordham, etc.

In the midst of the team's disappointing time, an incident occurred which was initially disturbing but soon became the humorous high point of the year. Herb Waller, an ex-marine and a reserve guard on our team, attended CCNY's downtown business school. He owned an old beat-up car that he sometimes drove to Manhattan from his Brooklyn home. Whenever he had the automobile at school, I would eagerly ride with him to practice. One afternoon, he parked the car at 137th Street, on the hill below Convent Avenue. That evening, when he went to retrieve it following practice, it was gone. He immediately filed a police report but had no success recovering the stolen vehicle. A few weeks later, after completing our usual subway trek, we were making the climb up that same hill. As we were walking, Herb saw his car being parked. Two men got out, locked the doors, and walked toward Broadway. We paused until they were out of sight. Luckily, Herb still had the car keys with him. He calmly strolled to the car, entered it, started the engine, and drove away. He then parked it at the south end of the CCNY campus, completing an unusual and exciting restealing of his own automobile.

My personal season was a productive one. I led the team in scoring averaging seventeen and a half points per game, which was approximately 30 percent of our low scoring squad's offensive output. I closed the season with a flourish, scoring a minimum of twenty points in each of our last five games, the best performances coming against nationally ranked St. John's (twenty-five points) and NYU (twenty-three points). I played close to the full forty minutes in most games, which was a problem in that I frequently ran out of gas in the second half. Coach Holman rarely took me out, and I was fearful of asking for a breather. The one time that I did, he forgot about me and left me on the bench for over ten minutes. For me, Holman was a great source of support and also a vocal booster. A sweet taste of his generous praise was evident in a *New York Times* preview of our team. The following was written: "Holman is high on Groveman, a junior whom he considers as accurate with a jump shot around the circle as anyone playing local college basketball." The accolades continued after a milestone triumph over St. Francis when Coach told the *New York Post* that "Marty Groveman is the ace of hearts in my deck." That St. Francis contest was Holman's six-hundredth as coach of CCNY. In it, I had the good fortune to overcome a one point deficit with eleven seconds left in the game. We were losing 63–62 when I was fouled as I drove to the basket. The referee called it a "one and one," ruling that I wasn't in the act of shooting. Fortunately, I made both shots, helping to cement a 64–63 victory. Incidentally, Holman's career record at that point was an outstanding 429 wins and 171 losses.

In mid-March, the icing on the cake for me came in the form of a wonderful surprise. The *New York Journal American,* a now defunct newspaper, informed me that I had been selected to their All-Metropolitan Basketball Team. I was invited to attend an awards dinner in which the local college and high school all-stars were honored. It was both strange and thrilling for me to be seated at the same table with such acclaimed players as Alan Seiden, Cal Ramsey, "Satch" Sanders, and my BRC pal, Tony Jackson.

The summer of 1959 was my last season in the Catskills. My Overlook busboy, Joel Jacobson, had a rating system for girls who he picked up in his Bensonhurst neighborhood. Girls' looks would be compared to the qualities of major league baseball players. A homely young lady would earn the name of a weak-hitting infielder or a pitcher with a losing record. Conversely, a very pretty girl would be labeled a "three-hundred-hitter" or a "twenty-game winner."

One Friday during the evening meal, he told me that "Hank Aaron" just walked into the dining room and was sitting at the station closest to the kitchen. Within a few minutes, I went into the kitchen and peeked to get a close look at the top-rated player. I immediately agreed with Joel's assessment. She was indeed an attractive girl. She was fine-featured and had dark brown hair and large expressive eyes. I learned that she was visiting the hotel under protest, having been dragged along to the Catskills by her parents.

I didn't approach her that evening but struck up a conversation after breakfast the next morning. Among other things I learned that her name was Helene. I asked her out for that night, and she accepted. We went with some of my lunatic Brooklyn friends to see a show at the nearby New Roxy Hotel. We had a great time, and I knew that I wanted to see her again. My only hesitancy was her age. She was entering her senior year at Jamaica High School and was not yet seventeen. In contrast, I was almost twenty-one years old and a college senior. Nevertheless, I asked for her phone number. As fate–or whatever one wants to call it–would have it, Helene and I did meet again. It was the start of a long and lasting relationship. We were married four summers later.

At summer's end, I was a little melancholy. I spent four wonderful summers in the Catskills. Like much of life's good things, it was not only fun but also a fabulous learning experience. As I said farewell to the Overlook, I knew that a special door was permanently closing. Real adult stuff lay ahead.

I had some important decisions to make. Firstly, by the end of the fall 1959 semester, I would have sufficient total credits and the requisite psychology courses to graduate. Unless I wanted to take all crap electives, which I would not do, January graduation was inevitable. Of course, I had every intention of playing my final year of basketball. I already did some groundwork and found out that it was permissible to take a concentration of graduate-level courses and retain eligibility. For me, this was better than perfect since I decided to apply for the CCNY master's program in clinical psychology. I loved every psychology class with the exception of Experimental Psychology, the research horror, and never attained any grade lower than A- in my major. It, therefore, made sense to pursue a career as a clinical psychologist. A slight hitch developed because the graduate program didn't admit students in midyear. In order to get around this detour, I agreed to register for the courses as a general studies graduate student. The gamble in doing this was that the credits would be worthless if I wasn't accepted to the master's program.

The great plan never had a chance. A large fly in the ointment appeared and put an end to the idea. That fly was the United States army. In actuality, the army's intent was good, as it was responding to a request that I put into motion. At that time, the country had a draft system for young, single, and able-bodied men. In an attempt to avoid serving two years, I, as did thousands of others, joined the army reserve. In doing this, the responsibility was to serve six months' active duty and receive the supplemental training for five and a half years in a reserve unit. I asked to have my number pushed up, figuring that I would be called to active duty in June following the school year. In my case, the army checked with CCNY about my status and learned that I would graduate in January. My luck, they then changed the original entry date and pushed the number up from June 1960 to the second week of February 1960, four months earlier and in the middle of the basketball season. My fate was firmly sealed.

Although it was late September and preseason basketball practice hadn't begun, I contacted Nat Holman and informed him of the situation. He reacted with disappointment but stated that he wanted me to play. My curtailed season would be fourteen games, ending on the last Saturday in January. Coach Holman brightened my mood when he informed me that I was his choice to be the captain of the team.

All signs pointed to a tough 1959–60 season for CCNY basketball. Aside from myself, only three returnees had significant varsity experience. These were Guy Marcot, Julio Delatorre, and Shelly Bender, a hustling but erratic front court player. A few that we were counting on for rebounding help dropped out due to academic ineligibility. A faint hope, however, was the arrival of three burly sophomores: Tor Nilson, Mike Gerber, and "Lefty" Cohen, all of whom played on Dave's very good freshman team. Aside from the experience factor, lack of size was the primary concern. Not a single player was taller than 6'5". Another positive addition was short and thin Teddy Hurwitz. He was a skilled ball handler, ferocious competitor, and a creative shot maker. His basketball intelligence, tenacity, and spirited personality all were significant factors in the team's performance. Many years after graduation, Teddy's dynamic personality and communicative excellence earned him the distinction of being chosen to serve as the commissioner of athletics for all of the City of New York colleges.

Once the season began, not surprisingly, we got off to a poor start. After seven games, we were two and five. We played hard and were never far behind but had a penchant for losing it in the closing minutes. Poor foul shooting, untimely turnovers, and committing foolish fouls–all indicators of an inability to deal with pressure–were some of the reasons for the disappointing record. Marcot and I were our two positive constants. Guy, in addition to his usual fine floor game, was averaging about fifteen. My shooting was consistently strong and were reflected in a more than twenty points per game average. Early on a December Sunday morning, my friend Shopper phoned me and had some shocking news. He heard on the radio that Nat Holman was taking an immediate leave of absence from CCNY due to illness. The report turned out to be true. At Monday's practice, Dave Polansky was once again the varsity basketball coach. I can't remember if Holman met with the team to offer any explanation or even to simply say good-bye. We also never learned the specific nature of his physical problem. We all knew, however, that this time, his departure was final.

Most of our players were happy with the change. For one thing, Coach Holman was tough on them. Secondly, many played for Dave as freshmen and liked his coaching style and personality. I too was a fan of Dave's but had no complaints, either about my treatment or what I had learned under Nat Holman. Right to the end he bestowed great praise upon me. In fact, to this day, I treasure the words that he said in the *New York Post*'s 1959–60 college basketball preview. Sportswriter Gene Roswell, quoting Holman, wrote, "Groveman was our Number One scorer last year and is even better now. He's a terrific shooter, as good as any around here now and would have made our past outstanding teams."

Nat Holman didn't fade away. He remained actively involved in basketball but in a new direction. He was highly instrumental in the development of the Maccabiah Games, the international sports competition for Jewish athletes. He spent considerable time in Israel and was as responsible as anyone for their emerging basketball fervor in Israel. He taught the game, gave countless instructional clinics, and spearheaded the drive to raise funds. His work was truly humanitarian. Monetary gain was not his motive. He was beloved in Israel and considered by many to be their basketball grandfather.

Through the years, I would sometimes meet Nat Holman at CCNY alumni athletic dinners and at other basketball functions. He always greeted me warmly, although there were times that he was slow to remember my name. Yet if he was with other people, he would always say something along these lines, "You see this lefty he could really shoot the ball." Frankly, I never got tired hearing such compliments.

Coach Holman lived to be ninety-seven years old. He spent his final years at a retirement residence where he sharpened his skills as a painter and produced some fine work. When I learned of his passing, out of respect, I felt it important to attend his funeral. I'm glad that I did. Many basketball luminaries were present, some delivering poignant eulogies. Nat Holman was far from perfect but contributed greatly to basketball and, in the bigger picture, was a historic American sports figure. I'm proud to have played a small part in his journey and to have been his last CCNY captain.

Dave stepped into the coaching spotlight without missing a beat. Amazingly, in a short period of time, he helped bring our record up to the breakeven level. It bugged me that I wouldn't be around to do my share to keep things going for the entire season. The army was just a few games away.

Under Dave's structured offense, the turnovers diminished dramatically. The guys no longer played scared or looked toward the bench every time a mistake was made or a shot was taken poorly. The sophomores, in particular, suddenly blossomed and were making positive contributions to the team. Tor Nilson got on a roll that was to continue for two more years as the college's star player. In fact, when he was finished, Tor's scoring and rebounding numbers were comparable to CCNY's all-time best.

Teddy Hurwitz began to get meaningful minutes and eventually started after my departure.

For reasons other than the contest alone, our game against Queens College was special to me. On the night that we played, Queens was dedicating its new Fitzgerald Gymnasium. Uncharacteristically, they also had an excellent team that season, supposedly the best of the New York City–run colleges. With our mediocre record and the noteworthy occasion, we were underdogs.

Minutes before game time, the gymnasium was packed and the atmosphere was festive. While warming up, I noticed someone waving to me. Much to my surprise, it was Helene, the Overlook's "Hank Aaron." She came to the game with her cousin, who was a Queens College student, and a few of his friends. I saw her a few times after the summer, and she knew that I was a senior at CCNY. What she didn't know was that I was on the basketball team. It just never came up in conversation. Anyway, standing there in my uniform, there was no time to make explanations. I enjoyed seeing her at the game and very much wanted to make a good impression. I was always motivated, but her presence was definitely added incentive to give it my best. There was to be no disappointment that evening. We played excellent basketball, and won an impressive victory. I had a hot shooting game and led the team in scoring. Helene's post game peck on the cheek prior to leaving the gym, was a fitting cap to a fulfilling and pleasant couple of hours.

The final game of my CCNY basketball career occurred on a snowy Saturday night, at our court against high-scoring Bridgeport University. I accepted the reality of my imminent entrance to the army and also that the game was the culmination of the realization of my boyhood fantasy. Yet on that momentous night, I was strangely emotionless. It was as if I was playing a role in a movie and what was taking place was not actually happening to me. A brief and unexpected pregame ceremony quickly changed all of that. It was announced that the game was my final one. I was presented with a gift and received a standing ovation from the large crowd. At that point, my emotions were fully awakened. It felt great but I had to bite my lip to keep from crying. It's a good thing I didn't have to speak.

The game was exciting and close. It looked for a while that we might upset the Tri-State League leaders. I had an outstanding first half scoring seventeen points on near perfect shooting. In the second half, Bridgeport made me the focal point of a "box and one" defense. I got a deuce within the first two minutes and was simply attempting to open things up for my teammates. Then, while getting back on defense a pass to a Bridgeport player went off his hands and bounded to the midcourt line. I had a good angle to the ball and dashed to pick it up. I succeeded and pushed it ahead to Marcot who took it on the run and scored an easy layup. In my sudden burst, I felt a sharp pain the back of my upper right leg. I knew instantly that I pulled the hamstring. I tried to play but I couldn't run, jump, or get free to shoot. I remained in the game for about five more minutes but was useless. My last game, which began so brilliantly, ended in a whimper. And to make matters worse, we lost by four. I finished with nineteen points and a pained heart that temporarily hurt more than my injured hamstring.

After the game, Dave and Max, our trainer, both congratulated and consoled me. They told me that I was in the select company of CCNY players whom they looked forward to watching. Dave added that I was a joy to coach and considered me as family. I received hugs and pats on the back from teammates and the managers. The best, however, was the reception I was given when I made one last walk from the locker room to the lobby of Wingate Hall. The assembled friends and families of the players broke into applause when they saw me. At that moment, all the pain was gone, and was replaced by the warmth of their affection. I exited the building confident that I had done a good job, not only that evening, but throughout memory filled years of basketball at CCNY.

As for my curtailed season, I was proudest of my consistency. My scoring average remained above twenty points per game and more importantly, I kept alive a streak where I scored in double figures in every game played during my career except for my sophomore Manhattan College debacle and the St. Francis box-and-one.

In terms of honors, which were definitely affected by playing a bit more than half of season, I received honorable mention for the All-Metropolitan and All-Tri-State League teams. Clearly, the most prestigious award, which I was not aware of until my discharge from the army, was my selection to the ECAC (Eastern Collegiate Athletic Conference) Scholar-Athlete Team. In a fall 1960 ceremony at CCNY, I was presented with a large gold medal that was encased in thick clear plastic. The medal depicted a young man reading a book. At his feet was a basketball. Getting it was quite a thrill. It stands to reason that it was also the award that meant most to my mother.

CHAPTER 5

In the Army

MY SIX-MONTH STINT in the Army began on February 13, 1960. As was the case for most inductees living in the northeast, I was stationed at Fort Dix. The post, located in New Jersey, was a major basic training center. I was assigned to F Company of the 2nd Training Regiment for the grueling eight-week combat preparedness program.

I pretty much got what I expected. The delightful package included being awakened at a ridiculously early hour, lousy food such as chipped beef on toast, better known as "shit on a shingle", low alcohol beer, and incessant marching and drilling. By far, for me, the constantly frigid weather was the greatest unanticipated nemesis. Fort Dix was no place to be in February and March, particularly if basic training was the primary mission. Unlike at home, you can't go indoors when the cold numbs your body. You stay out at the rifle range and continue the maneuvers until those in command decide it's enough. Most often, enough wasn't until dark. Even worse, lunch was usually served and eaten outdoors.

I remember eating ice cream in fifteen-degree weather. Not only did I eat it, but the wind would blow sand on the food, making it distastefully crunchy to eat. I was always so cold that returning to the dreary barracks was an answer to my prayers. It's funny how need makes one appreciate the tiniest pleasures.

By the fourth week of training, we were permitted to have Sunday visitors. That's when I knew that Helene really cared for me. Twice, she and my mother came down by bus from the New York City Port Authority. They brought me real food, the best of which was Hebrew National kosher salami. I shared it with Wilcox, my bunkmate from Arkansas, who had never before eaten kosher salami but quickly got hooked on it. The visits gave me something to look forward to and were wonderful morale boosters. However, after a month in the army, I felt as though I had been a soldier for my entire life.

Most of the sergeants in our company treated the recruits like dirt. One, however, definitely had a good heart beneath his crusty surface. His name was Hayes, and for whatever the reason, I knew from the start that he liked me. He rooted for me during the physical fitness proficiency tests and told me that I had a strong left arm after he saw me throw hand grenades. In reality, I was frightened of the darn things and, once pulling the pin, tossed them as quickly and as far as possible. Hayes would frequently get drunk when off duty. During these times, he would often lie on my bunk and talk about sports. One day, we were discussing basketball. I mentioned to him that it was my favorite recreational activity and that I played in college. He sat up abruptly and asked if I'd be interested in trying out for the 2nd Training Regiment Team. He said that the Fort Dix annual tournament would soon be held. I, of course, replied that I would be eager to play.

The next morning, Sergeant Hayes informed me that a tryout was arranged. Curious, I asked several questions pertaining to when it would take place and how I would get there. He told me that there was nothing to be concerned about and that I should just be ready to play. I wondered about what kind of basketball shape I'd be in. Until the army, I had never gone a month without playing basketball, not at least since Venty Lieb came upon the scene. More precisely, I never spent a week away from some basketball court. Peculiar, but perhaps in the back of my mind, I held some hope of playing a little hoops in the army because I brought along my sneakers.

That afternoon, I was picked up by jeep in the field during training. I was driven back to the barracks to wash up, change, and get my sneakers. From there, I was taken to a large field house that contained a modern gymnasium with an excellent basketball court. The Jeep driver introduced me to the coach, whose name I cannot recall. Warming up and at the beginning of the scrimmage, I felt heavy footed and totally out of synch. I didn't play particularly well and was obviously rusty but did eventually get a second wind. A feel for the game and a semblance of basketball movement also slowly returned. It was far from my best, but I made the team.

From that day forward, my army fortunes dramatically changed for the better. Although I wasn't picked up daily by jeep, I was excused early from field duty and driven by truck to the barracks to prepare for basketball practice or the games. Most often, I took an army bus from the 2nd Training Regiment to the gym. I guess I was the object of envy among the guys in my company because it was obvious that I was receiving favored treatment. Even so, I was never taunted by them nor experienced any hostile behavior. The worst that was thrown at me was playful questioning over the amount of money that I had to pay to get such a plush deal.

Although our regiment came in second in the tournament, my participation must have pleased some officers with clout. Initially, my MOS (Military Occupational Specialty), which was combat engineer, had me headed to Ft. Leonard Wood, Missouri, following basic training. However, newly revised orders called for me to be stationed at Fort Dix for the remaining months of active duty. Even more wonderful, I was going to be a mail clerk in C Company of the 2nd Training Regiment, a short walk down the road from my basic training unit. A mail clerk job for an army recruit is as good as it gets. The position, with the exception of one late OD per week, was an 8:00 AM to 5:00 PM responsibility, with no duty at all every other weekend. That meant a forty-eight-hour pass and a bus ride home twice each month. There could be no rational explanation for my extraordinary good luck other than basketball. It was definitely unfair to all my F Company buddies whose fate was determined by the usual impersonal army way. I, however, was not that principled to protest the sumptuous gift that I was given. I thanked Sergeant Hayes for starting it all. He gruffly pushed it aside but showed me a coy wink of the eye, which said so much without words. I also thanked God and was ever so grateful for my basketball fanaticism.

Only a day or two into my enjoyable mail clerk assignment, I received a phone call from a Sergeant Bill Volk. He said that he had seen me play in the post tournament and would like me to join a team that he was in the process of organizing. He further elaborated that he was to be its coach and that we would compete in the Mount Holly, New Jersey, summer league. We were going to represent the town of Browns Mills, a village located close to Fort Dix, where many career army personnel resided.

Our first practice was held in an old but adequate gymnasium on the grounds of Fort Dix. The team was loaded, easily as good as any squad on which I was a member. One of the players was a familiar face, someone whom I competed against in college and long admired throughout his illustrious high school and collegiate days. That person was NYU All-American Cal Ramsey. Cal, a shade over 6'4", had tremendous leaping ability and great strength. He was an equally fabulous rebounder and defensive player. He was also a prolific scorer, although not one regarded as a pure shooter. Like myself, Cal was a six-monther, eager to put in his time, freeing himself to continue pursuing an NBA career.

In that regard, I believe Cal got a raw deal. Flash forward from the army to civilian life, Cal played briefly for the Syracuse Nationals (the team that became the Philadelphia 76ers) and the Knicks. It's true that he was a "tweener," not really a guard and on the smallish side to play forward. Yet his excellent physical skills erased any size deficit when matched against taller forwards. In his short time in the NBA, he played well and shot respectably. I saw him at the Garden a few times and was impressed with his performance. Thankfully, Cal had other career options and elected to give up the elusive chase. For many years, he worked for the Urban League and, in time, became a respected radio and TV analyst for the Knicks and St. John's University. He also is employed by Madison Square Garden and works in a sports information capacity for his alma mater, NYU.

On our Browns Mills team, it was a pleasure to play with Cal Ramsey. He was as unselfish on the court as he was talented. In addition, his jump shot was a good one, certainly not the weakness that some basketball people claimed it to be. Off the court, he was a good guy, as was everyone on our squad. That formidable group featured 6'6" Lonnie West, a smooth and graceful former Boys High and Wagner College star and "Pappy" Baldwin and Bill Gray, two army sergeants whose specialties were dazzling ball handling and bone-jarring rebounding, respectively. Gray, at 6'3", had the defined muscles of a body builder but claimed that his sculptured build simply ran in his family. Others on the team who I still remember were Archie McCord, a long-armed athletic 6'4" forward and New York City friend of Cal Ramsey, and Ron Manwarren, a 6'6" free spirited Californian.

The team was outstanding, the best I had ever played on. We easily ran over the competition and finished the season with a perfect 15–0 record. As for my role, Pappy did most of the ball handling, making my primary offensive task to get to the open spots and be ready to shoot or to dish off when covered. I handled my responsibilities well as did my proficient teammates. We were the undisputed 1960 champions of the Mount Holly Mill Dam Park Summer League, New Jersey's premier park tournament.

As much fun as the games was the opportunity during the week to get off the base and do a little socializing. After each game, we would go for some beers and hoagies. The hoagie is the huge overstuffed sandwich which I, growing up in Brooklyn, knew as the hero. In southern Jersey and the Philadelphia area, it was called a hoagie. Those were good times, but not good enough to warrant remaining in the army. About a week or so after the summer basketball season, I happily received my honorable discharge and was headed home. I never again set foot in Fort Dix nor, with the exception of Cal, did I ever see any of my Brown's Mills teammates. At least two or three times yearly, I run into Cal at basketball-related functions. It's hard to believe that fifty plus years have passed since that pleasant summer of basketball and brews at Mount Holly, New Jersey. For both of us it is a blur that exists somewhere near the Twilight Zone.

CHAPTER 6

Back to the Real World

IN MID-AUGUST OF 1960, with the army behind me, I was back in Brooklyn. My priorities were Helene, graduate school, and a job. Basketball for the first time took a back seat to the realities of sudden adulthood. I was invited to work out a few times with the Scranton Miners of the Eastern Basketball League. I played okay but never hung around long enough to have a shot at making the team. Games in the Eastern League were played back to back on the weekends. I never considered making a serious commitment to play because I felt it would impede my nonbasketball lifetime priorities and goals.

I was accepted into the clinical psychology master's program at the uptown campus of CCNY. The graduate schedule made it possible to take a concentration of late afternoon and early evening classes. This enabled me to begin school no earlier than 4:00 PM, three days a week. Most important, the late start meant that I had time to work while attending the program.

I attained a substitute teaching license based on just six credits of education courses taken as an undergraduate. A high school friend who was already teaching at an elementary school told me about a vacancy due to a leave of absence for medical reasons. The principal preferred that the replacement be a male as the teacher who was on leave was one of the few men on the school staff. I interviewed for the position and was hired on the spot. I was now a fifth-grade teacher at PS 248, located in Bensonhurst, Brooklyn, just a few blocks from Lafayette High School.

The principal of PS 248, Florence Manbeck, was a stern and strikingly attractive middle-aged woman. At the start, I was by no means an accomplished teacher, but I was an instant hit with Mrs. Manbeck. This tough lady was sweet as sugar to me. My colleagues joked that I was the principal's pet, and indeed, I was her favorite. The other man on staff, Mr. Jacobs, was a fine teacher, about sixty years old. By contrast, my youth and vitality had to have been a factor in my favor.

In late fall, I joined an interesting basketball team. I began playing for the club representing Union Temple, one of Brooklyn's most prominent reformed synagogues. The temple was housed in an imposing high-rise building on Eastern Parkway, a wide tree-lined thoroughfare in the hub of the borough. It was directly across from Prospect Park, the Brooklyn Museum, the Botanical Gardens, and Grand Army Plaza, an architecturally heralded war memorial, which was the Brooklyn equivalent to France's Arch of Triumph.

Our team was headed by player-coach Kenny Kern, the temple's athletic director. Kenny also held the coaching position at Fort Hamilton High School, a picturesque Brooklyn school at the water's edge, overlooking Staten Island. In years to come, Kenny would make his mark as the high school coach of two of New York City's greatest players. These were future pros, the brothers Bernard and Albert King. As for Kenny's own basketball career, a 6'3" forward, he played for George Washington University. He was an effective unorthodox offensive player, possessing a sweeping hook shot which he could take on the run and an overhead two-handed pop shot. Personally, he was a handsome fellow with loads of charm and a good "rap" with the women.

For the first time in an organized setting, I was on the same squad with my good friend Syd Levy. Syd, an outstanding center at CCNY, graduated just before I began playing on the varsity. Long and skinny and just a shade under 6'10", Syd made up in good fundamentals what he lacked in natural ability. He was an intimidating defensive player and a formidable rebounder. Offensively, he took only high percentage shots and featured a competent baby hook and a short range angle jumper off the backboard. As an adolescent, Syd had some physical problems primarily involving his legs and didn't begin playing basketball until his senior year in high school. He attended Boy's High but, with raw skills and no experience, wasn't ready to play on this playoff contending team. Through persistent hard work and an aptitude for learning the game, he made himself into a fine player. A highlight among his many achievements was playing for the USA Maccabiah Team and winning a gold medal in the tournament held in Israel.

Syd is also one of the wittiest and, at times, zaniest people I have known. His sense of humor stretches from the tongue-in-cheek variety to extreme slapstick. He's the only one I've ever seen beat a street beggar to the punch by asking him for a dime for a cup of coffee. The confused unfortunate stared at Syd, collected himself, and said, "You're a nice guy, you big son of a bitch." Perhaps Syd's funniest bit was one that occurred at the Nevele Hotel in the Catskills. Syd was standing in the swimming pool in about six feet of water, which for him was about chest high. A little old man in his bathing suit approached the pool. In his thick Jewish accent, he called out to Syd, "How's the water?" Syd shouted back, "It's fine." The man then asked, "Is it deep?" Without missing a beat, Syd responded, "I'm standing." Hearing those words of encouragement, the man joyfully jumped into the pool near the spot where Syd was standing. The expression of horror on the poor gentleman's face as he sunk beneath the surface was something that I will never forget. Syd, of course, came to the rescue.

Lenny Sherman, another friend, joined our Union Temple team after finishing his playing days at LIU. A speedy 5'8" guard, Lenny had one of the best crossover dribbles in the metropolitan area. He also could hang in the air for what seemed to be an eternity, giving him excellent options to either shoot or pass the ball. In high school, at Jefferson, Lenny's role was to get the ball to Tony Jackson or to the other prolific scorers. As a result, it was a surprise whenever he took a shot. This was not, however, the case at LIU, where he averaged nearly twenty points per game and exhibited a vastly improved jump shot. This was added to his already fine floor game, and gluelike defense.

It was great fun playing for Union Temple. Our team had a winning record, and we had chemistry and camaraderie, both on and off the court. Kenny scheduled several games against military-affiliated teams. These were always challenging as the army guys were very physical and in tremendous condition. In one of our toughest games, which we lost by a few points, our opponent was West Point and was played at the army base at Fort Hamilton. We led for most of the game but were so fatigued by their relentless pressure that most of us didn't have the stamina to play offense in the closing minutes. I was one of the few still firing away while my teammates remained in the back court saving their waning energy for defense. In later years, when I'd run into Kenny Kern, he would tell this story about my one-man offense at Fort Hamilton.

In another memorable incident, we missed the ferry to Governor's Island, where we were going to play the Fort Jay team. We took a later boat, changed into our uniforms on the ride over, and got to the game about 10:00 PM. We were given about a minute to warm up and then began play before a very hostile crowd. Go figure it, we were terrific from start to finish and won easily. We celebrated with a couple of beers on the ferry ride back to Manhattan.

My first year of real adulthood turned out to be a good one. Helene and I became engaged in the spring of 1961 and were planning to get married the following June. Graduate school was going extremely well as my grades were almost all As. I greatly enjoyed the psychology course content, especially those classes in abnormal psychology and diagnostic clinical testing. At PS 248, I was getting the hang of teaching fifth graders and also liked the kids that I taught. The one thing about the job that irked me was the meager $4,800 annual salary.

In that summer of 1961, I was unable to obtain a permanent teaching assignment, but I worked sporadically as a substitute in the all-day public schools recreational program formally called Vacation Day Camp. This relaxed schedule afforded me much time to play basketball. It enabled me to become a regular on courts at Manhattan Beach, the 1960s most amazing outdoor basketball playground. It was clearly the mecca of Brooklyn summer hoops.

Manhattan Beach is located on the Atlantic Ocean, about a mile to the east of Brighton Beach and a shorter distance, directly south of Sheepshead Bay, the renowned Brooklyn fishing port. The Manhattan Beach community is residential, consisting mainly of expensive private homes and tree-lined streets. On weekends, from Memorial Day through Labor Day, street parking is prohibited. The beach parking lot is relatively small so that by 9:30 AM on a hot day, it would be filled to capacity. When this occurred, the beach crowd would either have to park in Sheepshead Bay or take public transportation and walk across the bay's foot bridge to Manhattan Beach. The basketball courts are situated about one hundred feet from the main entrance, on the west side of the concrete walk, leading to the sand and the ocean.

The basketball scene at Manhattan Beach was unlike anything that I had ever seen. On a typical weekend day, hundreds of people encircled court number one, the spot where the main action was happening. In the throng were players, spectators, scouts, and recruiters and lots of basketball groupies. Many arrived early, equipped with beach chairs, to get an upfront view of the games. It was as much a great social gathering as it was a wonderful place to play basketball.

In the morning hours, all six courts were so crowded that three-man half-court games prevailed. Full court would be played late in the afternoon when guys had enough of the sun and surf.

I rarely had anything left in my tank to go for a second helping of hoops. Losing on the main court generally meant a very long wait to get on again. In order to be successful, a team needed two good scorers and one "killer," someone who loved to bang bodies, could dominate the boards, and played intensive interior defense. I, naturally, was in the shooters category and learned to master the nuances of the beach baskets and the critical wind factor. On that court, in an attempt to lessen the effect of the wind, I became proficient at shooting the jumper off the backboard, particularly from the left side.

Manhattan Beach attracted the area's high-quality players. Most were prominent present and former New York City high school and college basketball stars. Among the regulars were Mark Reiner (NYU), Nick Gaetani (Brooklyn College), the Gecker twins, Leon and Harold (Seattle), Billy Galanti (North Carolina), Stan Feldsinger and Dave Newmark (Columbia), Richie Goldberg (Mississippi Southern), Tito Ades and Mike Levine (CW Post), Stu Kirsner (Providence), Mark Hassen (Utah State), Steve Karmiol (LIU), Mark Turenshine (St. Francis), and Neil Flamm and Hank Lam (Pace). I reacquainted myself and strengthened friendships with Charlie Hoffman and Mel Kessler (Muhlenberg College), whom I played with in the Catskills. Then there were the guys lacking name recognition, whose performances were among the best in the park. One of these players was "Duke" O'Connell, a brawny 6'4" New York City fireman whom I loved to have on my side. He got to the loose balls, seemed to capture every rebound, took only the highest percentage shots, and never made a mistake on the court. Lastly, there were the special weekend celebrities such as Connie Hawkins and Jack Molinas, who would put on a great show whenever they appeared.

It was at Manhattan Beach that I first met and played with my friend George Bruns. George, who is about eight years my junior, was a skinny kid from St. Augustine's High School, who would ride to the beach on his bicycle with a baseball glove usually dangling from the handlebars. At a slender 6'0", he possessed catlike quickness and multiple sudden shifts of speed. I believed from the start that he was going to be a good player at Manhattan College. He continued to shine in the Eastern League and capped it off by realizing his basketball dream as a member of the ABA, pre-Dr. J-led New York Nets. George played effectively when given the opportunity but was unable to crack the starting backcourt of "Super" John Williamson and Bill Melchionni.

Unfortunately, George was unable to truly show the extent of his marvelous offensive skills in the ABA. He was a great jump shooter with flawless mechanics. His ability to ready himself to shoot as he received the ball was equal to the very best. George had great range but was just as devastating taking the short jump shot off the dribble. He was uncanny at moving from full stride to a complete stop without ever being close to committing a traveling infraction. As a jump shooter, George was the ultimate picture of grace and square-up consistency.

I became friends with George when I moved to Long Island, where he also resides. In his nonbasketball career, George had originally been a teacher and then for several years worked as a broker in the stock market. He has since returned to the educational field and is a math professor at Nassau Community College.

In addition, he has enjoyed success as a coach, with several teams on a few different levels. One of these was developing outstanding women's basketball teams at Nassau CC. For over a decade, he has been the boys' varsity coach at Manhasset High School. Known as one of the premier lacrosse programs in the US, he has brought glory to Manhasset basketball as he has led his teams to two Nassau County championships.

George's multifaceted involvement extends to one more basketball-related activity. For almost forty years, he has been director of the Bruns Basketball Camp on Long Island. I have been fortunate to be on his staff for many of the summers and presently serve as the program's coordinator. We have both an excellent personal and working relationship. George Bruns was a terrific player and is an equally outstanding person.

On weekends, Helene and I would frequently be joined at the beach by Syd and Elaine Levy. We would pack lunch, fill a cooler with beer, and be off to Manhattan Beach by 8:30 AM. Once there, Syd and I would play first and then catch up to the girls and the beers in late morning or early afternoon. We maintained this routine even after Elaine gave birth to Howard, their first of three children. On one hot July day, we spotted our friend Shopper talking to a group of pretty high school girls. Shopper who was single and a nice-looking fellow, taught at a Flatbush junior high school. The young women were his former students. Syd, always the comedian, picked up baby Howard and walked over to Shopper. In an annoyed tone of voice, he blurted out, "Merv [Shopper's real but little used name], I'm tired of watching your kid. Please take him." With that, Syd handed Howard over to Shopper and walked away. Poor stumbling Shopper was beet red but regained his composure and explained that it was a prank. As for Howard, he too got over the trauma of being given to a stranger by his father. He grew up to be a wonderful man and an excellent basketball player. Howard, a 6'10" center, started on Princeton's Ivy League championship teams of the mid-1980s. He was on the Princeton clubs that gave major scares to UNLV and Georgetown. After college, Howard played professionally in Israel and Australia and was a longtime assistant to his Hall of Fame college coach, Pete Carril, at his alma mater. Even when Howard achieved success in business, he never lost his coaching fervor. At present, he supplements his primary job by being at the helm of the Mercer County Community College basketball team, a perennial high-quality New Jersey Junior College championship contender.

At summer's end, things were pretty much status quo. I continued the master's program in psychology at CCNY and returned to PS 248 for another year of teaching. I moved up a grade with the class that I taught the previous year. Now, they were sixth graders, preparing for graduation and the transition to junior high school. Mrs. Manbeck sweetened the job by providing me with the opportunity to teach physical education to the fifth- and sixth-grade classes. I never requested the assignment, although she knew that it was something that I would enjoy doing. On the relationship front, Helene and I set a June twenty-third wedding date and were shopping for furniture. I also obtained a driver's license, which enabled me to use Helene's car on a regular basis. She encouraged me to take it, especially on the weekends, in order save time traveling between Brooklyn and Queens.

Once again, I found a new basketball stage. At Manhattan Beach, Charlie Hoffman and Mel Kessler asked if I'd be interested in playing in the Bensonhurst JCH (Jewish Community House) Open League. Although I had never set foot in the JCH, I heard the basketball played there was of excellent quality. Sandy Koufax, a Bensonhurst native, prior to his baseball stardom, was a regular at the JCH. He had great jumping ability, and, in fact, went to the University of Cincinnati on a basketball scholarship. One of Sandy's JCH teammates was Sid Youngelman, a hulking lineman for the Washington Redskins who displayed surprising agility on the basketball court for a man of his girth.

As for me, playing at the JCH was the perfect situation. The open league games primarily took place on Sunday afternoons with a few held as special Saturday evening events. This schedule did not at all conflict with graduate school or the library research time that the program demanded. It also enabled me to gracefully sever my athletic affiliation with Union Temple. Those games entailed some travel and were played on weekdays. I enjoyed the Union Temple experience, but from a standpoint of available time, it was impractical for me to continue playing.

The JCH was far more than just an athletic club. The blocklong facility on Bay Parkway was a major center of athletic, social, and religious activities within the Bensonhurst community. From my limited perspective, it was a class operation productively serving an age range from childhood to senior citizen. Within the athletic sphere, there was a tremendous variety of programs conducted on a nonstop basis. The JCH's athletic director, Milt Gold, did a fabulous job of developing competitive leagues at varying age and ability levels. This was accomplished in the face of meager physical resources. The JCH had two band-box gymnasiums–the main one at basement level and an upstairs auxiliary gym which doubled as an auditorium. He was equally adept at public relations, as the JCH leagues were regularly written about in the local newspapers. "Coach" Gold as he was respectfully called by all at the "J" exemplified the pride felt at the JCH by its members. In my time spent there during the 1960s, it was a very special place.

I joined a good team in a top-level league. Each squad featured guys who played in college, many of whom I completed against at CCNY or knew from Manhattan Beach. My team's top players, other than Charlie Hoffman and Mel Kessler, were Nick Gaetani, Lenny Schroeder, Gary Kaufman, and Barry Epstein. I also brought Syd Levy along with me, who was able to make some of the games.

Gary Kaufman and Barry Epstein were all-city players from New Utrecht and Lafayette High Schools respectively, who in college got tainted in the Jack Molinas scandal. Neither Gary, a guard at the College of the Pacific, nor Barry, a forward at the University of Utah, completed their college careers, which were interrupted by their alleged association with gamblers. It was a subject that was never brought up in their presence, and they similarly refrained from talking about the blemish on their reputation.

Lenny Schroeder and Nick Gaetani were cocaptains at Brooklyn College. Lenny, a muscular 6'4" with a stoic game face, was outstanding at rebounding and defense. Nick, a 5'10" rubbery guard, was easily one of Brooklyn College's all-time finest players. He was a marvelous court general with tremendous speed, catlike reflexes, and excellent dribbling skill. Offensively, his forte was his slithery driving ability. He had a decent jumper, although the shot was not on par with the otherwise elite status of the rest of his game. Still, he belonged in the company of the best guards from major schools within the metropolitan area. For me, it was a joy to play with Nick Gaetani.

We won the JCH championship, beating out a team comprised of homegrown Bensonhurst guys from Lafayette and New Utrecht High Schools. Several of them went on to play for NYU and American University. I did well but never really felt completely comfortable. I was an addition and newcomer to an already established team that was deep in guards. Nick and Gary were an excellent backcourt duo that didn't need a third player, especially one with a scoring mentality, vying for time. Therefore, after the season, I decided that I wouldn't return. Happily, there was an opportunity to be a part of a new team, on which I would play for several years and have great fun and success.

I have no idea who it was that showed such a lack of imagination by naming our team the Cobras. Yet, the name turned out to be appropriate, as our bite was sudden and deadly. We were an awesome offensive team, frequently scoring over a hundred points. We played an up-tempo style but far more intelligent to be categorized as pure "run and gun." We deployed three guards, consisting of Mark Reiner, Julie Cohen, and me. Julie was an all-city player at Erasmus and started in the backcourt for the University of Miami, where one of his teammates was a pretty fair player by the name of Rick Barry. Once again, Charlie, Mel, and Syd came along for the new ride. A bit later, we added Anton Muhlbauer, a relentless 6'4" forward who was an excellent rebounder and an offensive force around the basket. He was one of the city's best at Lincoln High School and accepted a scholarship to play for the Wolfpack of North Carolina State. Unfortunately, as it happened to so many others that I have mentioned, his college career was truncated by scandal implication.

Some more needs to be said about Julie Cohen and Mark Reiner, two special players. Although not a particularly tall guard (about 5'10"), Julie was exceptionally strong. This power enhanced his ability to penetrate and mix it up with the big guys. It was most difficult to upset his balance or to jar him from the ball. He displayed great court vision, which augmented his superior passing skills. Julie was a fierce defensive player with quick feet and hands and was a master at coming up with steals. If Julie was a little more accurate as a shooter, I believe he could have made it to the professional level.

Mark was an exceptional offensive player, an innovator who could always create his own shot even though he didn't possess great speed or leaping ability. His game had the flair and the spontaneous originality of a poor man's "Earl the Pearl" Monroe. Unlike me who scored 90 percent of my baskets on jump shots, Mark hit on jumpers, one handers, hook shots, and an assortment of drives. For most other players, such shot selection would be considered to be mindless heaves. In his case, this array constituted high percentage chances. Mark and I were a highly potent one-two scoring punch. Finally, although his reputation was built on his offensive proficiency, Mark was mean and effective on defense.

Earlier, I wrote about Mark Reiner's scintillating personality. He was gregarious, always with a smile, a hearty greeting, and a good story. I often thought of him as a natural salesman, one who could make you consider buying shares in the Brooklyn Bridge. These qualities, along with his astuteness, were instrumental in his eventual success as a teacher and a coach.

Mark's profession was in the field of education, specifically a teacher of physical education at Canarsie High School. For many years, during the 1960s and '70s, he was also Canarsie's basketball coach and earned a reputation as one of the best in New York City. His teams at the relatively young Brooklyn high school were consistent playoff contenders and twice attained the ultimate distinction by winning the city championship. Some of Mark's outstanding players excelled beyond high school. The star of his first championship team was Lloyd Free (aka World B-Free), whose unique offensive wizardry continued in the NBA, primarily as a high-scoring performer for the Philadelphia 76ers. Smooth-as-silk Geoff Houston also became a capable guard for the Cleveland Cavaliers and the New York Knicks. Others such as Ty Ladson (Texas A&M), Curtis Redding (Kansas State and St. John's), and O'Neil Tarrant (North East Texas State) didn't make it to the NBA but were standouts at the college level.

In the late seventies, Mark's itch to move up the coaching ladder led him to college and the Midwest. He took a leave of absence from his teaching position, packed up the family, and headed to the hinterlands. Within a short time, he obtained a significant assistant coaching job at formidable Kansas State University. Mark quickly established a solid reputation there and was so highly regarded that he was named head coach when Kansas State's coach Jack Hartman accepted the top slot at Oklahoma State University. It wasn't, however, meant to be as Hartman had a change of mind and decided to stay at Kansas State. At that point, a very disappointed Mark Reiner felt it was no longer feasible to remain as an assistant coach. Once again, he and the family picked up stakes and returned to their Brooklyn roots.

Mark was no longer in the big time, but in 1981, he did land a college head coaching position. He took the job at Brooklyn College where the basketball program had been floundering at the Division III level. He immediately helped to turn things around as Brooklyn became a top team within the CUNY Conference (City University of New York) and in the general category of Division III Schools. In his best season, Mark led the Kingsmen to a national ranking of third in Division III. He also became a full-time member of the Brooklyn College faculty.

The true measure of Mark Reiner the man was poignantly revealed through his battle against cancer. With little warning, in his early fifties, Mark went from a healthy robust person who was running a few miles daily to a very sick individual whose life was imperiled by an unforgiving disease. A malignant tumor was found in Mark's abdomen. Attempts to quell the growth and spread of the cancer necessitated that he undergo arduous radiation and chemotherapy. He suffered great pain, significant weight loss and weakness, and the terrible bodily changes caused by the illness and the radical medical treatment. The cancer traveled and soon appeared within his lymph system. The prognosis for a recovery was bleak.

It is most remarkable that through it all Mark's spirit never sagged. As fragile as he may have sounded on the telephone or as ghastly pale was his appearance, he never gave up. I know in my case that whenever we spoke, he brightened my somber mood. He was so indomitable that he made believers out of those of us who were prepared for the inevitable.

Between his trips to the hospital, he also continued to work. Irv Bader, a dedicated friend, and the head of adaptive physical education for New York City's handicapped students, assigned Mark to a teaching position in special education. The job spared Mark some of the physical exertion ordinarily identified with the teaching of gym classes but made use of his proven expertise in the area of fine and gross motor development. His special students adored him, and Mark, in turn, remained productive and needed.

It is wonderful that Irv Bader was in a position where he could help Mark and at the same time enrich the adaptive physical education program. Years before, they became ball-playing buddies at the Williamsburg YMHA. Mark worked there part-time, and Irv was a regular in the ferocious Sunday morning workouts. Irv, in his active playing days, was outstanding at Erasmus High School and then became a basketball Hall of Famer at Yeshiva University. Of all his many achievements, perhaps his greatest contribution was his major role in the development of the Special Olympics for mentally retarded children. For many years, Irv chaired and coordinated Special Olympics involvement at the New York City Board of Education. He traveled extensively, helping to organize and conduct the games held throughout New York State and to promote the most worthwhile program, which has since attained national prominence.

Concerning Mark, his doctors attempted to locate a compatible bone marrow donor. When a match could not be found, it was decided that it would be worth a try to use some of his own healthy bone marrow. Against overwhelming odds, the delicate procedure worked. Mark slowly regained his strength and his vigor. Remarkably, all signs of the cancer disappeared.

For a few years, Mark remained in remission enjoying life to the fullest, particularly his daily round of golf. He decided to retire and savor more time to spend with family and friends. But the cancer did return, and this time, it was unrelenting. It spread and ravaged his physical being, although it could not damage his spirit. Mark died in the summer of 1997. At the darkest moments, Mark displayed tremendous courage, the kind we read about or see at the movies. For me, he was the ultimate role model, worthy of the highest admiration.

Getting back to the action at JCH, in the four years that our team, the "Cobras," competed in the open league, we won three championships and lost only once. That one defeat was in overtime in the final game of the playoffs. Although each team at the "J" was competitive and had players with college experience, our major rivals clearly were the Stars, a squad slightly younger than us and comprised of guys mainly from the Bensonhurst community. They were maniacal in their intensity, playing each game in suicide mission style. One of their better players and certainly their emotional leader was Dave Tawil, nicknamed "Ditto." He was the most combative opponent that I ever faced. A friendly and decent person off the court, he was a man possessed once the whistle blew. At 6'1" with a competent and versatile array of skills, he didn't really need the anger and provocation to be an effective player. Yet anytime we went up against Ditto, the mood was ugly and a step away from a brawl.

Ditto's teammates caught his fervor, played hard and rough, and sometimes became uncharacteristically hostile. The best of the Stars was Ed Mazria, a smooth and talented 6'6" forward. Ed had a terrific college career at Pratt Institute, a school renowned for art and engineering, not basketball. He, however, was so outstanding that he became a draft choice of the Knicks. Freddie Grasso, a hard-nosed 6'0" guard was another of the Stars standouts. He was a fine player at Lafayette High School and excelled in both basketball and football at Hofstra University.

The guys who did the digging under the boards and had a knack for getting the garbage baskets were Bobby Feinstein, a very good player at Lincoln High School, and LIU's hefty Ken Gershon. We prevailed over the Stars most of the time but not without battle scars. Our games were wars. When I think back upon them, I now have fond memories. Playing in the actual contests, however, wasn't always my idea of leisurely weekend fun.

CHAPTER 7

Marriage, a Few Career Decisions, and Parenthood

HELENE AND I got married on June 23, 1962. We lucked out with an apartment, as we were spared the task of hunting for a suitable place to live. We moved into the apartment occupied by my brother and sister-in-law who bought a home in Oceanside, Long Island. Our first nest was three and a half comfortable rooms in the upper floor of a two-family house on Avenue K, a short block away from Kings Highway, one of Brooklyn's busiest and best known streets. Our landlady was a pleasant eccentric widow who made no demands upon us and gave us ample privacy. All things considered, it was an ideal apartment for newlyweds.

My big decision entailed graduate school and my future as a teacher. Although I was closing in on the master's degree, clinical psychology had lost its luster. I was somewhat disillusioned by what I perceived as the absence of scientific objectivity within the field. In the advanced courses, I studied theories proposed by

Freud, Jung, Adler, etc. The concepts of one frequently clashed with the beliefs of another, and it was not uncommon for each to debunk or trash their rivals' perspectives. The field of psychology was great fun for me, but oh so subjective. I began to see much of it as a fascinating parlor game. I finally decided to make practical use of my training and knowledge of psychological concepts and become a school psychologist.

The position of school psychologist entails conducting psychological testing, providing counseling to troubled children, and recommending behavioral and instructional approached for difficult and underachieving students. I was temporarily enthused at the prospect of being assigned as a school psychologist within the New York City Board of Education.

The shift to school psychology was accompanied by a change in my teaching situation. It was most difficult for me to leave PS 248. I was treated like royalty by Mrs. Manbeck and the staff and also had great affection for the children. However, out of the blue, an opportunity arose to teach in a special education school, which was much more related to my academic preparation and targeted career objective. I accepted a teaching position beginning the fall 1962 semester at PS 617, a newly organized "600 school" for socially maladjusted and emotionally disturbed pre-adolescent and adolescent boys.

Interestingly, the person who got me the job was a childhood friend, Lew Burke. He taught in the "600 school" and was transferring to PS 617. Teaching was just an income supplement for him as he was a professional boxer. A little guy of 5'6" and 140 pounds, as an amateur, he was the New York City Golden Gloves lightweight champion. In his pro career, he was moving up and fighting six round preliminary bouts. Lew, as tough as nails, was perfectly suited to manage the rebellious antisocial 600 school students. These schools attempted to educate the most angry and violent kids in the city. All schools in this category were assigned a number in the 600 series. Each teacher and administrator assigned to such a school received an annual bonus of $600, which was popularly referred to as "combat pay."

The boys at our school would jokingly say that they would behave for Mr. Burke because "he is crazier than us." They knew that he could not be pushed. I, on the other hand, was unable to survive on brawn alone. For me, succeeding as a "600 school" teacher was a great challenge. At the beginning, I was tempted to throw in the towel, but I persevered, gained the respect of the students, and eventually made it work.

The school was located on Stagg Street in the Williamsburgh section of Brooklyn, a neighborhood that was not exactly a garden spot even back in the 1960s. PS 617 occupied the physical plant which previously was PS 36, a middle school. The building was considered too antiquated to continue operating as a mainstream school but was acceptable for our reject student population. Some classroom improvements, mainly in the form of additional industrial arts shops, were made. The renovations were designed to improve the instructional age appropriateness of the facility to meet the needs of our students. Regardless, it was to become my second home for more than fifteen years.

Basketball-wise, I entered a phase of afterschool teacher workouts. The runs were not up to the quality that I had been accustomed to in terms of the number of good players but were spirited, balanced, and competitive. Uppermost, they were convenient, generally beginning at 4:00 or 5:0 PM and ending about that time that Helene came home from work. For several years, when school was in session, I played in these games once or twice each week. Over the course of time, I was invited to participate in several school-affiliated workouts. It was also easy to avoid conflicts as each took place a different day.

The run that I joined in most regularly was at Junior High School 263, situated in the heart of Brownsville at the intersection of Sutter Avenue and Chester Street. Play was intense, frequently overly physical, and marked by heated arguments despite the off-court camaraderie of the group. Jerry Keitel, the guy who usually volunteered to guard me, ranked at the top of the "hatchet men." He clutched and grabbed and worked me over real good but rarely was successful at preventing me from scoring. Jerry, a former Brooklyn College player, was a good set shooter and was dangerous if left alone. His best assets, however, were his intangibles: his insane tenacity and refusal to accept defeat. I restrained my anger over his tactics, mainly because I felt that they were beyond conscious control and were incapable of being changed. Regardless of what occurred during the heat of battle, Jerry always shook my hand at the end of the workout.

Norm Wasserstein and Dave "Red" Tomberg, veteran teachers at Junior High School 263, also transferred to a "600 school." Our common interest led to the development of lasting friendships. Norm, a fundamentally sound basketball player of modest ability, is an outstanding tennis player. His career as an educator has been a distinguished one. For years, he was the supervisor of guidance and counseling for schools serving the severely handicapped. Dave, like Norm, excels at tennis but was considerably more skilled at basketball. He was deceptively strong and had a powerful inside game. It was too bad that he was just 6'0". Had he been a few inches taller, he could have played forward at a high-level program.

The run that was most difficult for me to make was clearly the one that featured the best players. Nick Gaetani invited me to play at a school in Manhattan, in the Chinatown area. Most of the participating teachers had college basketball experience. Nick, an indefatigable blur, set the pace for nonstop fast break basketball. The workouts were exhilarating but unfortunately were impractical for me. Driving to Manhattan from Brooklyn in late afternoon meant crawling through traffic followed by difficulty finding a parking space. It made sense to settle for lesser action closer to home.

Kenny Kern, my teammate and coach when I played for Union Temple, got me a two-evening-per-week recreational job at a Brooklyn Community Center. I was actually hired by the district supervisor of recreation. That individual was Norm Drucker, who was better known in his other work as a respected NBA referee. He assigned me to PS 11, which was on Washington Avenue in Bedford-Stuyvesant, a neighborhood that was a hotbed of basketball. By far, basketball was the center's most popular activity.

At the onset, I was somewhat uncomfortable at the school. I was the only white person there, be it staff or member. Jimmy Adams, the center's director and a kindly and perceptive person, recommended that I take part in the half-court games primarily to develop rapport with the attending teenagers. It was a great suggestion as it really helped to break the ice and overcame the unspoken barrier that I believed was present.

Through the language of basketball, I gained acceptance and respect. The center's young members called me Mr. Lefty, acknowledging my left-handed jump shot.

The district ran a league for high school–aged boys who were not on any organized day school team. Each school was involved and drew from a large pool of talented although mainly undisciplined athletes. Adams asked me to coach the squad at PS 11. Because of the tendency toward individualistic play, it was difficult to mold a unified team. Some of my potentially better players quit rather than to submit to the structure that I was attempting to impose. A few with good skills didn't grasp what the game was really all about. As an illustration, a player would shout "in your face," gloating over one blocked shot when the guy he has been guarding has dominated him throughout the game. In time, our PS 11 team did become a solid unit. However, we never won the district championship. Old friend Nurlin Tarrant at PS 31 was the most consistent winner. Also, in the hunt were the center teams coached by two of my basketball buddies, Tony Jackson and Solly Walker.

A funny thing happened on the way to becoming a school psychologist. Although I attained the master's degree and a school psychologist license, I never worked a day as a clinician or diagnostician. Instead, I took a slightly different yet similar route. My graduate studies and teaching experience qualified me to take the examination to be licensed as a guidance counselor. The salaries of counselors and psychologists were comparable. In addition, guidance counselors worked a shorter day and had more opportunities within the system for summer and after-school employment. Perhaps I viewed things from a narrow perspective, but I made my choice and soon passed the test and was issued a license as guidance counselor.

As my school did not have an available line for a guidance counselor, I was offered and accepted an assignment to an elementary school's special education program entitled Junior Guidance. I was set to reluctantly leave PS 617. It was flattering that my principal, Irv Goldberg, was upset at the prospect of my imminent departure. He appealed to the special education hierarchy at Board of Education headquarters and presented a case regarding the school's need for a second guidance counselor. It was definitely a long shot, but somehow, at the eleventh hour, a reprieve was granted. Our director, Sidney Lipsyte, approved the allocation and reassigned me to PS 617 as a guidance counselor. Naturally, I was overjoyed. Both Lipsyte and Goldberg told me that I possessed supervisory potential and should enroll in a certified graduate program in school administration and supervision. I took their advice, and once again, it was back to school.

Although I had little day-to-day contact with Mr. Lipsyte, whenever I did see or speak with him, he displayed a fatherly concern. Apart from board of education business, he was interested in my basketball background. He informed me about his son, Robert, who had a sports connection, not as an athlete but through his writing. Coincidentally, I got to know him as a fellow reservist, and we participated together in weekend training sessions. Robert Lipsyte worked hard at his craft and became a highly respected sportswriter for the *New York Times*. In more recent years, he has been freelancing and expanded his scope beyond sports. He is an award-winning writer, one of the best around.

At home, a most important event occurred. Our son, Jon, was born on December 7, 1965, Pearl Harbor Day. He was slightly jaundiced and had to remain at the hospital after Helene was discharged. We were sad and depressed when we left the hospital without our baby. Thankfully, our heartbreak was temporary. His condition soon improved, and we were permitted to bring him home. Jon was an adorable, bright-eyed infant who ate poorly and seldom slept. He was simultaneously a delight and a demanding chore. In his first six months, we were anxiety ridden and perpetually tired. Then we all finally got the hang of it and respectively, began to enjoy parenthood and his childhood.

Jon's arrival marked the first time that Helene and I were in conflict over my playing basketball. She understood its importance to me and encouraged my working out after school and in the mornings on weekends. What she protested were the Sunday afternoon games at the JCH. In the dead of winter, she would be stuck at home with the baby while I was out for several hours of recreational pleasure. Her frustration was exacerbated by my long weekday schedule due to the never-ending graduate school and evening community center employment, which kept me away from the family. I promised Helene that the 1966 JCH season would be my swan song. Logically, I accepted Helene's feelings and her point of view. Nevertheless, I truly believed myself to be the injured party, unappreciated for my diligent efforts to forge a better life for us. It wasn't until years later that I realized my blindness was because of my love for basketball. Helene was right. Once we had a child, our circumstances changed. She made some unpleasant sacrifices. Giving up the JCH hurt but was a reasonable price to pay as a husband and father.

By mid-1966, we made one of the biggest decisions of our lives. We decided to purchase a home on Long Island. It would take every penny of our modest savings to use for the down payment and some essential furnishings. Helene's parents graciously volunteered to assist while we were temporarily strapped. We found an ideal affordable split-level in East Meadow, a comfortable bedroom community in Nassau County about thirty miles from Manhattan. In March of 1967, this lifelong Brooklynite left his beloved borough and headed for a new adventure in the suburbs.

CHAPTER 8

Settling in Suburbia

THE TRANSITION TO suburbia was a smooth one. The only significant negative was the slow automobile commute, which at times, was worse than I expected. I quickly grew to like living on Long Island. My neighborhood was peaceful and uncrowded. Parks and the beach were close by. Best of all, I loved the feeling of the grass on my lawn gently tickling my bare feet. For me, it symbolized freedom, contentment, and a haven away from the tumult of the city. Despite the initial financial burden, I was happy that we made the move. It was definitely a good place to raise a family.

Some other very positive things happened soon after we bought our home. In June of 1967, my principal, Irv Goldberg, informed me that he had received approval from special education headquarters to assign me, in September, to the position of acting assistant principal. I had just attained provisional New York State certification in administration and supervision based upon the graduate courses that I recently took. I hadn't even served long enough as a guidance counselor to be granted tenure, yet I was being promoted to a higher level. The suddenness of it all was flattering but mind-boggling. A second important piece of good news was Helene's fall announcement that she was pregnant. Jon was almost two years old and ready to be a big brother to a new brother or sister. When we moved, one of the uppermost concerns in my warped mind was whether I could find adequate basketball activity on Long Island.

On evenings that I worked or attended school, the late afternoons were perfect hoops opportunities. I obviously lived too far from PS 617 to go home and return later in the day to Brooklyn. I, therefore, always had fresh workout apparel and sneakers in my car trunk, waiting to be used at the propitious available basketball moment. As for my ridiculous worries, I shortly learned that there was athletic life on Long Island.

Marty Adler, one of my Brooklyn after-school workout compatriots was a Long Island resident. He would soon gain prominence as the founder and director of the Brooklyn Dodgers Hall of Fame. He told me about weekend morning outdoor half-court games at Merrick Road Park just off the main route to Jones Beach and a ten-minute car ride from my East Meadow home. The first time I went there was on a Saturday morning in April. The park was bustling with basketball, tennis, and paddleball activity. I immediately noticed that the basketball players weren't young kids. They were men, most of them thirty years of age and older. As it was at Manhattan Beach, the highest-quality games took place on the court closest to the entrance.

A most pleasant surprise was that I saw people whom I knew from Brooklyn. In this group were two guys from Brownsville. These were Al Schiffman, a feisty little playmaker, and Sy "Nick" Gerstman, a rock solid rebounder with a distinctive sweeping backboard aimed hook shot. Another regular was Boston Bob Weinberg, originally from Brooklyn's Kelly Park who released his accurate one hander from his fingertips and played without a shirt even in cold weather.

Above all, the familiar face that I was most delighted to see was that of former pro Jerry Fleishman. He was one of the players that I admired and looked up to as a role model back at Lincoln Terrace Park. We became reacquainted, although his memory had to be stirred to remember our association from times past. Our meeting was to be the start of a wonderful ball-playing relationship that would continue over years in many places throughout Long Island. Jerry's skills may have diminished from his prime, but his competitiveness and his effectiveness against park competition never waned. His hands remained quick and strong, and he always retained that deceptive running left-handed hook shot.

Jerry was tireless and would often participate in a couple of sets of tennis following the basketball workout. He didn't possess a classical tennis style but used his superior athleticism to become a very good player. He was unique on the tennis court in that he rarely used his back hand. Unbelievably, he switched hands, and was fast and powerful enough to react to booming serves and hard hit returns. When I took up tennis, Jerry taught me to properly set my body and to stroke and follow through with my swing. Initially, even though he was far beyond my tennis ability, he would rally with me regularly. We eventually began playing singles together when my game dramatically improved. Without a doubt, he was the chief motivating factor in my tennis interest and modest development in the sport.

I quickly established myself as one of the featured basketball players at Merrick Road. I seldom had to wait long to get into a game on the main court and would be saved an open spot on a waiting team if I arrived a few minutes late. The games were intense and often acrimonious. Some of the better guys had short fuses and displayed bitterness to each other. It took no more than a hard foul or a questionable call to bring the anger to a boil. Stu Zimmerman (Michigan State), a prolific scorer with a great knack for shooting with his back to the basket, and Bill Jackey (Virginia), a versatile and creative offensive force, were two who constantly argued and showed little brotherly love. Billy Gordon (LIU), a tall and talented Long Beach product, was another who easily lost his cool.

I was definitely in the cluster of noncontroversial participants at boisterous Merrick Road Park. Among those who just played and avoided trouble were former fellow Brooklynites and good shooters, Jerry Feinstein and Steve Wilk. Another in this category was Herman Tibbs, a true gentleman who gave it his all every time he stepped on the court. A player of average ability but a top-grade individual was the park's second Jerry Fleishman. He was a prominent person in his own right, first distinguishing himself as a lawyer and more recently as a Long Beach City judge. However at Merrick Road, he took a back seat to Jerry Fleishman the basketball player. If someone was to ask, "Have you seen Jerry Fleishman?" the usual response would be, "You mean the real Jerry Fleishman?" Fortunately, the "judge's" shoulders were broad enough to accept his lesser status good-naturedly.

I learned from the group at Merrick Road that there was terrific summer basketball action at Long Beach, a Long Island resort community a few miles to the west of nationally renowned Jones Beach. The games of the half-court variety were played on weekends at Central School, which was on Park Avenue, Long Beach's wide main street. A few years later, the workout moved to a playground on the bay side of town at the site of a newly constructed indoor recreation center and ice skating rink. That rink, for a while, was the practice facility for the New York Rangers.

There was no comparison between the Long Beach competition and that at Merrick Road Park. Long Beach attracted hordes of present and former major college basketball stars. Locals such as Art Heyman (Oceanside High School, Duke University, NBA, and ABA), Larry Brown (Long Beach High School, University of North Carolina, ABA) and Kevin Joyce (Molloy High School, University of South Carolina, ABA) played regularly at Long Beach. Mike Riordan out of Providence College, whose game never stopped improving and made it in the NBA with the Knicks and Bullets, was a frequent participant. A very tall youngster from

New York City's Power Memorial High School, known then as Lew Alcindor, visited the Long Beach courts on a few occasions.

I was neither known well enough at Long Beach nor that much of a standout to immediately make it to the inner circle. Unlike most places in which I played, I had to endure a long wait to get on the court. Therefore, most often what I did was to play early at Merrick Road and then ride over to Long Beach. In that way, I already had my workout, and any additional run would be a bonus. Over time, I managed to work my way into the games and certainly never embarrassed myself. I shot well, earning the respect of my opponents but rarely played on teams strong enough to be victorious in the very formidable competition.

The winningest Long Beach players were Alan Seiden, Eddie Gard, and the combination of "Red" Blumenreich and Petey Meyers. They always played together, functioning as a smooth and powerful machine. Alan did 80 percent of the scoring. Eddie was the flawless consummate playmaker, and both "Red" and Petey did the dirty work, grabbing the rebounds and playing tough interior defense. In the close games, Alan made a foul call on every offensive move and shot. In the New York area, he definitely popularized the expression "and one," which he shouted as he released the ball. This term signified that the basket counts should the ball go through the net, and if not, it's a foul. It was practically impossible to get the ball a sufficient number of times to beat them.

I knew nothing about Petey Meyer's basketball background or formal experience. I saw at Long Beach that he was hard-nosed, rarely shot anything but a layup or tip-in and played much taller than his 6'2"/ 6'3" height. I also found out that he was the brother-in-law of Jack McMahon, veteran NBA guard and coach. I knew more about "Red" Blumenreich, who soon was to become a close friend. Red was similar to Petey in size and determination, but had a much broader spectrum of skills. He was a complete player, possessing talent, fortitude and wonderful basketball intelligence. The weakest aspect of Red's game was his shooting, yet his resourcefulness and deceptive strength resulted in an impressive number of points scored. I liken Red to a Bailey Howell in terms of style or, in more recent days, as a smaller but not quite as quick Bobby Jones. Red was a freshman at CCNY when the scandal broke. He transferred to Yeshiva University, one of the country's outstanding religious-affiliated colleges although not at all an athletic power. At Yeshiva, he played under the tutelage of another Red, Bernie Sarachek, who is considered by the basketball establishment to be one of the game's great innovators. "Red" Blumenreich was so dominant in his years at Yeshiva that he garnered the attention and plaudits of the local basketball community. He was just a step away from an NBA career.

Eddie Gard was the epitome of the thinking man's backcourt player. He was at best an average shooter, not a great dribbler and never attempted to be a Fancy Dan. What he had was great court vision, excellent passing skills, and unsurpassed ability in moving the ball and creating easy opportunities for his teammates. He was a maestro on the court, orchestrating the flow of the game, and ensuring that the most was made out of every possession. He was the mentor to Alan Seiden, as he was in his days at LIU when he started at guard and guided the development of the fabulous sophomores Sherman White, Leroy Smith, and Dolph Bigos.

I didn't get to play on Eddie's side at Long Beach, but I did have the pleasure of joining him later on in workouts at Hewlett High School and North Woodmere Park. He made it so easy for me. No one set a better screen, finished off with an over-the-shoulder drop pass than Eddie. I didn't have to shoot from far out as he would consistently get me open for short jumpers or layups off the pick and roll. Eddie constantly beat opponents with little mind games. If a new guy played him physically, Eddie would give his patented speech. He would say, "I don't put my hands on you. I don't expect you to put your hands on me." His lecture would be so sincerely convincing that the guy became reluctant to guard him closely. And of course, Eddie proceeded to have a party out there. In another situation, if Eddie saw that a player was out of control and was inclined to take poor shots, in the midst of the game, he would loudly warn his teammates, "Don't let him shoot." Within seconds, the fool responding to Eddie's false flattery would launch ridiculous bombs, damaging his team's chances to win. Other verbal code signals such as "I don't want it" or telling one of us on his side to "shoot the jumper," in reality meant the opposite. The talk relaxed and distracted the opponent, weakening concentration, while we were cutting to the basket or receiving a pass for a layup.

Prior to Long Beach, I became acquainted with Alan Seiden through playing against him in college and being in his company at basketball-related gatherings. Les Yellin, who gave me so much positive motivation in my awkward adolescent period was also one of Alan's closest friends. While I was receiving modest acclaim at CCNY, Alan was deservedly in the national spotlight. At St. John's, he won the Haggerty Award as the outstanding player in the New York Metropolitan Area and earned All-American honors in his senior year.

As years rolled on, I counted Alan among my best and most loyal friends. Back at Long Beach, however, I didn't like him very much. His on-court behavior was arrogant and frequently obnoxious. He wasn't a trash talker in the style of modern-day players, but his cocky body language and sarcasm were indicative of the delight he experienced when beating his adversaries and the disdain that he felt about them. Alan relished a good argument, primarily those related to disputed calls. He was stubborn and reluctant to compromise even in the face of long delays, while guys on the sideline waiting for the next game would be screaming at him to resolve the problem. In these squabbles, he was often blunt and insensitive to other players, demeaning them with unflattering evaluations of their basketball abilities. Alan believed he was fouled on every play in which there was contact. When he drove or posted up, almost every attempted shot was accompanied by a foul call. He never saw himself as the initiator of contact, even when digging his elbow or lowering a shoulder into the defender.

Physically, Alan had a trim solid upper body, but his true strength was in his thick muscular legs. Those legs had no business being on a 5'11", 180-pound guard. Added to the power that they generated was above-average speed and exceptional quickness. It was almost impossible for a player of Alan's size to stop him. He was relentless on offense, able to beat you off the dribble, or by hesitating or faking from the drive to get an opponent to leave his feet or lose his balance. He was extraordinary at both drawing the foul and possessing the strength to make the basket despite being hit. At St. John's, Alan averaged a remarkable ten foul attempts per game.

Alan was one of New York City's legendary high school stars. He was a rare four-year starter at Jamaica High School. When he graduated from Jamaica in 1955 after winning a city championship, he was New York City's all-time leader in total career points scored. His record has since been eclipsed but remains in the stratospheric scoring category. Alan didn't exactly stray far from home when he chose to attend St. John's. He's one of the few people that I know who lived in walking distance from both his high school and college.

Alan should have played in the NBA. He had no one to blame but himself for his ill-timed outspoken and foolish impulsivity, which short-circuited a promising career. Following his senior year at St. John's, he was the first nonterritorial draft choice of the St. Louis Hawks. The Hawks selected local St. Louis University star Bob Ferry as a territorial pick. In preseason camp, he did well but was unhappy and impatient over his perceived lack of playing time. The Hawks had traded for veteran playmaker Slater Martin, who was clearly on the downside of many years of excellence as a member of the esteemed Minneapolis Lakers. This was one source of irritation for young Alan who felt he was better than the aging Slater Martin. On an intellectual level, he understood the situation and the respect given to those who have earned the right to be in the NBA family, yet he couldn't bide his time. His general frustration escalated beyond the boiling point. He simply packed up and walked out of camp.

The next season he was invited to try out for the Detroit Pistons. Again, he did well, but this time was up against a crowded backcourt of contracted players consisting of Gene Shue, Don

Ohl, and Chuck Noble. Alan made it to the last exhibition game and was the team's second highest scorer in preseason. He knew, however, that the handwriting was on the proverbial wall. His friend and fellow St. John's alumnus, the gracious and gentle Dick McGuire, was the coach of the Pistons. Dick, hardly a master of language, was attempting to find the words to inform Alan of the bad news. He, in fact, was avoiding him. Alan spared Dick the unpleasant task. He sought him out and when he found Dick told him that he realized that he was cut. Not only did Alan console Dick, but he probably was the first NBA player to announce his own dismissal from a team.

Alan went on to play successfully for about a decade in the Eastern League and established a thriving business as a theater and sports ticket agent. In the pages ahead, I will write much more about Alan who died in his early seventies. In the last twenty-five years of his life, Alan became very heavy and paid little attention to his physical condition. It was remarkable that he was still able to play effectively despite the extra pounds and being terribly out of shape. He had an unsurpassed love of basketball, followed closely by an addiction to food and poker. He also was a fascinating extroverted character who treasured his many friends and treated them to countless meals and celebrations. On the other hand, once the ball was put into play, he became most annoying and exasperating. Although his basketball prowess was widely recognized and respected, his surface brusqueness and sarcasm impeded others from seeing his positive traits.

In the middle of the sweltering summer of 1968, our son Seth was born. He was bigger and rounder than Jon, which probably had something to do with his better sleeping and eating habits. From day one, Seth was a content and placid baby. Whereas he was inactive almost to the point of appearing to be in a vegetative state, he had the sweetest disposition and never cried. Developmentally, he was far behind Jon's early ability to crawl, walk, and talk. It's true that when Seth arrived, Helene and I were more experienced at parenting than during our anxious novice days of Jon's infancy.

However, Seth's inherent nature made the child-rearing task a relatively simple pleasure.

By the spring of 1969, whenever I played on weekend mornings, I would take Jon and Seth with me. It wasn't a chore or a distraction having them nearby. They behaved beautifully, never demanding my attention, didn't cry or complain, and not even once ran out on the court. They remained on the sideline, most often playing with the toys and balls that I brought from home or mingled with the children of other parents/athletes. Jon loved to imitate his television heroes and would run around with authentic replicas, pretending that he was Speed Racer or G. I. Joe. Once Seth was able to walk, he discarded the toys but never got tired of chasing a ball around. My friends would get a great kick out of this little tyke's efforts to dribble or shoot a basketball that was bigger than him. For many years, our going together to play ball was a wonderful ritual. Following the workout, we capped off the morning with a fast-food lunch at McDonald's, Nathan's, Pizza, etc. As the teen years approached, Jon went on hiatus from the routine, preferring to sleep late on weekends. Always one to exercise his independence, Jon would sometimes pull a surprise and decide to join us. On those occasions, he and Seth would play one-on-one or challenge other willing youngsters. Seth never stopped accompanying me and, to the delight of his proud father, eventually became a participant in the games.

Job advancement continued on an upward path. At the conclusion of the 1970–1971 school year, Principal Irv Goldberg announced his retirement. Our school was no longer PS 617 but reverted to PS 36, the original number of the elementary school that first occupied the building. The reason for the change entailed a federal court suit against the "600 schools." The major complaint contended that the "600 schools" stigmatized the students due to punitive and racially restrictive and segregated policies and practices. As a result of the landmark case, the "600 schools" were significantly revamped and subsequently eliminated.

Initially, Goldberg's retirement at the start of the 1971–1972 school year brought about the assignment of a nonspecial education supervisor. Irv Goldberg recommended me, but I never even received an interview. I was asked to remain as an assistant principal and to provide a comprehensive orientation to the selectee. He was considerably older than me and had expertise in curriculum but clearly lacked the patience and frustration tolerance to manage such an extreme student population. At the end of a difficult school day in late September, he simply packed up his scant belongings, shook my hand, and said good-bye. That evening at home, I received a phone call from Al Budnick, our superintendent for special education. He asked if I felt ready to be a principal. When I responded with an emphatic yes, he stated that I was assigned acting principal of PS 36 Brooklyn. He concluded that he believed that this was my calling. As for the individual who walked away from this job, he soon would become an elementary school principal in Brooklyn's Crown Heights and would do a fine job. I had to take additional courses in administration and supervision, pass the elementary school principal examination (there wasn't a special education principal's exam at that time) and was granted tenure in 1974.

Despite all that was happening in my professional career, I did not put basketball playing on the shelf. My friend and former high school teammate Don "Red" Goldstein came through in a big way. Don established his dental practice and residence on Long Island and first settled in Westbury but, with success, moved to Melville, a town on the western edge of Suffolk County. A school just down the road from his new home was to be open on Wednesday evenings for adult recreation. A group comprised of local residents, most of whom played competitive basketball, formed the core of participants in the emerging workout. It was to become a constant and a highlight of my 1970s basketball routine.

The full court Melville games were wonderfully hard fought and on a high skill level. In addition to Don who was still a tremendous player, the workout featured several guys with college experience. Some of them, the ones who were New York City natives, I knew from Brooklyn. Jerry Bloomberg was another fellow Tildenite. He was unappreciated by our coach Jack Krugman but blossomed into an outstanding defender after high school. I renewed acquaintances with Madison High School standouts Barry Multer and Gary Notice, both of whom I battled against at Manhattan Beach. Barry, smooth and possessing great hands, was a fine forward at the University of Rhode Island. Danny Russell and Harvey Pachter were rough and tough guards. Danny started on New Utrecht High School's 1954 city championship team, and Harvey was a regular at Jefferson High School and Adelphi University. I met and became friends with Gary Franklin, a Long Islander and an excellent all-around athlete who played football at Kansas University.

York Larese wasn't a weekly regular but frequently participated in the Melville run. He originally came to the workout through Don, who was his dentist. York was a great New York City high school star at St. Ann's and went on to excel for the Tarheels of North Carolina. After college, he had a stint in the NBA as a member of the Philadelphia 76ers. He also briefly coached the New York Nets in the ABA. York's strength was his offensive game. At 6'3", he was a deadly shooter and a versatile creative scorer. He was charismatic and charming, with a sharp tongue and fun to be around.

It was at Melville that I was introduced to Gary Wood, a remarkable athlete. Gary was just finishing his career as a professional football player. For several years, during the 1960s, he was the reserve quarterback for the New York Giants and later moved on to the Canadian Football League, where he gained prominence through his exciting style. Gary and his lovely wife, Jill, enjoyed the New York area and decided to permanently reside and raise their family on Long Island.

Although Gary's football height was listed at 6'0", he was closer to 5'10", certainly not the ideal size for a quarterback. Weight-wise, when I met him, he was a brick solid 190 pounds and also exceptionally strong. In college at Cornell, Gary was a triple threat tailback. He was, without doubt, one of the finest players in Ivy League history. His performance as a runner and passer was so impressive that despite the fact that Cornell played against less than football power competition, he received All-American recognition.

Gary's basketball skills were not equal to his extraordinary football talent. However, his speed, reflexes, toughness, and determination were all in the superlative range. A warm and gentle person off the court, he had no sympathy for his opponents during the game. It wasn't fun to be guarded by Gary Wood. Believe me, I worked my butt off and earned every point that I ever scored against him. He was a pressing, body-bumping, indefatigable whirlwind. His mere presence elevated our workouts to a higher level. Gary became a regular member of our basketball group and for years was a teammate in Long Island summer league competition. I loved playing with him and enjoyed the friendship that emanated from our athletic endeavors. It was a terrible shock to all of us when some years ago, this seemingly indestructible man succumbed to a sudden heart attack. For me, it was a harsh reminder of our fragile mortality.

The Melville Wednesday evening workout was the pathway for participation in the Town of Hempstead Summer League. I, along with Don, both Garys, and Jerry Bloomberg formed the nucleus of our team. We added Howie Bernstein & Paul "The Rope" Glass two other guys from the Wednesday run. Howie, a former University of Bridgeport player, had an awkward-looking but potent jumper, which was the Long Island version of the Knick's Dick Barnett's unique "fall back baby" shot. At 6'2" and 140 pounds, The Rope was the perfect nickname for the skeleton-like Paul. His best basketball asset was an accurate long range jump shot. His lack of bulk, however, put him at a serious disadvantage against stronger opponents. Still, for one more time, I was reunited with Charlie Hoffman and Mel Kessler, both of whom lived on Long Island. After our initial high school encounters and especially that tough loss to Madison in the playoffs, for twenty years we traveled the same basketball road in the Catskills, Manhattan Beach, the JCH, and now in the suburbs. Also on our roster, welcomed to play when their schedules allowed, were York Larese and the venerable Jerry Fleishman. Jerry at that time was fiftyish and could still get the job done. At the gentle urging of his wife, Isabel, who felt that enough was enough, Jerry retired from organized full-court basketball and dropped off our squad. This is not to say that he stopped completely as he continued to play half-court ball in the park and at the beach.

In the league, we were far and away the oldest team. Most of us were in our mid- to upper-thirties compared to the average age of mid-twenties for almost every other team. Many players were, in fact, fresh out of college. In an attempt to select an appropriate name for our club, I seized upon the age factor. At first, I came up with the Senior Citizens, which we were called during our first year. Not satisfied, I thought of a classier name within the same general theme. We therefore became the Elder Statesmen, a title that fit perfectly.

We played in the Town of Hempstead League for five years, and were champions for four of them. We finally learned that our time was passing when we were blown out by a younger, quicker, and much better conditioned team. The upstarts, all accomplished recent college players, were a Rockville Centre group that included two sets of brothers, Brian and Charlie Mahoney (both from Manhattan College) and Eddie and Peter Malloy (Rhode Island & Princeton university, respectively). Two other excellent players were Peter Crotty (Notre Dame) and Jim Hayes (Boston College).

Looking back, these were terrific times. Despite the ever-present mosquitoes at Seaman's Neck Park, the games were spirited, and the league was professionally administered. In the main, the officiating was competent even if a few referees weren't enamored with Gary Wood's humorous baiting and physical play. I distinctly remember a game where Gary sacrificed himself in order to remove a major obstacle that was blocking our path to victory. A skilled young guard from Canisius College was absolutely killing us. On that night, he was unstoppable. Highly competitive Gary was particularly frustrated by his inability to put the clamps on him. Gary decided to create his own lane to the basket and drove over, not around, the youngster. He was called for the charge, which left a sneaker imprint on the guy's chest. The violation was ruled intentional and Gary was thrown out of the game. Our nemesis, having just been run over by a steamroller, was on the sidelines, temporarily out of commission. From that juncture in the contest, the outcome was never in doubt.

Gary Wood was instrumental in starting an enjoyable postgame tradition. In the 1970s, Coors was unable to distribute its beer in the New York area. Gary had a brew connection and was able to obtain cans of Coors. He brought a cooler filled with Coors beer and ice to one of our games. After we finished playing and made our way to the parking lot, Gary invited us to share his treat. The cold liquid refreshment was the perfect thing to revitalize a group of thirsty and tired players. It was the start of a delightful weekly routine. Following Gary's lead, we rotated the responsibility for bringing the beer. Parking lot guzzling and gabbing became a high point, greatly enhancing our camaraderie. We then further enriched the social aspect of our summer league involvement by adding our wives to our game night repertoire. Dining together at a local Italian restaurant capped the postgame festivities. We felt it was well worth the expense of arranging for a midweek babysitter. It also led to the development of friendships among several of the women.

For seven summers, from 1969 through 1975, our family shared a cabana at Lido Beach, a Long Island resort on the Atlantic Ocean. The club, which was a ten-minute car ride from the Long Beach basketball courts, had a lengthy name. It was West Terrace at Nassau Beach Park. Nassau County acquired three privately owned Lido Beach clubs and opened them to county residents on a seasonal rental and daily admissions basis. Three sections–East, Central, and West–replaced the previously private operations. We were fortunate to obtain a cabana as they were in such great demand that it became necessary to establish a waiting list.

Our cabana partners were friends, Sid and Roz Chicofsky and their children and Glen and Lynn. My relationship with Sid began in Brooklyn and was initially one related to business. He was the insurance agent who sold us our first whole-life policy. Sid's recommendation, which resulted in our meeting, was sports-related. It came from my basketball buddy Lenny Sherman, who had a brief fling as an insurance salesman. At the conference where Sid made his presentation, I learned that he was a sports nut. Our common fanaticism and the warmth of his personality instigated a bonding that led to a close and enduring friendship.

Although by no means an accomplished basketball player, it's hard to find anyone who was more enthusiastic or took the game more seriously than Sid. For him, every game in which he participated was the final four or the NBA playoffs. On the court, he was emotion personified–grimacing, groaning, and expressing glee, anger, or disappointment depending upon his performance and the score. He exhibited the same behavior when playing tennis or challenging me to a two-man Olympics consisting of basketball, tennis, stickball, track and field, and fitness. It was good that resiliency is another of Sid's finest attributes. It lessened the negative impact of all those defeats.

The Groveman family loved the beach club. On sunny weekends and holidays, we would be there from early morning into the evening. Our cabana wasn't lavish but afforded us the comfort of a shower and a place to change to fresh clothes. It contained a refrigerator and sufficient space to maintain beach supplies, athletic equipment, and the kids' toys. Often, we would barbecue our dinner and leave for home long after the beach traffic had eased. We enjoyed the two pools, the ocean and its waves, and the broad expanse of beach. Jon and Seth had loads of playmates and never lacked for things to do. As they grew older, they would organize beach whiffle baseball games and, of course, induce their father to play basketball or throw high fly balls to them at the uncrowded rear of the beach. In between attending to the boys and chatting with club members, my favorite pastimes were tennis, three-man basketball, and hitting the cooler for a refreshing beer after working up a good sweat.

The basketball courts were far enough from the ocean to be relatively unaffected by excessive wind. We always made certain to have a broom handy to sweep away sand from the playing surface. Basketball was a popular activity at the club, attracting a large number of players and onlookers. Once again I had the pleasure of hooking up with Jerry Fleishman, who was a club member. We played together regularly, benefitting from the familiarity we had of each other's game gained from our basketball association in so many other places. Neil Rosenberg, a 6'4" leaper and an Adelphi University player, was our third man. He blended well with us veterans, completing a fluid and efficient trio that often dominated the beach club half-court games. Each August, we competed as an entry in the West Terrace three-man tournament. We either won or made it to the final round every year. My greatest joy during those contests was being cheered on by my young sons, Jon and Seth. Even today, I can clearly see them in my mind's eye, sitting in the sand bordering one side of the court, proudly rooting for their dad.

As the beach club was to our summer, so was Miami Beach to our Christmas vacation. In the 1970s, on the last day of school before the winter holiday break, Helene and the boys would drive to Brooklyn and pick me up at PS 36. From there, it was on to Route 95 and the long tedious drive to Miami Beach, Florida. Each year we would begin the trip with joyful enthusiasm at the prospect of fun and sun. However, by the time we hit South Carolina, we were grumpy, uncomfortable, and sick of the monotonous highway. Once in Florida, our collective mood would brighten, and we were again a loving family.

Those journeys signaled to me the deterioration of my right knee. After driving for a few hours, I experienced excruciating pain in my knee. I had to stop, get out of the car, and walk for a few minutes in order to alleviate the stress. Anytime that I was unable to fully extend my leg, the pain would return. My family doctor, who was not exactly an orthopedic specialist, minimized the problem and diagnosed it as tendinitis. The treatment was a few daily aspirins and the application of ice if the pain persisted. The throbbing was a constant that I just learned to endure.

Our specific destination was the Castaways Hotel in North Miami Beach, which was a free and easy place for singles, not exactly a resort catering to families. We, however, found the price to be right for our pocket. In addition, the location was attractive, and for the pleasure of Jon and Seth, there was an excellent balance between ocean water and plentiful swimming pools. Lastly, all of us liked the lively, youthful atmosphere.

Early each morning during our Florida vacations, the boys and I would head down to Flamingo Park in search of half-court basketball action. In those days, Flamingo was a hub of athletic activity. At Christmastime, the National Junior Tennis Tournament was held at the park. It also hosted the country's best four-wall handball competition. The basketball was not quite at that level but attracted vacationing players from all over the US. Our New York contingent, other than myself, featured Syd Levy and Marty Adler, who stayed with relatives while in Florida. Joel Silver, the first forward off the bench in his days at NYU and whom I played against in the JCH, was another park regular. At Flamingo, I became reacquainted with Eddie Hand, an old army buddy from Fort Dix, and Keith Kenner, an East Meadow, Long Island, neighbor and good shooter whose zest for basketball exceeded his playing ability. The final member of our group was a Jersey guy and former George Washington University player who migrated to Atlanta, Georgia. "Big Howard" was an amiable 6'5", near-three-hundred pounder. When he set his awesome body, no amount of contact could budge him. Yet he displayed grace and skill and a soft bank shot. The games at Flamingo added a special flavor to the Florida vacations and energized me for the cold New York winter that lay ahead.

As the boys moved toward their teen years and were refining athletic and other personal interests, Florida family automobile trips became impractical. In our last year or two in Miami, the Flamingo neighborhood was in a state of decline. An economically poor Cuban population replaced one that was upper middle class and predominantly Jewish. The snowbird" crowd in that area greatly dwindled and was similarly reflected in the suddenly half empty basketball courts. It was clearly time to close the door on my Flamingo Park basketball days. There is a very sweet postscript in that many years later, that section of Miami has enjoyed an unparalleled resurgence of economic life and high glamour. Flamingo Park is within walking distance of Miami's South Beach, one of the world's new playgrounds of the rich and famous and those striving to get there.

CHAPTER 9

Growing Up and Getting Older

THROUGHOUT MY PRINCIPALSHIP, given our antisocial and volatile student population, I sought diversity among staff members and a specific focus upon strong positive models for identification and emulation. While I didn't specifically advertise for basketball players, I believed that appropriately licensed teachers with athletic backgrounds correlated highly with the capability of relating successfully with the boys. It was gratifying that I was able to recruit a number of high-profile basketball stars.

Guidance Counselor Joe Gibson, a kind and exceptionally perceptive individual, was a star at Morgan State University. Bill Burwell, a hulking 6'8" stalwart at the University of Illinois, was the second half of Boys High's dynamic duo, where he played alongside Connie Hawkins. Jerry Davis, a 6'9" gentle string bean was a forward at Wichita State University. The first substitute teacher called to cover an absence was Dick Bunt, a smooth 6'0" guard from NYU who played briefly for the Knicks in the mid-1950s. Lastly, Hank Whitney was on the youth board staff, working intensively with Williamsburg's street gangs. Hank, a rugged 6'7", was one of the country's most prolific rebounders at Iowa State University and later played for the New York Nets in the ABA. Hank advanced to become a dynamic principal at the same junior high school that he attended years earlier. Bill Burwell, too, served as an administrator in the special education school headed by St. John's great Solly Walker and later became a principal on Long Island.

Basketball was perhaps my most effective tool regarding connecting and bonding with the boys. Whenever possible, I would spend time in the gym or the schoolyard, shooting hoops or joining in a game with them. On most Friday afternoons, I'd change from my business suit to shorts and sneakers and play some full court. Our new students at first found it hard to believe that an "old" principal could actually play. The veterans showed pride in my basketball prowess. In general, I believe my playing helped the students to see me as a real person. In turn, it made it easier for me to develop relationships. This enhanced communication and proved invaluable in attempting to mediate and resolve student problems.

During a New York City financial crisis of 1976, all summer school programs were cancelled. The prospect of a workless 1976 summer was disturbing. I prepared a resume and sent it to a few dozen day and sleepaway camps. I was surprised by the large number of quick responses that I received. I decided to go the sleepaway route as it would be the best thing for Jon and Seth. The most interesting offer came from Jerry Halsband, the owner/director of Raquette Lake Camp. He was seeking a full-time baseball coach for the camp's comprehensive hardball program. Although no Casey Stengel, I had played sandlot baseball, was an avid fan of the game, and was actively involved in Little League coaching on Long Island. Halsband's financial package consisted of a free eight-week camping season for Jon and Seth, a room for us in a staff house to be shared with two other married couples, a part-time job for Helene in the camp office, and a healthy salary for myself. As for the camp itself, Raquette Lake was one of the northeast's finest. Located in the majestic Adirondacks, three hundred plus miles north of New York City, it was comprised of distinct and separate facilities for boys and girls. The girl's camp overlooked huge Raquette Lake and was on the rustic but relatively modern mainland. The boy's camp, in a drastically different setting, was accessible only by boat. It was situated on an isolated peninsula, which had no roads except for those within the camps grounds, and was bordered on the land side by thick woods, mountains, and marsh. These circumstances necessitated that a miniferry-type service be the primary mode of transportation. The boats were used to transport trucks making deliveries as well as people. Intrigued by the uniqueness of the camp and impressed with the attractive business proposition, I accepted the position at Raquette Lake Boys Camp.

I spent one season at Raquette Lake Boys Camp as baseball coach and eight more as its athletic and program director. They basically were fulfilling and enjoyable summers despite bumps in the road, mainly in the form of philosophical differences with camp management. For Jon and Seth, it was a magnificent growing-up experience, exceeding our most optimistic expectations. They flourished athletically and made many friendships. Camping gave them the opportunity to visit Montreal and see the major league baseball all-star game. One summer, they lived for a week in a frat house at Syracuse University during the National Sports Festival. At the sports festival, the campers saw the best young athletes in the country compete in basketball, baseball, and track. It was fun and exciting watching regional teams comprised primarily of graduating high school seniors. The three that impressed me the most were Patrick Ewing (Massachusetts), Chris Mullins (New York), and Hershel Walker (Georgia). Much would eventually be heard from this special trio.

Another excellent aspect of the trips was barnstorming throughout the Adirondack, Berkshire, and White Mountains playing against the prominent sports camps in basketball, baseball, tennis, and soccer. Jon excelled in all but tennis, whereas Seth's main interest was in basketball, although his skill level was high in both baseball and tennis. Jon also developed a passion for true camping. Raquette Lake imbued Jon with a love for the unspoiled outdoors that continued to grow and remains even stronger today. He resides in Vermont and is a modern pioneer and an environmentalist. As for Seth, the only way he would go camping would be in a luxurious trailer.

For most of their years in camp, both Jon and Seth were among the smallest in their age groups. Of the two, Seth was more intense and competitive on the basketball court. Jon, in actuality, was a better natural shooter while Seth was more skilled at ball handling and driving to the basket. Seth developed a peculiar shooting style, which I now regret that I didn't attempt to change. Jon, although short and slight, always shot the ball from the center of his body. As he became stronger and progressed from taking a two-hand set shot to a jump shot, he simply moved the position of the ball from the chest on a straight line toward the top of his head. It wasn't the same for Seth. Beginning as a seven-year-old attempting to reach a ten-foot high basket, Seth released the ball from over his right shoulder in order to supply him with added power and leverage. Considering the weirdness of the shot, he was remarkably accurate, particularly from the foul line. I meekly suggested that he practice with a smaller lighter ball and shoot at the lower basket, which he vehemently resisted and dismissed as baby stuff. It was wishful thinking on my part that, in time, with size and strength, Seth would make the adjustment, change his release point, and learn to square up on the shot. Well, the full transition never occurred. He did move the shooting position from the shoulder to approximately the right ear but, unlike myself and his brother, was far from the standard jump shooter. To some degree, it hampered his consistency, largely due to the strange rotation of the ball, which impeded help from the front rim on his shots. Some coaches also gave him a hard time and misjudged the quality of his overall game based on his unusual technique.

Julie Levine and Norm Lefkowitz were Raquette Lake's two basketball coaches. They were veteran successful New York City high school coaches and moved on to the Division III college ranks within the CUNY (City University of New York) conference. Julie was about six years younger than me, while Norm was two years my senior. Both played collegiately, Julie at CCNY and Norm split time at the University of Cincinnati and LIU. They each had sons close in age to Jon and Seth, who were excellent athletes and at the very top in basketball. Norm's son Lew, in Seth's group, was a precocious player, confident as he was talented. Julie's boys, Jared and Russell, were two years apart. Jared was a bunk higher than Seth and Russell, a group below. Jared was the pure shooter and Russell the all-around player, a combination of skill and tremendous desire. At camp, all our boys were respected adversaries on the courts and playing fields and shared friendships at the close of athletic business. The dual relationships made for interesting dynamics among the three competitive fathers. Lew, Jared, and Russell went on to have successful high school and college basketball careers.

Norm and Julie differed greatly in their teaching presentation and methodologies. Norm's instructional style was comical, emotional, and animated. Julie was far more low-key, friendly yet somewhat more formal and serious. In their vastly different ways, both were highly effective and significantly enhanced the basketball abilities of the Raquette Lake campers. As for their own basketball participation, a chronic bad back forced Norm into premature retirement. Julie, on the other hand, in his thirties when he first came to camp, was in great basketball condition and played with the energy and the quickness of a much younger athlete.

Julie, about a dozen young counselors, and I played hoops at camp almost daily. During the rest hour following lunch, we would engage in tough full-court basketball. Most of the counselors were fine athletes, and several of them were either active or recently graduated college basketball players. We organized a staff team and competed after work against other Adirondack camps. In that mix, if Julie appeared to be a grizzled veteran, then I was absolutely ancient. Already fortyish and with damaged "wheels," it was a struggle to keep up with the young studs. However, I still could stick the jumper, and Julie did a beautiful job of getting me the ball at the right spot and moment. Year after year, we fielded excellent teams. Because of my advanced age and high-profile position within the camp, basketball made me a favorite and somewhat of a curious phenomenon among the campers.

Still vivid in my memory is the high-scoring game that I enjoyed at Echo Lake Camp. At that time, they were one of the few camps that had an indoor athletic facility. The court was shorter than regulation and rather narrow. Echo decided to play a zone against us, probably thinking that we would be hampered by the lack of space in which to beat the defense through passing. It didn't work out that way, as I positioned on the left wing and found it easy to free myself for open shots. My teammates consistently fed the ball to me, and I knocked them down for about forty points. Don Altman, our special events director, who was a zany character and a terrific multisport athlete in his college days at Hunter, was in attendance at the game. Just recently divorced, he got along well with Helene and was platonically attentive to her. Following our victory, he expressed amazement at my stellar performance, particularly in light of my age and physical limitations in contrast to the other participants. He made something akin to the following proclamation, "Keep playing. Your wife will soon be mine. You know you're going to have a heart attack out there and die. It's going to happen in the middle of one of your jump shots. And I'll be waiting on the sidelines ready to take over." I thought about it for a second but laughed it off and obviously haven't heeded Don's warning.

After the 1984 camp season in which Jon was a counselor and Seth was a senior camper aide, it was time to close the book on Raquette Lake Boys Camp. I had an opportunity to supervise the New York City summer schools for severely handicapped children, and the boys were ready to explore new vistas. We all were in agreement that taking the job nine years before at Raquette Lake was a wonderful family decision.

At home, from the time they were able to pick up a ball, there was a basket for Jon and Seth to shoot at by our house. At first, we put up a lightweight hoop on the side of our driveway. It was fine for shooting, but there really wasn't enough room to play a game. Therefore, we took the next step–cemented part of our backyard and made a legitimate good sized half-court. With the exception of the most inclement weather conditions, the boys used it daily. They invited friends over, often playing until dinner time. Jon and Seth engaged in intense one-on-one competition that frequently resulted in arguments and near brawls. Our antisocial next door neighbor, falsely contending that the games boisterously went on into the late-night hours, attempted to have the court legally dismantled. His actions were distressing from a humane standpoint and had a monetary impact, as we were required to seek a permit and hire a draftsman to obtain a Certificate of Occupancy from the town. In the end, we prevailed. Concerning our neighbor, I don't believe that he had the slightest misgiving over his mean-spirited behavior. We enjoyed our basketball court for many more years but never spoke with the Scrooge-like jerk in the next house.

Jon made the East Meadow High School basketball team and worked extremely hard to become a meaningful contributor during his senior year. He shot well but was a smallish guard (5'8") and was neither particularly fast nor strong. His coach, Bob Debonis, was an outstanding young mentor, equally skilled as a teacher and as a supportive communicator. Bob, in college, starred at CW Post, carrying on his family's rich basketball heritage. His father Joe and Uncle Dom both played for NYU. Bob Debonis's encouragement bolstered Jon's confidence, helping him to maximize his basketball abilities. The highlight of his modest career was coming off the bench and hitting four straight jump shots against a better team, sparking East Meadow to an upset victory. Upon graduating, Jon's formal basketball days ended. At Stony Brook and Binghamton, the two colleges that he attended, Jon confined his playing to the intramural tournaments.

Until his junior year in high school when he finally had a growth spurt, Seth was always one of the smallest on any team on which he played. As an adult, he is now about six feet, with a muscular build and near zero body fat. Actually, being short never deterred Seth. At the Police Boys Club and in junior high school, he was the best on his team. In a few instances, he was moved up to play with a group one grade higher than his age level. At East Meadow High School, he was a two year starter at point guard, where he amassed more than five hundred career assists and averaged twelve points per game.

Unlike Jon who greatly enjoyed the experience of playing under Bob Debonis, Seth had just a taste of Debonis's wise direction as a sophomore. Bob left East Meadow to accept the head coaching position at New York Tech, a local Division II participating college. His replacement at East Meadow, Jimmy Angelina, a youthful first-year varsity coach was brimming with enthusiasm and good intentions but clearly groping to find his natural style and identity. It was a difficult growing-up process for Jimmy and his team. As point guard, Angelina correctly demanded a great deal of leadership from Seth. He liked Seth a lot and respected his game yet frequently yelled at him when things went awry. He rationalized that Seth was better-equipped to take the verbal stings than his teammates because he was mature and stable.

The team had size and talent but also played in Nassau County's toughest A-school conference. The demanding schedule added to Coach Angelina's low frustration tolerance and unintentional impulsive outbursts. In the middle of Seth's senior year, the East Meadow team suddenly jelled. They went on a streak, where they won seven out of eight games, losing only to league powerhouse Hempstead High School. That game, played on the road, saw Hempstead come from behind to gain a dramatic victory in the closing minute. Hempstead eventually won the Long Island Championship and was the runner-up for the New York State Public School Championship. East Meadow made it into the playoffs and did well before bowing out in another squeaker.

Seth was recruited by Skidmore College, a Division III school, in upstate New York, with a fine academic reputation. Skidmore is located in Saratoga Springs, renowned for its natural mineral water and summertime thoroughbred horse racing. Seth was familiar with the college and the picturesque village, having visited the Saratoga Performing Arts Center as a Raquette Lake camper. He eagerly accepted admission to Skidmore.

In the late 1970s, the constant search to expand my weekend morning basketball menu led me to Hewlett High School and North Woodmere Park. The Sunday workouts basically drew the same participants, Hewlett being the indoor cold weather sanctuary and North Woodmere, the outdoor spring and summer place of choice. Hewlett and North Woodmere became the grazing pastures of so many old-time New York City basketball players who moved east and settled on Long Island. The half-court runs and the weekly gathering of friends were as much social happenings as athletic events. I know that I kept going there mainly because of the wonderful atmosphere and the nostalgic banter. The basketball action was enjoyable but was the undercard to the fascinating congregation.

The turf was familiar. The trio of Alan Seiden, Eddie Gard, and Red Blumenreich were regulars. I finally got the opportunity to play with and become friends of Phil Albert and Feeny, two admired guys from my Brooklyn teen years. Phil, whom I first met at Brighton Beach and then again in the Catskills, moved slower than ever but still skillfully used that ample body to screen opponents and position himself for his sweet baby hook shot. Feeny never lost those lightning quick hands nor his amazingly deceptive hesitation, fakes, and moves to the basket. It was also good to see Kenny Kern and the great Sid Tanenbaum, two others from my youthful basketball past.

Allie Rubinstein, Arnie Millman, and George Feigenbaum were three who stood out in the fifty-year-old category. Allie, a little set shooting specialist and a speed merchant, played for the University of Cincinnati and once held Kentucky All-American great Ralph Beard to a standstill. Arnie, a 6'3" rebounder and defensive specialist, is one of very few who played both for NYU and CCNY in their glory days. George Feigenbaum is an original and a legendary New York basketball character. The colorful and loquacious George had a game to match his personality. It was up-tempo, personalized, and stylish, featuring a variety of effective drives and shots. George's college meanderings took him to the University of Kentucky and then to professional ball in the early days of the NBA.

A few years younger than the above group was the multifaceted and always interesting Marv Kessler. Marv, a Brooklyn native, went from an outstanding back court career at Boys High to lesser success at North Carolina State University. It didn't stop there, for he had since achieved prominence as a coach and teacher of basketball. Outspoken and humorous, Marv built his lofty reputation through success at several levels. His high school teams at Martin Van Buren were consistent playoff contenders and among the best in Queens. He next moved on to attain similar winning results at the helm of Division II, Adelphi University. After retiring from college coaching, he coached professionally in Israel and South America. He later became an NBA scout and was actively involved in helping NBA draftees upgrade their skills. Throughout, he presented instructional clinics for other coaches and especially at the top-rated basketball camps. He earned the reputation as being one of the country's best. Howie Garfinkel, director of the renowned Five Star Basketball Camp, placed Marv in the elite company of Hubie Brown and Rick Pitino, two of basketball's most respected mentors.

It was at Hewlett/Woodmere that I met and later developed friendships with Ivan Kovac and Mark Rich. Ivan, a handsome, blond-haired poster boy–type was all-city at Queens' Bayside High School. He turned away scores of scholarship offers to remain local, choosing to play for St. John's. His Redman teams featuring Tony Jackson, Leroy Ellis, Kevin Loughery, Willie Hall, and Donny Burks were among the finest in St. John's long and proud history. Ivan's blazing speed and explosive first step to the basket were both exceptional attributes and still something to behold, even as he approached forty years of age. Mark Rich, a terrific outside shooter, is over a decade younger than me. A prolific scorer at Lincoln High School, he took his golden touch to powerful Southern Idaho Junior College to play under the guidance of Eddie

Sutton. His eligibility was completed at Adelphi University, where he never had the full opportunity to display his offensive prowess. At 6'2", he wasn't the purest guard in terms of ball-handling ability. His coach, viewing him as a small tweener, neither back court man nor legitimate forward, underused him, thereby discarding a brilliant shotmaker. Mark, like myself, was a special educator. The common professional involvement as principals, coupled with our affinity for the jump shot, were the ingredients for a close relationship. I'm flattered that Mark perceives me as both a friend and a mentor.

Sid Tanenbaum, in more ways than one, was the true star of Hewlett/North Woodmere. He was just as special a person as he was gifted on the basketball court. He was kind, gentle, and always sensitive to the feeling of others. He went out of his way to help the youngsters. I knew that firsthand from the attention and suggestions he gave to Seth. I previously wrote about Sid's storied All-American career at NYU and the awesome talent that I saw him exhibit at the BRC. This time around, at age fifty plus, his superior skills were still evident. It wasn't as much his deadly set shot or his graceful running one-hander as it was his quickness and darting movements without the ball. It was embarrassing to be beaten decisively by an old man. Sid hated to take advantage of inferior opponents. He felt uncomfortable showing up those who tried hard but weren't quality players. Sometimes he would even stop in the middle of an open layup and contrive a reason to start over.

In the mid-1980s, this prince of a man suddenly and tragically lost his life. He was stabbed by a woman, a drug addict, whom he had known and helped on several occasions by giving her a few dollars for some food. She was one of many drifters that hung out in the mean streets of Rockaway, near Sid's place of business. On that terrible day, Sid was alone and unable to call for assistance. In the pink of condition and a basketball player at age sixty, Sid bled to death. The following spring, the basketball courts at North Woodmere Park were officially designated The Sid Tanenbaum Memorial Basketball Courts. Furthermore, that

June marked the beginning of the park's annual Nassau County sponsored half-court tournament bearing Sid's name. These honors are testimonials to the esteem in which he was held by all who knew Sid Tanenbaum.

At Hewlett, a guy came across my nose with a forearm blow and broke it. There was no need for surgery as the injury didn't impede my breathing and, to begin with, my nose was far from perfect. I simply put on a comfortable softball catcher's mask and resumed playing. Shortly afterwards, a finger in the eye permanently ruptured my right pupil. My right knee was always stiff and sore, necessitating the wearing of some source of support whenever I played. Perhaps because of overcompensating for the poor condition of the knee, I continuously pulled calf and hamstring muscles on my right leg. Long and careful stretching helped a bit, but the strains continued to occur with cyclical regularity. Through all the pain and temporary setbacks and the reality that things would not improve with age, I never seriously considered hanging up the sneakers. I loved the action and, as I would frequently say, needed it more for my head than for the exercise, which I could get through a variety of less physically demanding activities than basketball. The game was my addiction, and I wasn't seeking a cure.

Raquette Lake basketball coach and friend Julie Levine taught physical education at Samuel Gompers High School in the Bronx. Gompers was located in the tough South Bronx area that attained considerable notoriety as a result of the movie *Fort Apache*, which starred Paul Newman as a policeman. On Saturday mornings, Julie opened the gym and hosted an outstanding full-court workout. The majority of the participants were well-known black players from the Bronx and Upper Manhattan, with a few white guys sprinkled in the mix. Ironically, one of the prominent Caucasians in the run was Alan Seiden, who seemingly crossed paths with me anywhere basketball was played. Our meeting at Gornpers brought about a level of communication between us beyond the court and transformed a polite acquaintanceship into a lasting friendship.

At most, my attendance at the Gompers workout was a twice a month thing. I never became a true regular there and generally had to wait to get a game. On the court, I attempted to blend and didn't look to create my own shot with the aggressiveness that I would ordinarily exhibit in a comfortable Long Island run. I definitely felt like a guest at Gompers and treated the invitation with respectful appreciation. Despite the self-imposed restraint, the games were fun and challenging.

A large reason for going up to Gompers was the opportunity for Seth to see and play with Julie's son Jared. As the Levines lived far north of Long Island in Rockland County, it was logistically difficult for the boys to get together. Gompers became the convenient meeting ground, where they would find a side basket and spend the morning engaging in a shootout.

Alan was drawn to Gompers by the presence of Stacey Arcenaux, someone he played with and against for many years in the Eastern League. Stacey, a legendary New York City high school scoring machine, was all-city in the early 1950s at Taft High School. He was one of the very first to make the jump from high school directly to the NBA. Stacey, without a day of college ball, played briefly for the St. Louis Hawks before moving on to a long and successful career in the Eastern League. I can't explain his short stint in the NBA, but I can state with certainty that the 6'5" wide-bodied forward had the shot to match anyone in the big show. Stacey's jumper was soft, smooth, and highly accurate. His shooting range and ability to get it off quickly were equally impressive.

Most of the guys at Gompers were big and exceptionally strong. Just bumping into them often brought about pain and the realization that it was best to tread lightly. Eddie, the brothers Tom and Scoop, and Milton, a martial arts expert–all of them hulks–took delight in crashing the boards and banging bodies. Even the guards at the workout such as Miles Dorsch and Russell, with his shaved head, were Herculean physical specimens whose raw strength augmented their excellent basketball skills. On occasions, New York Knicks Mel "Killer" Davis and fan favorite

Hawthorne Wingo added their imposing physical stature to the run. Bob Keller, a formidable Eastern League forward, originally from Brownsville and Harlem Globetrotter Bob Hunter were two others who helped enrich the play at Gompers.

Alan was his usual exasperating, foul-calling self. His stubbornness generally resulted in his winning most of the arguments, primarily because the other guys, eager to get on with the game, would weaken and finally submit. There was, however, one hilarious yet scary time when Alan didn't prevail. On that morning, Alan and a player by the name of Mike were involved in a heated dispute. Both stuck to their point of view and refused to bend.

Mike suddenly, without explanation, left the gym. He returned within a minute or two, carrying a pistol. Looking directly at Alan, he calmly asked, "Whose ball is it?" Alan, with absolutely no delay, responded, "No problem. It's your ball." With no other words exchanged, Mike put away the gun and took the ball out of bounds. The game resumed without further incident or hint of the earlier hostility.

At the end of the June 1978 school term, the doors of PS 36 closed forever. As planned, the building was torn down to make room for the ball field of the new Eastern District High School. PS 36 continued to exist in name with me as principal but without a main facility. Our students and teachers were dispersed to a number of Brooklyn and Queens special education schools. The reorganized PS 36 consisted of a cluster of seven smaller programs for emotionally handicapped children, six housed in regular elementary and junior high schools and in a plant that previously was occupied by a Catholic parochial school. I was told by board of education authorities that PS 36 would again have a home base when a suitable and affordable building could be found. It was made clear that the facility would not be a newly constructed school.

A complication was that none of the schools accommodating the PS 36 programs had enough space to provide us with an office for myself and secretarial/clerical staff. Marge Louer, a dynamic special education principal, and a good friend carne to the rescue. With the approval of the board of education, she offered a room, not exactly spacious but adequate for our basic administrative needs. She also graciously would allow us to share her large basement supply rooms and threw in a walk-in closet opposite the proposed office. Having no other option even close to what Marge was willing to do for us, the offer was enthusiastically accepted.

Marge Louer's school, situated in Bedford-Stuyvesant, was Sterling High School, a former "600 school" (prior to the court-mandated transition) but still an institution that served the most difficult adolescent and young adult male student population in New York City. All the students were certified severely emotionally handicapped and were placed at Sterling as a court of last resort. Almost every one of the pupils was known to the judicial system, police, and/or psychiatric treatment facilities. Intellectually, many had the cognitive ability to earn a high school diploma. Sterling's academic program, therefore, paralleled that of a non-special education school.

Basketball was a major interest of Sterling's students and some of the faculty members. Solly Walker, prior to his appointment as principal to a similar-type school in Manhattan, was the Sterling assistant principal. Percy Watson, Eddie Barnett, and Embra Sease, three of the school's most respected teachers, were outstanding athletes, all of whom played in college. Knowing of my own basketball involvement, they drafted me to compete in staff-student games and other special events. As my office was in the building, I qualified and was accepted as one of the Sterling faculty. Similar to the response at the original PS 36, playing against the students was a tremendous icebreaker in terms of gaining respect among the boys and being seen as one of the homies. The Sterling players ran faster and certainly jumped higher than us, but we beat them with smarts, better ball control, and most often, my outside shot. The games were more than just fun. They enhanced morale by bringing staff and students closer together.

Eddie Barnett, following a weekly tradition begun by Solly Walker, obtained approval to keep the Sterling gymnasium open after school on Fridays for adult basketball. Every Friday, a group of significant names from my Brooklyn past would assemble at the school for hours of basketball and socializing. In addition to Solly, Eddie, and sometimes Percy, other regulars included Hank Whitney, Ed "The Eel" Willis, and the wonderful Viceroy/Brownsville crew consisting of Danny Culley, Jake Jordan, Arnold Branch, Karl Walkes, etc. Every once in a while, Tony Jackson would make an appearance. I participated several times and had a ball, partly reliving my youth at Betsy Head and other terrific Brownsville playgrounds. The one deterring factor was the time of the workout. It was supposed to start at 4:30 PM but rarely got underway before six o'clock. Not only would the guys drift in late, but the friendship and bonding aspects of the gathering frequently overshadowed the basketball action. From a family standpoint, getting home well into the night on Fridays would be insensitive, especially considering that I played hoops at other times during the week. For these reasons, I discontinued attending the nostalgic Sterling workouts.

From the day I moved to Long Island, I had more indoor basketball options on Sunday mornings than I did on Saturdays. Of course, there never was a problem when it was warm enough to comfortably play outdoors. There was a point, however, in the mid to late 1970s that unless I went to Gompers or to Manhasset High School (a place that I have yet to mention) some of my Saturday mornings were basketball-less.

The need for a basketball fix led me to Nassau Community College. The school, then in its infancy, was developed on the site of the recently closed Mitchell Air Force Base. A gymnasium was established in one of the vacated airplane hangars, which I heard was also the scene of perhaps the best workout on Long Island. The word was that "Dr. J", Bill Bradley and Phil Jackson competed at Nassau.

Jon, Seth, and I set out one Saturday morning to see firsthand what was happening at Nassau. The school was located little more than a stone's throw from Nassau Coliseum and Hofstra University. As there was more than one airplane hangar on campus, it took a while to find the one that was transformed into a gym. The place was immense, large enough to use for football. There were at least a dozen baskets on concrete surfaced courts. And then there was the main court, which was something to behold. It was regulation size, above ground level on what could be accurately described as a platform or a stage. The floor was all wood, a replica of the court at Madison Square Garden, right down to the dead spots on the weak boards and near the seams. It was a marvelous place to play.

Although I sometimes shot around at the big court at Nassau, I never got into a game. It was obviously a closed workout that drew a crowd of players, generally numbering between fifteen and twenty and necessitating a wait for several of the regulars. There was no way that I, uninvited, would attempt to push myself into that type of situation despite the burning desire to play. Most often, I would work with the boys on the side basket and watch a bit of the excellent activity in the prime time game.

Erving, Bradley, and Jackson were long gone from the workout when I arrived at the Nassau gym. The quality, however, was still first rate. In my opinion, the best was George Bruns, whom I hadn't seen in person since the Manhattan Beach days. I followed his fine progress from Manhattan College to the ABA but never crossed paths with him. Initially, we made eye contact and nodded in a mutual show of recognition. Yet we didn't speak until much later. There were some others whose play immediately caught my attention. One of those was ex-St. John's great prolific shooter and a former Net Billy Schaefer. I also was impressed with the skills of Fairfield star and innovative scorer George Groom and Pete LaMantia, another former St. John's player who was a deadly long range bomber and a tenacious defender.

Two outstanding players who are also very special people that I now count as good friends are Lou Roethal and Larry Kaufer. Lou was the 6'6" center on St. John's NIT and Holiday Festival Champions of 1959 (e.g., Seiden, Jackson, Alfieri, Engert). Not blessed with superior running or jumping ability, his game was one of intelligence. Lou was a terrific passer, boxed out beautifully to gain rebounding position, and could hit the open shot. Off the court, he is a most warm and caring person. Larry Kaufer is a slender and fit 6'4" forward with a terrific deep standing jump shot. In college, he played at Adelphi University and then had an exciting stint on the hardwoods of Israel. Larry's game is full of fire and unrelenting determination. He has a nose for the ball and a knack for grabbing weak side rebounds. His nonbasketball demeanor is in direct contrast to his athletic aggressiveness. Like Lou, he is a sincere, community-spirited individual.

The workout in the converted airplane hangar ended when the permanent construction of a modern Nassau Community College was undertaken. Most of the old Air Force structures were razed and replaced by functional school buildings. The games, however didn't die but were moved to a new location at Freeport High School. Two of the players, outstanding-jump-shooting-and-quick Jerry Jackson and strong-on-defense tenacious rebounder Ernie Kyte, were graduates of Freeport High School and were influential in obtaining permission for us to use the gym. In addition, Ernie eventually became the school's principal and doubled as the girls' high ranking basketball coach. Jerry was a standout at both Nassau Community College and CW Post and has been enshrined as a Hall of Famer.

My desire to get into the workout kept increasing and at last was satisfied. Some of the guys were dental patients of Don Goldstein. Don was invited to play and, after his first appearance, was hooked by the quality and intensity of the games. He then asked if he could bring me along. Naturally, I was ecstatic when the OK was given. I immediately echoed Don's feeling about the competition and the prevailing atmosphere of good fellowship. The workout was officially dubbed The Saturday Run. This title was printed on the reversible blue and white tank tops that were worn during the games. The shirts had an illustration of a cartoonlike character in a basketball uniform sitting with a beer in his hand. Sharing a few brews following the workout was a rewarding and refreshing Saturday Run tradition. Once I became acknowledged as a regular, a shirt was ordered for me, carrying the inscription "Wheels." This was a warmhearted but cutting reference to the ever-present bands on my knees and the obvious declining foot speed brought about by age and injury.

In general, the nicknames on the shirts were personally relevant and clever. The one that most intrigued me was "Senor Madre," Spanish for Mr. Mom. It applied to Walt Szczerbiak, who rejoined the workout in the 1980s after his retirement from a notable professional basketball career in Europe, most of it spent in Spain. When he returned, Walter did much of his work as a representative for the Spanish professional leagues from his home while his wife, Marilyn, was out selling real estate. When his children were small, he shared much of the daytime responsibility as co-homemaker. Hence, he was jokingly referred to as Senor Madre.

Walt was a 6'6" forward, who played considerably taller primarily due to his extremely long arms. Born and raised in Pittsburgh, he left the Iron City to play his college ball at George Washington University, where he was one of the leading rebounders in the country. His next stop was the ABL upstart league, the father to the ABA, with the red, white, and blue ball; he played a season for the Pittsburgh Condors. Although drafted by the NBA's Buffalo Braves, he chose to accept a more secure long-term contract offered by Real Madrid, one of Europe's premier teams. That decision turned out to be an excellent one as Walt's stellar play made him a favorite in Spain and was a key factor in Real Madrid's three European championships. In his best season, Walt averaged an awesome thirty-two points per game. He is considered to have been one of the finest Americans to play in Europe.

Walt is one of the best that I have ever played with. He is also one of those rare guys whose unselfishness and all-round excellence elevated the performance of his teammates. Offensively, he never wasted a dribble or a movement. Everything he did was purposeful and economizing. Neither a great leaper nor a speed merchant, he got the job done with deceptive strength, a rubbery body, and above all, basketball intelligence. He was a tremendous jump shooter, just about automatic from the baseline and foul line extended. He had good range, a quick release, and shot smoothly and efficiently without having to put the ball on the floor. Defensively, he intimidated with his reach and was much quicker than he appeared. I firmly believe that had Walt been given the full opportunity to play in the NBA, he would have easily made the grade.

Lou Roethel grew up as best friends and practically a brother of John Kresse. John, a former assistant basketball coach at St. John's and also in the ABA in the brief time that Lou Carnesecca coached the Nets, migrated to Charleston, South Carolina, to accept a position as head coach at the College of Charleston. When John arrived there, the school had a mediocre basketball program and competed in the NAIA category. It is an understatement that he helped to turn things around. The College of Charleston's basketball fortunes blossomed dramatically and soon enjoyed consistent winning records. Basketball at Charleston under John's direction was elevated to the Division I level, where their winning teams captured the attention of the American college basketball community. John's reputation as a coach grew dramatically as the College of Charleston became a top mid-major, capable of competing against the very best.

Getting back to Lou Roethel and his connection to John Kresse, Lou got the brilliant idea to organize a long weekend basketball excursion of our Saturday Run group to Charleston, South Carolina. The plan was to do it in April after the basketball season, when John Kresse could accommodate us with a gym, free of conflicts due to scheduling and time constraints. John embraced Lou's request and was eager to host our traveling basketball caravan. Quickly, airplane, hotel, and auto rental arrangements were made. I and the bulk of us were off to Charleston. The 1980s experiment was a smashing success and became an annual spring ritual for old basketball players, golfers, and gourmets.

I went four times and enjoyed each trip immensely. Charleston is a wonderful, culturally rich, and genteel southern city. It is a warm and friendly place with outstanding restaurants, old-world charm, and tremendous history. For many of the group, basketball has become the supplement to the plethora of excellent Charleston area golf courses. I'm not a golfer, so for me it was hoops, southern sunshine by the pool, pumping a little iron in the health club, considerably more imbibing than I do at home, and lots of laughs spent with a great bunch of guys. John Kresse, who has a home on Kiawah Island, a nearby resort, made arrangements for us to spend a day of fun and assorted athletic activity at the beach. The annual visit to Kiawah was always one of our highlights. Of players that I have written about the regulars on the Charleston shuttle were George Bruns, Lou Roethel, Larry Kaufer, Don Goldstein, and Jerry Jackson. Other Saturday Run participants who made the trips were Jimmy Burke, Joe Hoffman, Steve Nisenson, Stu Klein, and Kevin Finneran.

Joe Hoffman was the life of many a party at Charleston. A gregarious fellow in a perpetually good mood, he loves to laugh, shoot the breeze while downing a couple of cold ones, and hang out with the boys. As for basketball, I first met and played with Joe at Long Beach where he lived. He was tough 6'5" forward who rebounded very well, was a good shooter, and was specifically adept at using the backboard. Collegiately, Joe played at Belmont-Abbey in the early coaching days of Hall of Famer Al McGuire. At Charleston, Joe usually roomed with Bill "Bud" Boyd, another bruising forward who now lives in Boston but reserves time in April to hook up on the road with his New York cronies.

Steve Nisenson is one of Hofstra University's all-time greats. When he played there during the 1960s, he was among the highest scorers in the country and, in fact, one year lead the nation in free throw percentage. Steve had a chronic back problem, which fortunately didn't interfere with his golfing but could no longer take the strain and pounding that occurs on the basketball court. His silky smooth backcourt game and feathery touch, however, remains very vivid to me. As a person, he is low-key, mild-mannered, and a pleasure to be around.

Stu Klein, for close to twenty years, had been the men's basketball coach at Nassau Community College. A terrific high school guard at Martin Van Buren, where his coach was the dynamic Marv Kessler, he next went out west and played at Northern Arizona University. Stu's uncanny crossover dribble and fast hands were the hallmarks of his classy game. At Charleston, he mixed basketball and golf and invariably was limping about after two days of hoops. Stu is friendly, easygoing, and a good communicator, all qualities that his players recognized and appreciated long after their basketball days at Nassau was over. Interestingly, one of Stu's closest friends and his former Nassau assistant (and a Van Buren guy) is respected coach Tom Pecora. Tom had outstanding teams at Hofstra University and later was at the helm at Fordham University.

The Don Juan and most eligible bachelor of our crew was Kevin Finneran. Kevin is 6'2", handsome and charming, and many years younger than most of us. Time and time again, Kevin demonstrated his ability to attract the young and pretty women of Charleston. When I and others were tucked away in our beds, Kevin was out enjoying the city's vigorous night life. He always managed to save a little something for the basketball court, where his athletic ability was evident. Kevin is a former Nassau Community College player who later coached there, both as an assistant and briefly as interim head coach.

A Charleston regular who was in a category of his own is Mike Candel. Although he gave up active playing many years ago, his association with basketball was as strong as any of us. Mike was an outstanding sportswriter for *Newsday*, the award-winning Long Island newspaper. As a reporter, his assignment included covering basketball on the college and high school levels. In his capacity as sports columnist, he had written countless feature stories. Apart from *Newsday*, Mike taught math at Nassau CC and previously coached its men's basketball team. On the trip, Mike was one of the golf enthusiasts. Personality-wise, he is articulate, outspoken, opinionated, and always interesting.

Literally, Jim Hegmann was a huge addition to our Charleston entourage. Jim, an original Saturday Run player, is a former Niagara University center. At 6'10" and more than three hundred pounds, he is an imposing figure both on and off the court. It is a blessing that given his size and strength, he is gentle and good-hearted. In business, Jim distributed meat and cold cuts to restaurants and delicatessens and found it difficult to get away from the job. Once, however, he made the commitment to arrange his schedule to attend the trip, he knew how important the few days off was to his revitalization. Aside from basketball, where he demonstrated an extraordinary soft jump shot for a big man, he was one of the group's best golfers. As expected, he got great distance on his drives but also showed that good touch in his short game.

I recruited two close friends with whom I played in other Long Island workouts to join us in Charleston. They were both hooked after the first visit. These guys were sweet-shooting Mark Rich, my Hewlett-North Woodmere protégé, and Joel "Swimmer" White. My relationship with Joel went all the way back to basketball in the East New York section of Brooklyn and at CCNY, where he was a standout on the swimming team. Joel was an athlete rather than a pure basketball player and was in excellent running condition for a man in his fifties. Like me, Mark and Joel were nongolfers. As our interests in Charleston coincided, we roomed together and shared the same rental car during the fabulous minivacations.

Don Goldstein continued to find new places for us to play basketball. In the early 1980s, he received a phone call from Neal Wichard, a Long Islander who he originally met at the University of Louisville. Neal and Don hadn't been in contact for many years but still felt a mutual bond of affection. In that conversation, Neal told Don about a Sunday morning workout at CW Post College that he had a hand in coordinating. He wanted Don to participate and to bring along additional guys to compete in an informal full-court game against those who regularly played at Post. That first time, we came with a team of six–Don, me, Gary Wood, Gary Franklin, Howie Bernstein, and Paul "Rope" Glass. It wasn't, however, to be our last appearance as it marked the beginning of a very long running show.

Neal Wichard didn't graduate from Louisville, having transferred and eventually earned his degree from CW Post. At Post, he played baseball and had remained active and philanthropic in the school's athletic programs as an alumnus. Several years later, Neal's brother Gary attended Post and became its most honored athlete. Gary achieved Division II, All-American recognition as quarterback and in his senior year led all US college quarterbacks in total passing yardage. He was invited to play in major college all-star games and was drafted by the NFL's Baltimore Colts. After working briefly for an automobile dealership, Gary shifted business gears and served an apprenticeship under a prominent sports agent. He then set out on his own and quickly established himself in this field of specialization. Initially, he was best known for his representation of the charismatic football star Brian Bosworth. Later on, a few of his high-profile clients were all-pro tight end Keith Jackson and certain future Hall of Famer Miami Dolphin defensive end Jason Taylor. Closer to home on Long Island, Gary became the agent for a young man who is the son of a friend and someone he had known since childhood. That person was sweet-shooting NBA forward Wally Szczerbiak.

The basketball setup at Post was a half-court game at one of the main baskets and full-court across the other side of the gym. Naturally, playing across the floor shortened the length of the court by approximately twenty feet, which was ideal for old warriors like us. Our Post debut was highly successful. Having the benefit of playing together so many times, we performed smoothly and efficiently as a team in contrast with the makeshift squad thrown together by Neal and Gary. The winner of each game was determined by the first team to score eleven baskets. On that morning, we won them all.

The Wichard contingent had some guys with college basketball experience. There was Judd Rothman, a strong and hefty 6'8" center who played at Louisville a few years after Don Goldstein, and Charlie Vachris from Yale, a 6'2" hard worker with an effective baseline game. Other lesser names but tough competitors were Jeff Rubinstein, fundamentally sound and a good shooter, whom I remembered from Brooklyn's Williamsburgh YMHA, and Richie Mandor, a scrapper and fierce defensive specialist who played with reckless abandon. Two eager participants, a cut below in ability, were Keith Kenner, whom I hadn't seen since Miami's Flamingo Park, and Seth Rotter, an accurate shooter with otherwise marginal skills.

Neal and Gary were tremendous competitors and compelling personalities. Neal made up in effort what he lacked in talent. At 6'0" and much stronger than he appeared, he rebounded well and relished banging against bigger players. In the heat of battle, Neal would often become emotional and angry. Opponents knew to watch out when Hurricane Neal began to blow. Afterwards, when calm, he would seek reconciliation with the source of his irritation. He enjoyed organizing the Post workout and took his "commissioner's" responsibilities most seriously. He definitely demonstrated leadership qualities. It was easy to see why Neal was such a success in business. Gary too had the intense determination, which no doubt was crucial to his high standing in the sport's agent field. On the negative side, I felt at times, he exhibited over-the-top emotionality when things weren't going his way. Athletically, he was physically gifted. A rock solid 6'2", he was fast, could jump, and was always in excellent condition. His shooting and ball handling were erratic accompanied by sporadic hot and cold streaks. Despite the checkered results, Gary's confidence level was remarkably high. He wanted the role of go-to guy and never faded in the background when the game was on the line. In my opinion, he would have been a far more effective basketball player if he better understood how to utilize his skills within the context of the total game. Like his older brother Neal, he would blow off steam, erupt, and then forget about it by the next time he stepped on the court.

Neal, convinced that our participation enriched the workout, invited us to become regulars at Post. It would not, however, be an "us against them" situation as it was decided that the games would be of the choose-up and make-fair-sides genre. I asked Neal if I could bring Alan Seiden to the gym. Alan was looking for Sunday full-court action, which wasn't the mode of play at Hewlett-North Woodmere. Neal, knowing Alan by reputation and through his past press notices, was eager to have another quality player in the run.

Alan's first time at Post was memorable. Luck would have it that on that particular morning, a leaking roof prevented us from using the whole court. A few remained, but most left, unenthused about playing half-court. Alan and I challenged Gary Wichard and his client, Jet's quarterback Richard Todd, to a game of two-on-two. While I was shooting from the outside and hitting with consistency, Alan was going to the hole with much success against the two taller opponents. As was his habit, he also called many fouls on Wichard and Todd. They were crazed, frustrated at losing to two older players and angered by their perception of Alan's cheap calls. A war of words ensued wherein Alan refused to back down. They cursed at him while he calmly commented about their lack of basketball ability. In truth, Todd wasn't much of a basketball player. As for Gary and Alan, that was the start of a long stormy athletic relationship. Each had respect for the other's toughness and, at times, declared a temporary truce. However, the clashes of two aggressive and obstinate personalities were inevitable.

Word of mouth about the excellence of the Post workout quickly spread. Many of our ball-playing friends soon joined the mix. Others close to Neal and Gary also began to attend with regularity. Stu Goldman, Tony Licata, Roosevelt Jackson, and Jim McKinstry were all guys from the Wichard connection. Stu and Tony, both former CW Post hoopsters, added their hustle and hardnosed styles. Roosevelt, a leaper and former Long Island high school scoring sensation, was young and a man of a thousand moves. Jim McKinstry, an immovable 6'3" forward, was both a New York Titan and an original New York Jet tight end. Jim's incredibly powerful and sure hands were his best basketball assets. In high school, he was one of Nassau County's finest rebounders.

Those who came to the workout by way of Don and me included Ivan Kovac, "Red" Blumenreich, Joel "Swimmer" White, Chuck Kaufman, Mark Groothius, Bob Sack, and Al Schindler. I've already said much about Ivan, Red, and Swimmer. As for the newcomers, Chuck and Mark, both guards excelled at moving without the ball and displayed good court sense. Chuck played collegiately on Dartmouth's Ivy League Championship teams of the late 1950s that featured Rudy LaRusso. Mark's college ball was at William and Mary and NYU. Bobby Sack, a 6'3" forward from Hunter College, was slow and a bit overweight but got it done through fundamentals, crisp passing, and a deadly one-hander. Al Schindler, an addictive park player whom Alan Seiden knew from his youth in the Queens schoolyards, could run all day, had a fine driving hook shot, and jumped remarkably well for a middle-aged man.

In our second year at Post, George Bruns, Larry Kaufer, and Lou Roethel became occasional participants. Later on, Walt Szczerbiak, Jim Hegmann, and Mark Rich came aboard. Walt also introduced his friend Mike Griffin, a Harvard point guard with dazzling head fakes and spin moves on the run.

For me, a highlight of the early years at Post was having the pleasure of playing with and getting to know several of the professional athletes who were clients and/or friends with Gary Wichard. From the Jets–Darrel Ray, Jerry Holmes, and Lance Mehl played regularly after the football season ended. Ken O'Brien and Rocky Klever are two other Jets who later participated in the workouts. The lone baseball player in our group was relief pitcher Neil Allen. All were terrific guys and capable basketball players.

Darrel Ray was an outstanding safety before repeated shoulder separations became a permanent obstacle to hard physical contact. Darrel, at 6'2" and two hundred pounds, had movie star looks and an unbelievable, sculptured body. On the basketball court, he played great defense, ran like a deer, and was a strong rebounder. He also had a nice shooting touch but was reluctant to let it fly. Off the court, he was charming and articulate and loved hanging out with city slicker Alan Seiden.

Jerry Holmes, a 6'2" respected veteran cornerback, had the body and grace of a greyhound. Jerry's strongest suits in basketball were his lightning reflexes and quick jumping ability. He would go up and down twice before most guys were setting themselves to jump. He also had a good first step to the basket. Jerry Holmes was a wonderful, sincere, and warmhearted person. When my son Seth played in high school, Jerry came to see a few of his games.

Lance Mehl was another who attained all-pro status until successive devastating knee injuries prematurely ended his football career. Never the biggest, strongest, or fastest linebacker, his acumen and discipline at Penn State and for the Jets made him one of the best. His skill, intelligence, and team play were similarly evident on the basketball court. He wasn't flashy but did everything extremely well, He could shoot, handle the ball, and play good defense. As a person he was quiet, sensible, and friendly.

I link Ken O'Brien with Rocky Klever because they always came and left together. Having heard so much about Kenny's slowness on the football field, I was surprised by the athletic ability he demonstrated in basketball. True, he was no gazelle, but of all the Jets at Post, he was the most skilled player. Almost 6'5", he was an excellent shooter and a smooth and proficient ball handler. Ken was a bright, polite, and genuine individual. I felt badly about the hammering he received toward the end of his days as quarterback in New York. As for Rocky, his game matched his flamboyant, extraverted personality. The 6'3" tight end possessed great athleticism and a body to match. He played up-tempo, loving to run, gun, and apply the pressure. Occasionally, he would get out of control but always maintained the smile and took constructive suggestions good naturedly.

Neil Allen was a fun-loving character and an enigma. He had one of the premier curveballs in baseball and for a few years was one of the game's best relief pitchers. His confidence, however, was easily shaken, and there were times that he doubted his superior tools. We saw that on the basketball court where he would deprecate his ability if he missed a few shots or lost the ball. Neil, in fact, ran well, jumped high, and had a good jump shot. Yet he frequently, realistically dismissed his performance. Whenever Neil showed up at Post, there was laughter and lighthearted conversation. He often brought a baseball, a fielder's glove, and a catcher's mitt and would pitch to Neil Wichard or my son Seth. The break on his curve was awesome.

Ex-NYU standout Dom Debonis played just once at Post. He hadn't seriously picked up a basketball for over ten years when he decided to get back to the game. Already fifty years of age, another impediment was his fairly heavy smoking habit. The day he came, we held him out until later in the workout, giving him time to stretch, loosen up, and shoot around. When he got in, he played in a frenzy, defending his man nose to nose and pressing from end to end. Within fifteen minutes, not only was he completely breathless but lost all color in his face. We sat him down and considered calling for emergency medical assistance, but he resisted, mainly because he quickly felt better and began breathing normally. Tragically, Dom didn't get the message from that scare. About a month later, he attended a reunion of friends from his old neighborhood and again attempted to play basketball. This time, there would be no reprieve as he suffered a fatal heart attack.

I cannot emphasize too strongly the great risk to older guys who return to the strain of basketball after being away from the game for a considerable period of time. I personally witnessed two other basketball deaths due to heart attacks. In both instances, the victims foolishly put their lives on the line. At Merrick Road Park, Bert–big, out-of-shape, and a smoker–suddenly dropped in the middle of the game and never regained consciousness. He knew how to play, but skill is no substitute for minimal fitness.

The second tragedy occurred at Manhasset High School, where I would occasionally play with Dick Martino. Dick was one of Merrick Road's finest outside shooters and an unabashed self-promoter. On that Saturday morning, we were playing together in a three man game. The fellow taking me was much younger, thinner, yet clearly in poor basketball condition. He was breathing heavily and exhibited distressed body language. I immediately whispered to Dick, "I'm going to run this guy until his tongue falls off." I then put my plan into action—cutting, changing direction, and remaining in constant motion. Without any distinct sign of imminent physical difficulty, he gasped and fell backward, hitting his head on the floor. Initially, his eyes were open, and he was obviously conscious. He got to his feet, began walking to the sideline, and again collapsed. This time, he didn't get up. The horror was worsened by the presence of his young son who accompanied his dad to the gym.

For days, I felt guilty about my overly competitive behavior, which perhaps contributed to his death. I asked myself whether I should have recognized the extent of the problem and insisted that he stop playing. The answer that I eventually accepted was that I had no way of truly foretelling such a nightmare. A player looks for an edge. When I saw that he was out of shape, it was an opportunity to gain the upper hand. I, therefore, attempted to take that advantage.

The Wichards grew up in Glen Cove, Long Island, and befriended the town's recreation director, John Maccarone. John, an older man, was a warm and caring individual, dedicated to family, friends, and his job. He loved sports and was successful in developing a wide range of athletic activities and competitive leagues in Glen Cove. One of the things that he was widely acclaimed for was the formation of an advanced open basketball league at Friends Academy in Locust Valley. The tournament attracted the finest former college players on Long Island.

Neal and John got together and came up with a concept for a late fall/winter league for older players. The idea became the reality of the Glen Cove 38 and Over League. It originally was going to have a bottom age of forty, but John made the change when he learned that George Bruns, high-profiled and one of his favorites, was only thirty-eight.

All the regulars at Post were eager to play, as well as a high percentage of guys still active, who resided on Long Island. I immediately reinstituted the Elder Statesmen, a name that was even more appropriate this time than in the days when I played in the Town of Hempstead Summer League. As a mock reward for reviving the Statesmen, I was drafted to be our team's player-coach. We had a formidable roster featuring George Bruns, Don Goldstein, Larry Kaufer, Lou Roethel, Stu Goldman, Gary Franklin, Howie Bernstein, and Mark Groothius. Our part-time players, on call to fill in as needed, were Neil Flamm, Shelly Rokeach, and Frank Russo. Neil was someone I first met way back at Manhattan Beach and later befriended when he worked under my supervision at the board of education. Crisp passing and gluelike defense were Neil's specialties. Shelly, another from Brooklyn days but at the Williamsburgh "Y", had a dynamic post-up game for a guy just 6'1". He enjoyed being mentioned as an Adrian Dantley type. Frank, a Saturday Run regular, was strong, intense, and could hit the long shot.

Hank Cluess was part-time only because his job as a policeman and supplemental involvement as a high school basketball referee prevented him from making the bulk of our games. Hank, an ideally built 6'7" forward, was an excellent all-around player with multiple skills and no discernible weaknesses. Hank was the oldest of four talented basketball playing brothers. He, Gregg, and Kevin all starred at St. John's. Tim, the youngest, began but transferred to Hofstra where he enjoyed success.

The Cluess family, strong and close knit, has endured and overcome tremendous heartache. Both Gregg and Kevin, vibrant young men in the prime of their lives, were stricken with blood-related cancers. They battled valiantly but eventually succumbed to the deadly disease. Hank, Tim, and the other members of the Cluess family are healthy, productive, and always perform deeds to honor the memory of Gregg and Kevin. They are models of resiliency and unshakeable faith.

Tim is the coach of the Cluess clan. His career in this aspect of basketball has been meteoric and exceptional. Tim has won big in every level that he has coached. In high school, his teams at St. Mary's of Manhasset, Long Island, were among the best in the US. At St. Mary's, his most celebrated player was Danny Green, a star at the University of North Carolina and a key member of the San Antonio Spurs. His success at St. Mary's was followed by championships at Suffolk Community College and Division II CW Post. He then moved up to his current position at Division I mid-major, Iona College, where he has taken them back to three NCAA tournaments. Tim is considered one of the rising stars in the college coaching firmament.

Most teams in our league were represented by former college standouts. Among those that I played with previously were Alan Seiden, Ivan Kovac, Joe Hoffman, Red Blumenreich, Billy Gordon, Billy Burwell, Bob Sack, Judd Rothman, Tony Licata, etc. Other highly skilled players who were first time opponents were Luther Green (LIU and NY Nets), John Mathis (NY Nets), Dan Mascia (St. John's), Dave Stewart (St. Louis University), and Wandy Williams (Hofstra and the NFL's Denver Broncos). Two other impressive players were Ralph Willard and Jerry Powell.

Ralph was to have a distinguished coaching career compiling impressive records at Western Kentucky, Pittsburgh, and Holy Cross. More recently, following retirement as a head coach, he returned as the top assistant to his Long Island buddy, Rick Pitino, at Louisville. Jerry Powell was one of Lenny Wilkens assistant with the Atlantic Hawks. The Wilkens-Powell story is a wonderful one, as they played together well over fifty years ago at Brooklyn's famed Boys' High School.

In the tournament's first year, we breezed through the regular season with just one loss. Bruns, who retained the quickness of a collegian along with his flawless shooting stroke, was clearly the league's outstanding player. Don Goldstein, although no longer the magnificent offensive force, was still superior defensively and off the boards. The rest of us contributed significantly, adding to a whole that was better than any of its individual parts. I was in and out, depending upon the extent of muscle strains and ever-sore right knee. When able to get open, I drained a good percentage of my jumpers.

In the final game we faced Ivan Kovac's squad. Although we were out in front from the start, and never lost the lead, it was a competitive contest. In addition to Ivan, Bob Sack, Red

Blumenreich, and Dan Mascia, they were bolstered by the play of Sam Stern (Yeshiva University), Jack Gibbons (Georgetown University), and John Doran (Manhattan College). Sam, who was also an excellent college coach, was a clever guard. Jack had a strong and versatile post-up game, and John was a ferocious rebounder and supreme "garbage" man. We prevailed in the end, capturing the Glen Cove Old Gray Hair 38 and Over championship.

That season's most humorous moment was, of course, provided by Alan Seiden. As many times as he went to the free throw line, it wasn't enough for Alan. If he didn't make the shot, it had to be because he was fouled. One of the referees who had little patience for Alan's antics was Jerry Loeber, a former NBA ref. In a close game, Alan drove to the basket, faked, and shot. When he released the ball, he reflexively shouted, "And one," which was his patented "I was fouled" statement. Jerry's quick response was "And one on you." Not only was Alan not awarded the foul shots, he was assessed with a technical. I can't remember if it was vital to the outcome of the game.

The next season was the league's last one. John Maccarone was upset over several instances where teams used ineligible younger players. Another thorn was the increasing number of requests to change the schedule due to player job conflicts. The complications pushed John over the edge. As much as he enjoyed the involvement and the surprising local publicity, administering the league became an overdemanding burden.

Stu Goldman left the Elder Statesmen to join a team with some of his close friends. He was replaced by Stu Klein, who did a great job for us in a time of need. We were thin in the backcourt early in the season as my physical condition had me on the shelf for at least half the games. More importantly, George Bruns's workload and family obligations caused him to be unavailable during the first part of our schedule. Our record was still respectable, but we were far from dominant.

The team came alive in the second half of the season, primarily due to George's increased presence, and made it into the four-team playoff. We easily defeated Joe Hoffman's Long Beach squad in the semifinals and were pitted against the Oyster Bay Baymen in the championship game. This is when things became muddled. The date of the scheduled game wasn't acceptable to the Baymen and was changed at the last moment. John Maccarone selected a revised date without ascertaining its convenience to us. It so happened that we were to be hampered by the absence of Don Goldstein and Gary Franklin, who had planned to go on vacations. I appealed to John, requesting the game be played a week later. He turned me down but listened to my suggestion concerning the use of Hank Cluess as a replacement. Hank was on our roster but hadn't played the requisite five-game minimum during the regular season. John agreed to waive the rule, and permitted Hank to play.

The day before the elusive game was to be played, the floor of the Glen Cove Middle School gym where our games were held buckled from water damage. John again was forced to postpone the contest. Within a few days, he arranged the game at Friends Academy. This third delay enabled Don to play as he has just returned from vacation. I, however, was out, this time as a result of whiplash sustained in an automobile accident. I mentioned to John that it would be fair for Hank, whom he already approved, to now take my place. He nodded in apparent affirmation.

When the game was finally played, it was absolutely no contest. We routed the Baymen, winning by over thirty points. At the conclusion of the game, Allie Lizza, the Baymen's fiery, pugnacious player-coach, filed a protest concerning our use of Hank Cluess, an ineligible player. Unbelievably, John Maccarone upheld the complaint and declared them to be the champions. He contended that when I spoke with him, he was still under the assumption that Don wouldn't be back in time to play. This clearly was not the case, but my argument fell on deaf ears.

John attempted to soften the blow by awarding us trophies as the overall two season winner of the soon-to-be-defunct league. He knew it would be insulting to have the trophies inscribed as second place. I never truly understood why he gave in to Lizza but could tell that he genuinely felt bad about his misguided decision. He was basically a very good guy, which is why we soon forgave him and remained friends until his untimely death at a relatively young age. Our group and hundreds of athletes who crossed John's path attended his funeral. Chris Mullins, one of John's favorites, who lived off-season on Long Island, sent a beautiful floral arrangement and wrote a poignant message expressing sympathy and respect.

CHAPTER 10

Lots of Changes and Adjustments

AS I CLOSED in on age fifty, Bill Jesinky, a longtime special education colleague, asked me to leave the PS 36 principalship, and join his administration as supervising principal. Bill was the superintendent of Citywide Programs, the New York City Board of Education's central district responsible for the education of children with severe handicapping conditions. The students in the more than fifty "special" schools under Bill's aegis ran the gamut of developmental, intellectual, physical, and emotional disabilities. I accepted the assignment and, for the first time in my career as an educator, changed my working address from a school building, to the austere Board of Education Headquarters at 110 Livingston Street.

Bill and I were acquainted from the basketball courts before we seriously embarked upon our professional pursuits. Bill was from Park Slope, and frequently played at the St. Francis Lyceum, one of Brooklyn's fabled church gymnasiums. He was friendly with local standouts such as Brendon McCann and Mal Duffy, who both played at St. Bonaventure and Ed Aquilone and Jack Prenderville from St. Francis. Bill's organized ball stopped after high school, but it was plain to see that his on-court cleverness and toughness was the product of CYO (Catholic Youth Organization) basketball training. Our common bonds, which strengthened a close working and personal relationship, were the concern for the total growth of our students and the unspoken language of basketball.

The new job was challenging and enjoyable. My chief responsibilities were the supervision of the schools' instructional programs and the provision of supports to facilitate their smooth and efficient operation. I was the Division of Special Education's liaison to all of the schools that were totally comprised of disabled students. Visiting the programs and talking to people came easy to me. I felt most comfortable in a role that entailed constant face-to-face communication.

Many principals, who knew about my basketball interest and background, invited me to play in student-faculty and fund-raiser benefit games. The old guy, with the bandaged legs, who somehow could get up and down the court, became an added attraction to the events. So I kept the sneakers, socks, and shorts in the car, and when the schedule allowed, made guest appearances. It's funny, but participating in those quasi-basketball games definitely brought me spiritually closer to the students and staff. The greeting would always be warmer the next time I visited the school.

In the spring of 1985, I received notification of the greatest honor of my life. I was selected for induction into the CCNY Athletic Hall of Fame. It was almost inconceivable that I was to be in the esteemed company of the college's very best basketball players. For someone who worked so hard, and initially experienced such meager success in the sport, it was the ultimate reward. I was bursting with pride and joy.

The ceremony was held at a dinner-dance on May 17, 1985, at Leonard's, a huge catering hall in Great Neck, Long Island. In that year, I was the sole basketball player among the six inductees. There, on my behalf, sharing that unforgettable evening, were Helene, Jon, Seth, my mother, brother, sister-in-law and about twenty-five friends. The day's emotional importance was further heightened by the presence of my two CCNY coaches, Nat Holman and Dave Polansky, and many fellow basketball Hall of Famers, most notably friends Syd Levy and Jerry Domershick.

The CCNY Athletic Hall of Fame's creed wonderfully expresses the meaning of the tribute. It reads: "To honor in perpetuity those who by their participation and in association with athletics at the College, and by their demonstration of character, sportsmanship and service to the community, have won personal distinction and brought honor and glory to sports and to the City College of the City of New York."

At the dignified ceremony, I was presented with a plaque which outlined my athletic accomplishments and cited the Hall of Fame selection. It was also announced that my name was to be inscribed on the Wall of Fame at CCNY's Nat Holman Gymnasium. The official program contained bios of each of the inductees. I was very impressed by the words that capsulated my basketball career. The following is the exact flattering description:

MARTIN GROVEMAN '60, Basketball

> A member of the varsity from 1957-58 through 1959-60, he was the team's starting guard throughout his career. He led the team in scoring in each of his years and was selected as team captain in 1959-60. His career field goal shooting percentage was 46%, his foul shooting percentage 82% and he scored in double figures for 30 consecutive games. His statistics rank among the top in CCNY basketball history. He was selected for the All Metropolitan team; the ECAC Scholar Athlete All Star team; and the Tri-State League-All League team. For his outstanding accomplishments, he received the Tunick Award for the Most Valuable Player; the Cohen Award for the highest foul shooting percentage; and the CCNY Special Merit Award. He was regarded by Nat Holman as a "terrific shooter" who would have made

any of his acclaimed past teams and by Dave Polansky as the smoothest player on the squad. Professionally, an educator, Martin has been a principal in New York City's Division of Special Education for the past 14 years. In you, Alma Mater takes pride.

My boys were moving toward adulthood. Jon began college at Stony Brook, spent two years there, and then transferred to the University Campus at Binghamton. He earned his bachelor's degree at Binghamton, and went on to Law School at the University of Bridgeport. He completed the demanding three-year law program in 1991. Throughout the duration of his higher education, Jon's interest in sports, and his participation, primarily for purposes of fitness, remained strong. His other equally enthusiastic avocations were music and women.

As planned, in 1986 Seth went to Skidmore to pursue his education and college basketball ambitions. He made the varsity in his freshman year, and received considerable playing time. He was somewhat inconsistent, mainly on offense, but overall showed promise and progressed noticeably as the season rolled on. I made the two-hundred-mile drive several times and also drove to Massachusetts for the games against Williams and Amherst. For me, it always was a special thing to be there, cheering on my son. There is no doubt that my anxiety level was higher, as a spectator, watching Jon and Seth play, than any nervousness that I felt in most of my games.

In late spring, Seth was selected to represent the United States in the Pan American Maccabiah Games, to be held in the summer in Caracas, Venezuela. The USA squad consisted of twelve active college players, all Jewish Americans. The team was coached by the respected, dynamic Marv Kessler. Our entire family was ecstatic over this wonderful honor, and proud of Seth's accomplishment. He was thrilled, and eagerly anticipated the experience of his young life.

The team trained at Kutsher's Country Club in the Catskills, and was guests of the hotel. I drove up to see a practice and was delighted to run into my old Brownsville friend, Cookie Wolkoff. His son, David, a forward at Harvard, was on the team.

Another Brooklyn guy, Kenny Fiedler, who played at Wingate High School with Roger Brown, and was himself an outstanding high school coach at Springfield Gardens, was also at Kutsher's. Kenny's son Scott, a member of the team, was a starting guard at the University of Washington at St. Louis.

His younger son, Jay, became an outstanding football player. In college he was an Ivy League all-star as quarterback at Dartmouth. Then against, most experts' assessment of his potential made it to the NFL where he was a long-term backup and eventually progressed to the starting quarterback job for the Miami Dolphins.

The stage was perfectly set for the excitement, fun, and the limelight. Then, what we thought was just a small cloud began to block the sun. Seth, and a few of his teammates, became sick with some sort of intestinal bug. We assumed it to be the twenty-four-hour variety. Seth, however, had it the worst of the group, and was unable to practice.

At the games, things went from bad to worse. Seth attempted to practice, although nausea and weakness returned. Whether drinking the Venezuelan water or eating their food exacerbated the problem was subject to conjecture.

He played briefly in two early round games, but lacked the energy and even the concentration to function adequately. However, regardless of the cause, Seth's physical condition deteriorated rapidly. He was soon confined to bed, and the attending doctor thought it might be best to fly him home early, so that he could receive competent medical treatment in New York.

We were planning for this to occur when he suddenly began to feel somewhat better. His fever broke and he began to regain a bit of his appetite. Naturally, he immediately expressed his desire to remain with the team and cheer them on. So he got out of bed but was unable to participate.

As for the conclusion of the tournament, the USA in a failed protest lost to Brazil by one point in the gold medal game. It was a farce likened to the historic turnabout in our defeat to the Russians in the 1972 Olympics. Despite the nightmarish circumstances, he had no regrets. Seth cherished the rare opportunity and the distinction of representing his country. He came home with a silver medal and fifteen pounds lighter.

In the Hollywood script, having overcome great adversity, Seth would undoubtedly go on to glory. That's not exactly what happened. Firstly, it took him a few months to fully regain the weight and his strength. Secondly, trying to make up for lost time, he worked furiously during Skidmore's preseason to be in top shape by the October 15 official practice date. The urgency was heightened by the change in coach. Glen Begly, the man that recruited Seth, was surprisingly replaced by someone far more aggressive in personality and demanding as a coach. Seth got to know and like Begly when he coached the Echo Lake Camp team, and Seth competed against him as a Raquette Lake camper.

Again, bad luck struck. Seth tore ligaments in his ankle in a full-court pickup game. Impatient to impress the new coach, he came back prematurely. He couldn't run or cut and had limited stamina. At the most critical time, he was unable to perform to his usual standard. The coach, already unimpressed with Seth's peculiar shooting form, cut him little slack. He decided that Seth should begin the regular season on the JV. Feeling insulted and disrespected, particularly in view of his successful varsity play as a freshman, he refused to accept the demotion. He left the team, and made a decision to transfer to Binghamton at the conclusion of the school year.

In the fall of 1988, Seth transferred to SUNY Binghamton. A second player, 6'6" forward, Perry Medviner, Seth's good friend and a Long Islander, also transferred. They would be roommates throughout the remainder of college. Another positive was the opportunity for Seth and Jon to again attend the same school. In the short time that they were together at Binghamton, the brothers became closer than ever.

Seth and Perry tried out as walk-ons and made the talented Binghamton squad. The coach, Dave Archer, liked Seth's quickness and toughness but seemed to grapple over using him ahead of his recruited players. By the middle of his junior year, Archer began to give Seth significant playing time, particularly against the faster teams that played full-court pressure defense. Seth didn't disappoint, coming through with several fine performances. Seth consistently got the ball to the team's high scorer, Chris Jackey, who had excellent two-guard skills. Interestingly, Chris, another Long Island product, was the son of Bill Jackey, a guy I played with and against, for many years, at Merrick Road Park and the Nassau Beach Clubs. As young children, Seth and Chris would sit in the sand watching our games.

Overall, Binghamton's teams didn't play up to their talent level. They teased with brief flashes, but rarely sustained the strong efforts. Morale and team unity were frequently lacking. Coach Archer, a good person, was not a decisive leader. He was also overly influenced by recruitment pressure and parents with political clout. There were times that after a fine performance, Seth would receive reduced minutes given to a former local high school star. Still Seth was content that he came to Binghamton and was given the opportunity to satisfy his college basketball ambition. Most significantly, he enjoyed the school and graduated with academic honors.

By the late 1980s Neal Wichard passed the Post workout commissioner's baton to me. Both he and Gary were leaving the East Coast and heading for California. Neal gave up his New York business, and went to La Jolla, where he established a chain of moderately priced buffet and salad-bar-type restaurants. Gary settled in glamorous Malibu and continued to flourish as a sports agent. Being the commissioner is often a headache, not an honor, nor a blessing. Neal saw me as the one best suited from the standpoints of patience and temperament, to do the thankless job. Seeing no other logical alternative, I reluctantly accepted the responsibility. It fell upon me to arrange for the use of the Post gymnasium; to be the liaison to the college's athletic department; to make fair and balanced sides during the workout; and to help resolve disputes over turnovers, and a myriad of alleged violations.

It is a conservative estimate to say that Alan Seiden was at the core of 70 percent of the arguments.

All our professional ball-playing friends also left the workout when they retired or were traded to other teams. None of them remained in the area, although a few visited when they were in New York. In their time in the workout, Jets Darrel Ray and Jerry Holmes became regulars at one of our great lasting traditions, the post-workout gab sessions at the Sea Crest Diner.

Every Sunday morning and Wednesday evening, following the run, a gang of us retreated to well known Old Westbury eatery to dine, discuss the highlights and low points of the day's games, and to tell new stories and retell old ones. Our steady group, which averaged about twelve in number, at times swelled to as many as twenty participants. Alan, which was to be expected, generally took center stage and was the leader of the pack. Our entourage was good-naturedly boisterous, eccentric in our food orders, but very good customers—which is why the diner's management put up with us.

In the diner, outstanding performances were acknowledged, but in no way got the attention and mock ridicule that bestowed upon those who played poorly. Alan headed the self-appointed evaluative tribunal, always dishing out more abuse than he received. He did poke fun at his expanding waistline and was accepting of jibes about his girth and his physical condition. Yet he had a clever way of turning being overweight into a pat on his own back. He often said, "If I play this well when I'm so fat, imagine how I'd dominate if I was thin."

Darrel Ray loved to instigate Alan's mischief making. They were an unlikely duo, who strangely complemented each other in social settings. Although basically a straitlaced guy, Darrel enjoyed being around Alan, and even occasionally accompanied him to his New Jersey poker games. Alan saw Darrel as his good-luck charm, and claimed that he never lost when Darrel was present. At the diner they would team up to poke fun at the idiosyncrasies of the guys, and collaborated to create nicknames for them. Assigning nicknames was a specialty of Alan's. Many were appropriately descriptive of the individual, and have endured the test of time.

Neal and Gary Wichard known for reckless, physical play were likened to tag-team wrestlers, and were dubbed by Alan as the "Bushwackers." They took it with good humor and had T-shirts printed with "Bushwhackers" and a basketball on the front. Gary wasn't as accepting of another nickname given to him by Alan. He referred to him as "Tragic Johnson," the antithesis to the great basketball I.Q. of Ervin "Magic" Johnson. Richie Mandor, a hands-on, suicide squad type player was renamed "Buck" for his supper aggressive style of defense.

Among the Seiden nicknames, those that caught on and stuck were "Swimmer," "Nouveau Riche," and "The Glove." Joel White, whose athletic reputation was made in the pools at Jefferson and CCNY, is widely known in local basketball circles as "Swimmer." Alan constantly derided "Swimmer" for his poor shot selection and careless passing. Seth Rotter, a lawyer who came from humble beginnings, but made it big and lived a fairly lavish lifestyle, was "Nouveau Riche." Seth incurred Alan's wrath for his soft play and one-dimensional game, which is his shooting ability. Mark Rich, respected for his excellent shooting, not his defense, is "The Glove." The name was given when Mark claimed that he put the defensive lock on Alan. On the court, Alan referred to me as "Possum," emphasizing that I was most dangerous when injured, or pretending to be hurt. In my case, this label is confined to the gym. Jules Epstein, who was a hard worker, had a propensity for blowing layups and shooting inconsistently. He joined the workout when the movie *Jewel of the Nile* was a hit. In a play on words, Alan called him "Jules of the Vile." It got laughs and caught on.

The last of the nicknames that I'll touch upon is that of "Morty Joe Mason." His real name was Morty Goldberg, and he can most aptly be described as the mascot of the CW Post workout. Back in the 1950s, Morty was a neighborhood friend of Alan's and avidly followed his basketball exploits. When St. John's played against Bradley University, Morty developed a fascination for the versatile play of one of their stars, Bobby Joe Mason. Bobby Joe went on to become a member of the Harlem Globetrotters, and Morty Goldberg, thanks to Alan, became "Morty Joe Mason." Morty and Alan, for unclear reasons, drifted apart. Morty took a twenty-year hiatus and then suddenly resurfaced. When he returned, Alan revived the legend of "Morty Joe Mason." Morty Joe was in no shape to play in a ful- court game, so he practiced shooting from long distance. Morty was in the cookie business and generally brought cookies, pretzels, and assorted sweets to the gym–just what we needed for nutrition and energy.

Some of the diner's best ongoing, adversarial banter was between Alan and Walt Szczerbiak. The close friends argued incessantly about basketball philosophy and strategy, player evaluations, and most of all which of them made the worst calls during the workout. Alan playfully ridiculed Walt's precise preparatory routines, especially when Walter found excuses for substandard performances when diverting from his usual habits. Walt strongly believes that his attention to routine and structure contributed significantly to his consistency as a top level player. In our workouts, the culprits that he contended adversely affected his shooting efficiency included haircuts and hot showers on the day of a game, not getting eight hours of sleep, forgetting to drink orange juice in the morning before playing, fatigue from walking the dogs, etc.

Neal Wichard and John Maccarone, in the 1980s, were responsible for starting another wonderful basketball tradition. Over a five-year period, our old-timers participated in fund-raisers held at Glen Cove High School, against the New York Jets and New York Giants. The causes that inspired the games were noble, the crowds were large, and the exhibitions hard fought and lots of fun. Most amazingly, considering our ages compared to those of younger, active professional athletes, we won them all. Our victories were the results of better team play and superior shooting, not because of sympathy or lack of effort by complacent opponents.

The Jets quality players were basically the guys that were our friends from the CW Post workouts. As for the Giants, I was impressed with the grace displayed by the very beefy Leonard Marshall, and the excellent basketball skills of Lawrence Taylor. He was, hands down, the best of the football players. Lawrence drove by us and shot over us, almost scoring at will. His personality, however, left something to be desired. He snarled throughout the game, totally ignoring the goodwill purpose of the event. Moreover, he showed no recognition or warmth to the hundreds of adoring youngsters in the stands, who came to cheer on one of football's greatest stars. It was poetic justice that we beat the Giants, on a jumper by George Bruns, in the closing seconds.

All but one of those special benefit contests were festive occasions. The exception was the memorial scholarship fund game played in honor and memory of Ivan Kovac, Jr. The young man, who tragically died in an automobile accident, while home from college, was the son of our friend and fellow ballplayer, Ivan Kovac, Sr. Young Ivan, a freshman at Lehigh University, was handsome, personable, and an all-around outstanding individual. Athletically, he was a fine guard at Glen Cove High school and had aspirations of playing for Lehigh. As he matured, he was invited to take part in our workout. At the gym Ivan Jr. became friendly with my son, Seth. They attended the same session of the prestigious "Five Star" Basketball Camp, and were bunkmates. The thoughtful basketball tribute to Ivan Jr., in addition to our game, featured a court battle between two younger teams, representing New York and New Jersey. An impressive array of prominent players turned out for the heartfelt event. It was a display of great respect for Ivan Sr., and a show of affection for a special person who is gone, but not forgotten.

Ivan Kovac Jr. was one of many offspring of our basketball group members that participated in the Post and Freeport/Nassau workouts. As the kids grew taller and got better, they slowly integrated into the games. Being on the same court with your son, and witnessing his transformation into a player, is a marvelous feeling. Whenever possible, we attempted to match our children against each other, or, at the very least, pit them in opposition to guys with youthful legs.

The father-son pairings were me and Seth, "Red" Blumenreich and Scott, Judd Rothman and Eric, Mike Candel and Lou, Bobby Sack and Jon, Howie "Edels" and Brett, and Al Schindler and Andy. Scott played at Brooklyn College under Mark Reiner; Eric at Lutheran High School and then briefly for the University of Rochester; Lou was a starter at Amherst college; and Jon was a standout at Emory University. The younger father-and-son tandems were Jim Hegmann Sr. and Jimmy Jr., Mark Groothius and Steve, John Randazzo Sr. and John Jr., and Walt Szczerbiak and Wally.

Jimmy Jr. played on championship teams at St. Mary's High School and then was a star center and captain at Western Maryland University. John "Daz," an all county high school guard and fabulous three-point shooter, continued to make a splash at Sacred Heart University. And last but certainly not least, Wally became one of the greatest players in Long Island High School history. He went on to enjoy a sensational All-American career at Division I Miami of Ohio, followed by eleven years in the NBA. During his prime, Wally was an all-star for the Minnesota Timberwolves and upon retiring was one of the leading three-point percentages scorers in NBA history.

Lastly, two father-daughter combos played in the Freeport workouts. Jerry Jackson's daughter, Sheila, was a dynamic all-purpose guard who was all-Long Island in high school and a star at C. W. Post. Samantha, a 6' power forward, was both all-Nassau County in basketball and track and field and continued to shine in college. "Sam" is the daughter and sister of Jim Hegman Sr. and Jimmy Jr.

For several years, I and others from our crew were involved in another worthy basketball related fund-raiser. In July, we would make the journey to Kutsher's Country Club for the annual Maurice Stokes Games. With the exception of Alan, George, and Walt, who, as former professionals, participated in the old-timers game, the rest of us contributed to the cause and attended as spectators. For us, the preliminary old-timer's exhibition was more enjoyable and meaningful than the main event that featured present-day players. Former NBA stars, all Hall of Famers, that I met and saw play in the Stokes benefit, including Oscar Robertson, Dolph Schayes, Dick McGuire, Bobby Wanzer, and Pete Maravich.

The person most responsible for bringing the marquee players to Kutsher's and for coordinating the Stokes extravaganza is Zelda Spoelstra. For years, she has been one of basketball's outstanding behind-the-scenes volunteers. Zelda's tireless and competent endeavors have earned her the honor of selection to the New York City Basketball Hall of Fame, for service as a "contributor." For many years, she was an employee of the NBA and has also been associated with the game, in a benevolent capacity, since the league's inception. My bond with Zelda is particularly strong, as her closest college association was with the players from the CCNY double championship team. Floyd Layne is one of her very best friends, as were the late Ed Warner and Ed Roman. I and many former CCNY athletes consider her to be an honorary alumnus of our alma mater. At Kutsher's, she always saw to it that our gang was treated with the utmost hospitality.

We had great times on those trips to Kutsher's. We'd arrive early in the afternoon and hang out by the pool, soaking up the sun, have a few beers, and shooting the breeze and enjoying some laughs with the retired NBA stars. One of the pool regulars was the humble Dick McGuire. Through Alan, who enjoyed a tight friendship with him, I spent many pleasurable hours with Dick.

He was much admired for his genuineness as a human being, as he was for his excellence as one of basketball's supreme playmakers. Dick came to our Post workout a few times, and despite his advanced age, still displayed the flawless passing skills and magician- like hands. Alan got me invited to some of Dick and his vivacious wife, Terry's, summer barbecues. They were wonderful hosts, providing poolside fun, good company, and fabulous food. Each year, Alan instigated a three-man game on the McGuires' court. With his directing hand, they somehow ended up more competitive than originally intended.

The two most memorable Kutsher's excursions occurred when Alan rented a limousine and chartered a bus. The year of the limo, Alan took me, his lady friend Barbara "Square" and "Red" Blumenreich along for the luxurious ride. It was quite a spectacle when the limo pulled up to the door of the Clair Bee Arena prior to the old-timers game, and Alan and Dick McGuire, in basketball uniforms, stepped out of the car. The puzzled throng of onlookers thought it was the arrival of royalty.

The long day and night of the bus ride was absolutely hilarious. As was his magnanimous custom, Alan did it all at his own expense. The bus contained almost every player from the Post workout, and an assortment of Alan's card-playing cronies and social acquaintances. The warmth and camaraderie of the large gathering of friends, in the unique manner that we were thrown together, was very special.

The bus driver and bus itself were a major part of the show. Clinton, the driver, was one of those unfazable people who simply shrugged his shoulders in the face of impending disaster. The well-worn bus had a faulty starter, which "died" during the trip. The only way to make it to the Catskills and back was to leave the engine running. This, therefore, is what Clinton did for over twelve hours. Of course, this essential adjustment consumed considerable fuel. Our problem was worsened because the taciturn Clinton didn't attempt to refuel until we were on our way home, well after midnight. So there we were searching for an open gas station, scouring the roads of Middletown, New York. Somehow, we made it back to the City, exhausted, yet teary eyed from laughter.

Through all the excitement of that wild adventure Alan contends that George Bruns's ability to sleep under any conditions was the most amazing aspect of the trip. George slept peacefully on the bus and at the pool, and in between, used his stored energy to perform with gusto on the basketball court. Walt Szczerbiak's amusing comments and reaction to marijuana smoke was another highlight. One of Alan's New Jersey friends, "Shorty" was a nonstop pot smoker. That sweet, easily identifiable odor permeated the bus on the ride up to Kutsher's. In the opening minutes of the old-timers' game, Walt uncharacteristically missed a wide open layup. Afterward, he attributed the errant shot to a residual contact high from the marijuana. He added that the effect was psychologically intensified when he sighted Shorty in the stands, as he drove to the basket. Walt's blown layup and his unintentionally funny explanation was something that Alan would never let him forget.

At my job, Bill Jesinkey, with support from Ed Sermier, the executive director of New York City's Division of Special Education, promoted me to the position of deputy assistant superintendent of "Citywide Programs." It was a major upgrade from my status as Supervising Principal. My responsibilities remained the same, although the salary was substantially greater, and the title itself carried a high degree of authority and respect. It enabled me to work more effectively within the bureaucracy, as doors that were previously closed were now open. I also had access to people of influence, with the clout to facilitate positive change, particularly instructional program improvements.

I worked harmoniously for four years with Bill and Ed Sermier. Our team disbanded when Ed went to work for Mayor Ed Koch's administration and Bill opted for retirement. Ed and Bill were replaced by Eddy Bayardelle and Bill Rojas. Eddy continued to be supportive of my efforts, but hardnosed Bill Rojas was another story. He had a personality, manner, and work style vastly different from mine. In a short time, it became apparent that we were professionally incompatible. I also realized that I was inherited, not chosen by Rojas, and that it was typical for new administrations to make changes, especially regarding cabinet level personnel. Still, it was a shock to me when Bill Rojas informed me that he was terminating my service as deputy superintendent. It was fruitless to fight it, but I did vent my anger over what I considered to be an unjust shafting. For one thing, he made no attempt to shift me to a parallel position. More personally, it was the first time in my life that I experienced that kind of rejection. I understood it from an intellectual standpoint, but it really hurt.

As a tenured principal, I had the job security of being assured of a return to a school in a principal's capacity. It was at this point that Bill Rojas did me an enormous favor. He assigned me as Principal of P.S. 256 Queens, a school comprised of three residential treatment centers, uniquely under the jurisdiction of The New York City Board of Education, serving adolescent students with severe emotional and social problems. The three components were St. John's Home for Boys, Wayside School for Girls, and St. Mary's Children & Family Services, also housing a male student population. St. John's is located in Rockaway Beach, Queens, whereas Wayside and St. Mary's are on Long Island, situated in North Valley Stream and Syosset respectively.

The change occurred in fall 1990, and over time would be welcomed by me as a blessing. Firstly, as a Nassau County, Long Island resident, my office, at St. Mary's, was twenty minutes from my home. For nearly twenty-five years I made that horrible commute to the city, spending countless hours battling traffic and contending with adverse elements, such as never ending road construction and weather related delays. Secondly, my new staff and the institutional personnel were terrific people. They, along with the challenging students, reenergized me. It was so good to be back in a school setting. Thirdly, the organization's assistant principal, Stanley Goldstein, was outstanding. He eased my transition tremendously and from the start, helped me to feel completely at home. He is also the person most responsible for developing the school at St. Mary's into one of the finest of its kind in the USA. St. Mary's, as a residential treatment center, parallels the quality of the school, and is at the very top of enlightened, comprehensive institutions for troubled youths.

Ironically, the assignment was vital to my physical well-being. In the late spring of 1990, my right knee fully surrendered to the stress and strains of too many years of basketball. It folded under me as I came down from shooting a jump shot at the Post workout. I limped off the court, knowing that this latest injury was something out of the ordinary. The diagnosis made by Dr. David Dines, a prominent orthopedist who for several years was the New York Mets head doctor, was a severely torn quadriceps muscle. The quadriceps tendons that attach the large thigh muscle to the knee were almost completely torn away. He placed me in an ankle-to-thigh immobilizer, holding out little hope that a sufficient recovery could occur without surgery.

My turmoil at work made things more complicated, delaying my decision concerning an operation. Within a few weeks, I was able to switch to a smaller, lighter-weight brace. This enabled me to move about with some ease that was previously restricted by the immobilizer. However, I had limited mobility, and basketball was out of the question. I soon came to the realization that surgery was a necessity. If I was lying on my back, I couldn't lift my leg by its own power. I had to place my hands under my right knee to raise it. It was similarly as difficult to move my leg from the bed to the floor.

The operation, performed by Frank Hudak, an excellent orthopedic surgeon, took place in October 1990, a month after my reassignment to PS 256. It couldn't be done arthroscopically and required five days of hospitalization. The reconstruction entailed the utilization of a cadaver's tendon in place of my irreparably damaged one. I was fitted for an elaborate soft cast and adjustable immobilizer, which I wore for eight weeks. A few weeks into my recuperation, I began a comprehensive program of physical therapy and rehabilitation to rebuild the weak and atrophied leg muscles, and to regain range of motion in my knee.

My Long Island assignment enabled me to return to work quickly, something I could not do if I retained the deputy superintendent position in the city. Stan Goldstein and other staff members did everything possible to assist me. Bud Schtiernan, my guidance counselor, neighbor and a friend was wonderful. He picked me up at the hospital, helped me to get around by car, and was simply there for me throughout the ordeal. Bud, an outstanding athlete and a former college basketball player, was a true sports nut, which was a major reason for our close relationship.

The independent "homework" aspect of rehabilitation motivated me to join a health club. Unable to run or jump I began to look at the arduous leg extensions, leg presses, and hamstring curls, not as treatment alone, but as my new workout.

I never resented doing it or considered the hard and often painful work as punishment. It aided my relative speedy recovery and a resumption of normal activities. Furthermore, while in the gym, I decided to alternately condition my upper body. The lifting, pulling, and pushing weren't exactly fun, but the results evidenced by bigger muscles, increased strength, and overall improved fitness confirmed the value of the effort. For years, I was reluctant to accept Helene's recommendation that I attempt some weight and resistance training. Today, I am a converted advocate of regular health club gymnasium participation.

I resumed playing full-court basketball in June of 1991. My return was triumphant in the sense that, at almost fifty-four, I would regain sufficient mobility to participate in such a demanding activity. My friends marveled at my determination, and the fact that I could still do enough in the game to avoid being an embarrassment. Yet, physically, I was half of what I used to be prior to the injury and the subsequent surgery. I played with a large and intricate ACL knee brace that provided great support, but obviously could not help me to run faster or jump higher. Thankfully, I was pain free and able to run straight ahead with an adequate degree of fluidity. My lateral movement, however, was permanently hampered. Cutting, reversing direction, and making sudden movements, like going after a loose ball, were things that I did pathetically. The difficulty moving laterally robbed me of my high level of proficiency at shooting a jump shot off the dribble. Defensively, particularly because it was difficult for me to shuffle backward in response to the forward movement of an opponent, I played clutch and grab, using my arms and upper body, instead of my legs.

The things that remained constant were my knowledge of the game and a good shooting touch. More than ever, I had to rely on basketball intelligence to function productively. Moving the ball crisply, sharp passing, and knowing where to *be* on the court are skills that *I* continued to possess. As for shooting, using screens and picks, and getting to the open spot became more important than ever. My range was curtailed, as I no longer had enough leg strength and leverage to be effective from distances beyond seventeen feet from the basket. Past that point, it was a throw, not a shot. There are delicatessen restaurants that feature "kosher"-style cold cuts. These eateries are not officially kosher, but their cuts of meat are close, if not exactly certifiably approved. I refer to my postoperative shooting as kosher-style jump shots. It's identical to the real thing in technique, except that I do not leave the ground. It's also amazing that the many years of being a jump shooter was so reflexively ingrained in me that my unconscious instinct on the court was to prepare to shoot in this manner. It took the most intense concentration, which felt totally unnatural, for me to shoot a standing one hander instead of a jumper.

After graduating from Binghamton, Seth found it difficult to obtain a job in the field of marketing research, his college major. He took an extended Florida vacation, visiting my in-laws in Delray, who were delighted to have him there. He liked it so much that he decided to remain. Initially, he worked as a waiter and a bank teller, and enrolled in graduate school. He didn't seek my advice about his new career objective, but entered the master's program in special education at Florida Atlantic University. He felt that I didn't do too badly working with problem children, and had pleasant memories of his days spent with me at PS 36. He attained the advanced degree, and by 1993 was a full-time Florida special education teacher.

Helene, who for years thirsted to get away from the New York winters, was further motivated to head south by Seth's enthusiastic endorsement of life in the "Sunshine State." We put our home up for sale in the winter of 1992, and were completely out of it by September. I rented an apartment in East Meadow and Helene found a lovely place, 20 feet from a tranquil and scenic man-made lake in Boca Raton, Florida. The sudden dramatic change from the predictable stability of our Long Island life, over the last 25 years, marked the beginning of a new era. It was also the start of my New York to Florida shuttle.

I turned fifty-five in September of 1992, which made me eligible for retirement, and a fairly decent pension based upon thirty-three years of service in the New York City school system. The sale of our home, combined with establishing a residence in Florida, drew me to serious consideration about packing in the career. After much gut-wrenching, and privately debating the pros and cons of leaving versus continuing, I decided it was in my best interest to retire. My plan was to work through the entire 1992–1993 school year, making it official on September 1, just prior the start of the fall term. My three years at PS 256 were wonderfully fulfilling and tension free, but it was the right time to get out. Something else was to occur that would make my decision seem even wiser.

In June, while getting out of my car on a rainy morning, I slipped and twisted my left knee. The left was my good knee, unlike the right one, which bothered me for so many years before the surgery. Immediately following the mishap, it was swollen and stiff, and hurt considerably if I attempted to move it too boldly. Having been through this kind of thing, I iced it, put on a rubber knee support, and took some leftover, prescribed anti-inflammatory tablets. I rested for a few weeks, refraining from playing ball, jogging, or riding a bike in the gym. The self-treatment seemed to do the trick as the symptoms disappeared. I returned to my usual athletic routine.

Seth flew into New York, in early July, to spend his vacation with me and Jon. I arranged some basketball workouts for him, and on his final day in town took him to our run at C. W. Post. We were playing on the same side when Swimmer, whom I was guarding, drove to the basket. On his move our legs became entangled causing us to fall to the floor. My left knee folded under me, hyperextended and twisted. I felt something tear and had to be helped to my feet.

I knew immediately that it was serious. As much as it hurt, my greater concern was for Seth. His anguish over my physical condition was worsened by the fact that he was leaving for Florida that afternoon. I attempted to minimize the extent of the injury, but he recognized that I was disguising the discomfort. It was a Sunday, and impossible to contact Dr. Hudak or my family doctor. What I did was to get out the immobilizer and stabilize the leg.

It wasn't the correct fit, but it provided imminent support and prevented further damage.

On Monday, I took an MRI. It clearly showed that once again I tore my quad, but also the ACL on the left knee. The number of tendon strands separated from the knee was less than the first time, but surgery was the strong recommendation. The odds against sustaining torn quadriceps in both legs are monumentally high. Dr. Hudak held the strong opinion that some constitutional weakness played a part in this rare occurrence. My vulnerability was exacerbated by my basketball addiction and stubborn refusal to act according to age.

I balked at the horrifying thought of another operation. At first, I intellectualized that with rest and physical therapy, I could be satisfied with a sedentary existence wherein there would be nothing more strenuous than a walk in the park. It wasn't that simple, as my left leg became an unpredictable folding chair. Pain was not a factor. It was the inability of the leg to support my body. Without a brace on, and with no warning, the knee would frequently collapse. Over the summer, it must have happened a dozen times. Dr. Hudak spoke with me regarding his concern over the great risk that I was taking. He pointed out that falling while crossing the street could result in my getting hit by a car. Reality was eventually faced, and surgery was done in September 1993.

This time Dr. Hudak was able to reattach the torn tendons of the quad. He referred to it as using my own "equipment." The one drawback was that the connection would be shorter than the original, thereby reducing flexibility and range of motion. He further stabilized the knee by inserting a temporary pin, which was more like a rod. I was astounded at its length when it was removed several weeks after the operation. My hospital stay was 4 days. The ensuing recuperation took place at the home of my brother and sister-in-law, who were so gracious and attentive to my needs. I couldn't care for myself in the apartment, and Florida was not an option due to the weekly evaluative visits to Dr. Hudak.

Basically, the 1993 rehabilitation duplicated the therapy of 1990. The condition of the left knee was better to begin with, so progress was commensurately rapid. As soon as I could walk, I returned to my honorary status as "commissioner" of the Post workout. Playing competitive basketball was another thing. My attitude had definitely changed after the second surgery. I never formally announced my basketball retirement, preferring to gracefully fade into the background. For a few years, I was content to shoot around, dribble by myself, and stay connected to the scene of the action.

Time and injury had taken their toll on more than just me. Several of my friends were permanently on the sidelines. Don Goldstein's and Bobby Sack's knees betrayed them. "Red" Blumenreich, Howie Bernstein, and Lew Roethel had also been forced to stop playing for varied reasons. Red had a chronic Achilles tendon problem, Howie tore his rotator cuff, and Lew Roethel suffered a detached retina. With each passing year, our ranks continued to dwindle. Even the seemingly "indestructible" great ones, Walt Szczerbiak and George Bruns, broke down. Walt, suddenly close to death, survived an excruciating nine-hour operation to reroute his aorta. As for George, all those hard stops and cuts damaged his hips, necessitating their replacement.

I previously mentioned that the youth in our workouts were our children. As we grew older the blend became increasingly important to the maintenance of the vitality and quality of the games. Two decades ago, St. John's awarded a basketball scholarship to Sergio Luyk, a young man from Spain. Sergio's father, Cliff, is an American, who played at the University of Florida and went on to have a fine professional career in Europe. Playing in Spain, he met and married a native, and settled there. Cliff is a friend and former teammate of Walt Szczerbiak. When Sergio came to St. John's, after completing high school in Kentucky, Walter happily took on the responsibility of godfather. Sergio welcomed having a surrogate family so far from home, and as a result of his relationship with the Szczerbiak's began playing in our workout. He delighted in the old-timers' raucous milieu, our obvious love for the game, and best of all, the nuttiness at the diner. He developed a closeness to most of our group, but none greater than his friendship with Alan Seiden. Alan treated him like a son; taking him places, paying for his meals, and issuing to Sergio an open invitation to his home. There is no doubt that Alan was most responsible for Sergio's enjoyment of his time spent in New York.

Sergio's career at St. John's had its good moments, but overall didn't meet expectations or his potential. At 6'8 ½", Sergio was an extraordinary outside shooter. He had great range on his jump shot, and a quick release. He was very agile for someone so tall and was adroit at passing to the low post. On the mediocre side of the ledger, his foot speed was just adequate, and against Big East competition was not a strong finisher. Following his graduation from St. John's in the spring of 1996, Sergio returned to Spain and played professionally. After a few years, his career was halted by the horrifying onset of stomach cancer. Right to the end, he remained outwardly upbeat. He was gone before his thirty-fifth birthday.

Sergio's presence hastened the development of Walt's son, Wally. Before Wally had the size and strength to go up against Sergio, Walt and Eric Rothman generally took on the difficult assignment. By the time Wally was a high school junior, and about 6'4" (he grew to 6'7") the task was imposed upon him. At first, he held his own offensively, but got destroyed on the defensive end by the bigger, stronger, and more experienced Sergio. The dramatic change occurred during the summer, prior to his senior year. Wally was Sergio's equal, and in fact, surpassed him in several aspects of the total game. Wally played with greater intelligence, was a more accurate shooter, displayed a better shot selection, and was more team oriented than Sergio.

At the conclusion of his final season at Cold Spring Harbor, Wally was named Long Island's "Player of the Year." He definitely was one of the Island's all-time greats. He averaged thirty-seven points per game, and was as good a shooter as any high school player that I had ever seen. He scored from everywhere, but was most phenomenal with his three-point shooting. Singlehandedly, he carried Cold Spring Harbor, not a traditional power, to the finals of the B school category for the New York State Championship.

Ironically, his team was beaten by a deeper, more athletic Peekskill squad whose star player was Elton Brand. Elton became an All-American at Duke and an elite NBA player.

As written previously, Wally became a legendary player for Miami of Ohio. Best of all was his fantastic performance in the NCAA Tournament during his senior year. He carried his team to the "sweet sixteen" with thirty-plus games in upsets over Washington and Utah, before bowing out to Kentucky. Following the tournament Wally's stock soared and he became the Timberwolves first round draft choice. After a decade of fine play, on account of persistent injuries, most notably "bone-on-bone" deteriorating knees, hastened his retirement.

Today, Wally is a highly respected studio analyst employed by the Madison Square Garden and CBS Sports Network. He is best known for his work on the Knicks pre- and postgame shows. He and his beautiful wife Shannon have five children and reside in Wally's hometown, Cold Spring Harbor.

As a preteen, at our workouts, Wally usually spent hours sitting atop the folded bleachers, observing the games. His routine of watching and studying amazed us. Obviously, he got a great deal out of it, and successfully applied things that he perceived to help shape his own play. "Red" Blumenreich, who was relegated to the permanently disabled list, often tutored him individually, as did Walt. I could tell from how difficult it was for me to beat him in "horse" that he was going to be an outstanding shooter.

As Wally's Long Island high school championship game against Center Moriches, the Suffolk County crown holders, we were sitting close to their rabid fans. Alan Seiden got into a verbal duel with a deranged Center Moriches supporter who, at the beginning of the contest, was denigrating Wally's ability. He kept shouting "Wally Who?" whenever he touched the ball. Alan seriously pushed the guy's buttons by rubbing it in every time Wally scored. And Wally did score frequently. In the second half, as Wally proceeded to sink the Center Moriches ship, the man, during a brief stoppage of play, menacingly strolled onto the court, moving directly toward Wally. Thankfully, before he could get to him, he was ushered away by the police. Cold Spring Harbor won the game, with Wally ending up with 42 points. At the games' end, the irrepressible Alan gleefully began chanting, "Wally Who?–got 42." Of course, he incurred the animosity of the dejected Center Moriches crowd. He loved it, and took his new slogan to a step that only he was capable of doing. He ordered special T-shirts, and distributed them to our inner circle and the Szczerbiak family. On the front was inscribed, "Wally Who?" The number 42 was boldly printed on the back of the shirt.

The Wally-Sergio duels were expanded to include the involvement of other young players. All–Nassau County guard John Randazzo began to attend with regularity. This was countered by my asking Peter Ruh, a thirtyish, deft point guard who formerly played at Adelphi University, to join the Post run. Peter was already a regular in the Freeport-Nassau games. Wally's friends from Cold Spring Harbor, Teddy and "Stackhouse" and Mike Holland, a Long Island all-star center, were also added.

Wally also brought twin brothers, John and Jim Vlogianitus to the workout. At 6'5", both were athletic, strong, and extremely hard-nosed competitors. They had outstanding "small college" basketball careers at Brockport State. Three of our players' sons, Scott Blumenreich, Jon Sack, and Jimmy Hegmann Jr., also made it whenever possible.

The competition was strengthened most by the arrival of Rob Hodgson, the 1993–1994 Long Island Player of the Year. At the time he joined us, Rob, a versatile 6'7" was on his way to the University of Indiana. He, his dad, Bob, who was his high school coach at William Floyd, and his younger brother, Rex, came to our workout through the invitation of former Jet, Jim McKinstry. Rob, intermingled with Wally and Sergio, elevated the games to another level. He also contributed significantly through his personality and character, and was an exemplary young man. On the court, Rob was best described as a slasher and opportunist. He was a scorer, but not the purest of shooters. His quick hands and sharp passing skills were two of his other superior attributes. In his freshman year, Rob was redshirted at Indiana. He elected not to remain there, transferring to Rutgers University, one of the new entries in the Big East. He became eligible in late December of 1995, and worked his way into the starting line-up.

Rob's success and progress at Rutgers was continuous. He was a coach's delight at small forward. In addition to his double digit scoring, he played excellent defense, moved beautifully without the ball, and exhibited keen court awareness. His shooting had also markedly improved. He was one of the Big East's best from the free throw stripe and he became proficient from beyond the three-point line.

Following graduation, Rob played professionally in the European Scandinavian countries eventually becoming a player-coach in Finland. He returned home to Long Island in 2009 and assisted his dad at William Floyd High School. Unbelievably and again tragically, at the Long Island Championship game held at Hofstra, Bob Hodgson suffered a heart attack. He coached an entire game, went to the hospital, and died the next day. Bob and his family were all terrific generous people. He is greatly missed.

So many outstanding players joined our workouts. Not all of them were able to become weekly participants, but were there when schedules afforded the free time. Those who were terrific three-point shooters include Peter Ruh, John Henry, Terry Tarpey, Chris Eldredge, Andrew DeLoia, and Jack Ryan. Peter and John, stars at Adelphi University and Nassau Community College, have unlimited range. Terry is NYU's all-time total points leader. True, he played in the period when the school went from Division I to Division III; however, his later success in Europe proved that he had top-level ability. Chris Eldredge is simply a very gifted offensive player. He is an instinctive creative scorer who features a running teardrop shot equal to basketball's best. The 6'2" shooting guard started as a freshman at Hofstra University, but fell short of fulfilling his promise due to relationship problems with renowned coach Bill Van Bredakoff. As deft a long-distance shooter as Andrew DeLoia is, the former Hobart standout has made his greatest splash as a high school coach. In his very first year as coach of his alma mater, Northport High School, his team won the AA Long Island Championship.

The guy whose story is at the least worthy of a Lifetime Channel bio is Jack "Blackjack" Ryan. For much of the first thirty years of his life, he was an unstable, carousing "good time Charlie." He drank much, slept little, and was thrown out of countless schools. At an athletic sturdily built 5'11", he possessed marvelous basketball skills, especially his rapid fire releases of deep shots and a ball-on-a-string handle. Every time he was on the brink of making it, he somehow got sidetracked. When he met his then girlfriend, now his wife and the mother of his adorable basketball wunderkind daughter, an epiphany occurred. I'll save all the details for perhaps another book, but today Jack, or "Blackjack" as he is called, is one of the USA's foremost basketball entertainers. Handsome, tanned, and in his fifties, Jack puts on a fabulous show featuring twirling several basketballs all at one time using his fingers, feet, nose, and head. His great shooting dexterity is also on display. Jack, the ultimate extrovert, has great rapport with his youthful audiences and always utilizes the kids in his act. He does minishows at NBA and college halftimes and presents longer performances at fund-raisers, camps, school assemblies, bar and bat mitzvahs, etc. As far as the level of his three-point shooting ability, he has won countless contests with the most prestigious one being crowned as the national champion in the Chicago competition. Jack's journey is truly inspirational.

Another special basketball showman considerably older than Jack Ryan with a constant twinkle in his eyes is George Schauer. George played in college at the University of Minnesota during their glory days (Kevin McHale, Dave Winfield, Ron Behagen). Persistent injuries and considerable weight gain prematurely ended his active hoops participation. However, with his magnetic personality and an impressive array of ball-handling skills, he became a basketball entertainer and named himself "Crazy George." His act, which is nationally known, is participatory, comical and loaded with "shtick." His most enthusiastic audience is children from ages seven to thirteen. They are mesmerized by

George's energy and the continuous action. George Bruns invites him to perform at every camp session. An interesting commentary on a sad trend in our country is that with all the "crazies" acting violently, he recently changed his name to "Generous George."

As age steadily gave way to relative youth, several talented payers, not specifically known for three-point shooting, excelled in the runs. The oldest, Jim Signorile, in his sixties, is indefatigable. He always wants to extend the workouts to "one more game." At a slim 6'9", without exaggeration, he is still among the best classic hook shooters in the entire world. He is deadly with both hands from the post on the move and even from the baseline. He was one of NYU's last great players prior to the school's temporary hiatus from basketball. His high games of the Garden was fifty points. After graduation, he enjoyed a lengthy career in Europe, much of it in France. A. J. Wynder, a 6'2" point guard, has the hands of a "cat burglar," keen passing skills, and awesome court vision. He followed a brilliant career at Fairfield with a short stint with the Boston Celtics where he was part of a championship team during the Larry Bird era. Today he is the respected coach at Nassau Community College. Jim McTigh, a former star junior college guard, is quick and high jumping, and possesses a fine pull-up jumper. He is also a slasher, particularly from the baseline, where he makes difficult reverses look easy. In his blended family, there are seven children (six boys, one girl), all athletes. Rick Pichinick has the athleticism of an Olympian. He has amazing speed and agility, and is a suicide-type competitor. Had he selected football as his primary sport, he would have been an outstanding cornerback or safety. Once, while attempting to save a ball going out of bounds at the Island Garden, he dove over two rows of benches, tapped the ball to a teammate, and avoided certain injury by completing a perfect forward roll. Of course, without missing a beat he hustled back to the count. Rick played both basketball and soccer in college. Brian Davis at 6'5" is all muscle and hustle. He is a prolific rebounder and defensive player blessed with a lithe, strong body. His unselfish game makes those around him better.

East Meadow Long Island, where my boys grew up, is not a hotbed of basketball. However, the town pool and adjoining small park named "Prospect Park" (not the famous one in Brooklyn) hosted the best full court pickup games on Long Island. It is where my son Seth learned to play. It wasn't for me however because it was asphalt based, and too tough on my knees. Guys that I had already mentioned that became integral to our indoor workouts were part of the Prospect mix and looked out for Seth when he was a neophyte. I refer to the ultra-efficient Peter Ruh, Rick "The Rocket" Pichinick, and the explosive Chris Eldredge. Two other primetime payers who both Seth and I first met at Prospect and then joined the runs at the Island Garden and Lutheran are Barry Millhaven and Paul Barrett. When I first saw Barry play, he was tall, thin, yet square shouldered. At that time, he was a high school all-star from Port Washington. He really blossomed as he added great strength to bolster an excellent all-purpose game. Few thought that Barry could make it at the highest college level, but he certainly did. He wasn't a highly coveted recruit, but became a solid contributor at St. John's. We all cheered this good guy's success. Paul Barrett, after high school ended, practically lived at Prospect. At 6'3", he always played bigger than his measurements. He literally is an outstanding small forward from perspectives of defense, rebounding and midrange jump shooting. He's so fundamentally sound and a great teammate. Personality wise, Paul can be characterized as a good humor man. In college, he excelled at Alfred University.

No matter where our workouts were held, there were many basketball enthusiasts for whom playing into middle age and beyond was worth the pain and suffering that lingered for days after competing. Jimmy Sullivan, one of the originals, began as an elusive 6'3" post and baseline marvel, to a player whose injury-riddled body necessitated all his court intelligence to remain productive. The former St. Francis College standout is no longer a force, but is always a contributing role player. Jimmy Burke, finally on the shelf, battled to keep his weight down while remaining remarkably shifty and innovative against younger and fitter components. Five-foot-ten senior citizen John Hogan still plays. A product of Brooklyn CYO leagues, his game is one of perpetual movement and quick passing. Another guy whose effectiveness stems from continuous movement, primarily on the baseline, is a space creator and an efficient corner shooter is Chris Jones.

Two close friends, Jerry "King Kong" Kornbluth (another Alan Seiden nickname) and Harris Insler, got the most out of their modest abilities. Jerry's strength was outside shooting, whereas Harris' forte was based on quickness, driving ability, and hustle. A third player, Phil "Flinstone" (Alan again), had an effective pull-up baseline game, is "Bruising Buck" Mandor's brother-in-law, and was instrumental in procuring basketball figurines for the bewildering Mr. Seiden.

Three men significantly younger than Jerry, Harris, Hoagie, and Sully started playing at Freeport and then migrated to all our locations. I refer to Peter Vlogianitus, Brian Flatherty, and Dave Taylor. Peter is the eldest of the Vlog brothers. At 6'2", he is shorter than John and Jimmy, but shares their competitiveness and is far more emotional on the court. His constant chatter motivates his teammates to push their efforts. Offensively, he is a streak shooter and an opportunistic rebounder. Brian Flaherty (aka Bway) is perpetually loquacious and upbeat. His ball hawking elevated his modest talent level. In general, he is a delightful, lovable person. Dave Taylor is on par with Rick "The Rocket" as an athlete. He is an explosive driver to the basket and has amazing hang time. His frequent injuries, some of them quite serious, are football, not basketball related ones. One of the best receivers on Long Island, he has a "jones" for football that won't allow him to quit.

For different reasons, I have been ambivalent about two of the older originals from the Freeport High School Nassau CC runs. Rodney Friedman, who brought into the games by Jim Signorile, his best friend. A 6'3" a loose-limbed, unorthodox player, Rod outperformed his physical abilities. Through a love of the game, the most stubborn, determined Rodney competed while battling against malignant stomach cancer. Over many years, through numerous surgical procedures and continuous intensive treatments, he played regularly despite the suffering he endured. Not only did he never complain, but he was always pleasant and gregarious. He got on the court almost to the end, finally losing the fight in 2007. Rodney was admired and respected by all of us.

The person who I am truly reluctant to write about is our oldest member, Abe Weinstein. His circumstances are also sad, but the gloom surrounding him lacks the nobility associated with Rodney. Abe, now in his early eighties, was clearly the least skilled participant that ever participated in our workouts. With the exception of his lung power, which he developed on the track at Brooklyn's famed Lincoln High School, to be kind, he displayed the most rudimentary basketball skills. Yet the longtime college professor, who ascended to a vice president's position at Nassau Community College, was much respected and embraced by all of us. He strongly believed in the strong correlation between athleticism and potential academic and career success. In order to accomplish his practical hypothesis, he brought former college athletes into the classroom at Nassau. George Bruns, Larry Kaufer, and Lou Roethal are just three of many who became outstanding professors in Nassau's Math Department. Apart from their effect upon the general student population, they, as role models, furthered the development of many talented athletes, helping them to refocus and stay on the academic and career track. Abe's beliefs, through the years propelled hundreds to gain matriculated status and earn college degrees. With all of the good, what bad could have happened? A shock to everyone, he was arrested and found guilty of fraud and misappropriation of college resources and services. He was sentenced and spent time in a "white collar" prison. And then, a few years later, was again arrested, convicted, and incarcerated. For myself and most of the guys, it seemed inconceivable. How and why does someone go from the top to the bottom? Does Abe's fatal flaw negate all the good he did? For me, it doesn't, but I no longer feel that he is a friend. I hear that he has volunteered to do many acts of contrition; however, he is not part of our inner circle.

A version of a popular saying is that "only death and taxes" lasts forever. Therefore, like almost everything else, basketball workouts eventually end. Our CW Post runs ended when a new sports center was built. With Neal and Gary Wichard in California unable to exert their influence, we were not allowed to use the new facility because we weren't authentic members of the post alumni. A ridiculous decision was made even though we had contributed thousands of dollars to the college athletic department. A few years later we were banished from Freeport due to a single complaint from a *community trouble*maker and the "closed" nature of our early Saturday morning competition. He claimed he was denied the opportunity to participate when, in truth, he wasn't skilled enough to shoot a proper layup. The school board terminated our permit and even took mild punitive action against the custodian.

At the time that the banishments occurred, most of the originals were *in age-* and injury-related basketball retirement. Yet we wanted the tradition to continue to be carried by the younger players who were integrated and added to the decreasing veteran corps. With persistence and our status as being known and respected in the Long Island basketball community we migrated to the Island Garden (where the Nets once played), Portledge School (an exclusive private school on the North Shore of Nassau County), and finally to Lutheran High School (where Mark "Glove" Rich coached). As I write this, only Lutheran and Portledge remain active places to play.

Wally's NBA status affected the format and players in the evolving workouts. During the off-season, especially at Portledge, the older guys would play from 8:00 AM to 9:30AM. Then Wally and the high flyers would take over the court. If the numbers were low, our group would be sprinkled into the games. I played a bit and, if left unguarded, could still make a midrange shot. Of players who came over from Post, the best were John and Jimmy Vlogiantius and John Randazzo. The best newcomers were Jason Hernandez, Jim Moran, and Brad Wysczbiki.

I wasn't looking to make new friends, but that's what's happened when we were expelled from CW Post and shifted Sunday runs to

Portledge School. Harvard's Mike Griffin and our Earl Monroe, a spin-and-shift clone (but with more turnovers), swung the deal that enabled us to gain entry to this perfect facility. It was just the right length for aging hoopsters. The 8:00 AM–10:30 AM time slot was also ideal. My reference to new friends pertains to the need to recruit additional players for full-court basketball. With most of our originals participating in the Saturday morning games at the Island Garden (which transitioned to Lutheran High School), only few had the time and/or the physical resiliency to play back to back days. Therefore, it was either bring in other guys or get out of the commitment. It turned out we successfully accomplished our recruiting goal, both in terms of numbers and the quality of the people involved. I made Portledge my primary venue and continued as commissioner. Mark "Glove" Rich then became the coordinator of Island Garden/Lutheran.

Those that made the change to Portledge were Walt Sczcerbiak, Jim Signorile, Jeff Rubinstein, Jerry Kornbluth, Harris Insler, and Mike Griffin. The main additions, all of whom enriched the play and were well known in basketball circles, were John Pitts, Sean O'Leary, Mark Marshall, and the Atkinson brothers. As written awhile back, Wally and his contemporaries also came aboard mainly because they liked the later start time.

Jason Hernandez, at Hofstra University, was paired with the terrific Speedy Claxton, as one of college's basketballs best backcourts. Jason was a terrific defender with lightning-quick hands and an amazing stepback jump shot. Jim Moran at 6'7" was strong and versatile with great skills and smarts to match. He excelled both at William and Mary and in Europe's top league as a standout for Canary Island. Brad Wysczbiki, 6'3" and unrecruited at Queens College, became a Division II All-American and one of the country's highest scorers. He is an excellent jump shooter and can "stop at a dime." All three: Jason, Jim, and Brad are wonderful, high-character young men.

John Pitts is a 6'7" legend out of Long Island's Hempstead High School. Sound in every aspect of the game, his passing, rebounding, and defense play were elite. Offensively, not only could he shoot effectively with both hands, but he is also able to wait until the last moment to decide which hand presents the best opportunity to score. John's good friend and college roommate at Centenary is Robert Parish, "The Chief." Through John, a few of us get to meet the former Celtic great when he was in town. A second tall player who frequently went head-to-head against John is Sean O'Leary. At 6'6", Sean's defense and defensive rebounding are his strengths. Offensively, he is inconsistent, often missing short shots and layups because his body's orientation to the basket is poor. Sean is the habitual late arriver in our group and takes a fair amount of kidding for his pattern. At times, Sean will shoot and make a jumper with perfect form, which make those flubs even more mystifying.

Mark Marshall is a graceful and smooth 6'2" guard with a small-forward-type dynamic offensive game. He retains remarkable athleticism for a person in his fifties. His fadeaway and step-back jump shots from the baseline are illustrative of a dazzling elevation and great accuracy.

The Atkinson family is Long Island basketball royalty. Three of the gifted brothers were part of our Portledge runs, while a fourth whose job duties kept him away is, basketball-wise, the most accomplished. I refer to Kenny Atkinson, who for many years had been an NBA assistant, most of it under Mike D'antoni and most recently with the Atlantic Hawks. Well, Kenny has finally made it to the top. In the spring of 2016, he was selected as head coach of the Brooklyn Nets and is preparing for the 2016–2017 season. As a player, a 6'1" all-purpose guard, he was one of the finest ever of the University of Richmond and then enjoyed a stellar pro career in Europe. Brothers Mike and Tom, now gone from our workouts due to relocation and job changes, contributed high-level and spirited play. Mike, another guard, is a cerebral player with a fine outside shot. A subtle coach on the court, he has extensive successful coaching experience in high school and college. Tom, 6'3", is a tenacious high-jumping forward and a dynamic creative scorer. The best of the Portledge's Atkinsons is Dave, a wonderful player and person who is still one of the mainstays of the games. A slender six-footer, Dave is a blur of perpetual motion. His off-the-ball movement is reminiscent of Bill Bradley and Rick Hamilton. He creates space for himself to facilitate getting open to shoot his deadly midrange jump shot. When defenses overplay him, he is eager to display his pretty scoop drives to the basket. Always in great condition, even doing wind sprints at the conclusion of the workout, he strangely is prone to pulling his calf and hamstring. However, he always returns.

Several more players, most over fifty, came and went quickly. A few were not able to play at the level of the games. Some could play half-court, not full court. An even larger number injured themselves and had to drop out. However, with our numbers down, a bunch of guys came aboard, revitalized the Sunday morning games, and now are basically the core of the run. I refer to Brad Samuels, Matt Baltrus, Mark Friedberg, Peter Eichler, Conner Lynch, Kevin Mauro, Mike Ladisa, Frank DeRosa, Rich Schwam, Jason Allan and Charlie Prizzi.

A transplanted Midwesterner, Brad, at 6'3" has his shooting touch is his primary weapon. He can hit it from deep especially when given time. Matt, 6'2" has so upped his game since coming to Portledge. He is an explosive driver and has the ability to elevate to get open. Both his accuracy and ball handling have raised him to an elite level. Mark, a 6'4" Bostonian, is all maximum effort. He sprints in transition from defense to offense exceptionally fast. He also is able to rebound and still beat his man to the basket for layups. His awkward shooting style violates many principles and is the least of his skills, yet he does come up with clutch baskets. Peter "the Road Runner," is a track star sharpening his basketball abilities. Speed and jumping ability are his best assets, and he keeps learning and getting better at the finer points of the game. Conner is a 6'5" banger with a soft touch. It is extremely hard to move his big body when he is down low. Intermittently injured, Kevin, 6'1" and big shouldered, is deceptive moving toward the basket and consistently hits the outside shot. Little Mike, a 5'7" Italian leprechaun, is bullet fast and never gets tired. He wears out defenders, especially me. Mike is also a highly respected tennis coach. Young Frank DeRosa (in his twenties) is a combination point-2 guard, speedy (naturally), and opportunistic with an improving jumper. Rich, whose wife, Zoey, is a Co-AD at Portledge, jumps high and has the ability to stop on a "time" and is lightning quick to the basket. Jason, a high school coach at Sewanaka, despite a few severe injuries sustained when he was a Division 1 recruit at Wagner College, shows flashes of shot-making creativity that makes him so difficult to defend. Lastly, the newest addition is long, rubbery Charlie, so quick to rebound and to loose balls. Offensively he's an indefatigable slasher.

At Portledge, the tradition of fathers bringing sons continued, but on a much smaller scale than in Post's glory days. Stu Goldman's son Michael, whom we know since he was a toddler, blossomed into a fine player. Late to develop physically, he grew to be 6'2" and is blessed with a special ability to strip opponents of the ball and to also make steals through keen passing-lane anticipation. He was all-county at Jericho High and then created more havoc at Hobart. Another lifer at our workouts is Robbie, son of the man of few mistakes, Jeff Rubinstein. Robby, very fast and a dangerous scorer, played at Port Washington, but is far more reckless than his dad. Our two current prodigies are Steve and Dylan, the sons of Brad and Matt. They are making great strides and are looking forward to contributing to the program at Cold Spring Harbor, the school that Wally Sczerbiak put on the basketball map.

A person that I haven't yet mentioned, Roy Horowitz, brought his equally tall son, Dylan, to Portledge. Dylan at 6'6" had a totally different skill set than his thicker-bodied father. Dylan, graceful as a young deer, has superior leaping ability and at Half Hollow Hills High School was Suffolk County's premier shot blocker. It is a total mystery why he stopped playing at Ithaca, his college of choice. A most interesting aside regarding Roy is his lack of efficiency at making layups. Leave it to Alan Seiden to put Roy's weakness into embarrassing perspective. After a poor Sunday performance, Alan sat down next to Roy and asked the question: "Roy, does your wife know that you can't hit a layup?" It was a few months before Roy reappeared.

Walt Sczcerbiak, whose body was in basketball decline a few years before his aorta failed, occasionally brought his younger son Will to both Post and Portledge. Once he was on the sidelines, Wally induced Will to play in the active "youth" run. Will is 6'4", very strong and a competent three-point shooter. He started at Cold Spring Harbor, but didn't have the fervor of the rest of the family. He is, however, a bright, respectful, and caring person. Incidentally, there is another basketball playing Sczcerbiak. That is 6'2" all Long Island, sister Wendy. Do you get the pattern of W's in the family? It flows from Walt, to Wally, to Willie, and to Wendy. Only mom Marilyn breaks the string of Ws. Lovely and charming Marilyn is a star herself. Getting back to Wendy, she played for Division I Lehigh, but truncated her college career as a result of chronic severe knee deterioration. Wendy could have been a factor in our workouts, but resisted playing because "men are too sweaty." Had she competed, the ladylike Wendy would have impressed with her great hands and soft shooting touch.

Two players who made the transition from CW Post to our newer venues and are no longer on the scene are Matt Hanson and Kip Manfra. Matt, tall blond, and slender, could be the All-American model for a Norman Rockwell illustration. When we first met Matt, he was playing with Pat Daly's (Pat is Gary Wichard's brother-in-law) bruisers on the second full court at Post. We identified Matt's superior talents and invited him to play with us. Every major aspect of this former Dartmouth College lacrosse player just kept on improving. His progress was so dramatic that Wally Sczcerbiak had him take another step up to play with the younger studs. Even an ACL tear couldn't stop him. I've never seen anyone come back so quickly without losing any mobility, jumping, or running skills. It was a significant loss for our workout when a business opportunity necessitated Matt and his terrific family to move to New Jersey.

Kip Manfra, 6'2" and wide shouldered, had to stop playing due to multiple chronic injuries. Kip, a gregarious guy, shows excellent range and explosive streakiness in his shooting. Although not basketball related, but certainly the main factor of Kip's priorities was to rebuild his home that was destroyed by Superstorm Sandy. Even in his absence, the standing joke in our run is that if Kip was on the court, its odds on that he would take the game's first shot. Kip has happily rebuilt his home and vows that he will be back.

A late bloomer to the workout is someone that many of us knew from the eighties at East Meadows Prospect Park. He's also the person who's hardest to miss. This individual is delightful, witty, 7'0" native-born Irishman John Burke. He wasn't very good when he first arrived at our shores but, over time and with experience, has become a versatile outstanding player. He played here at South Hampton and Hofstra but achieved the potential as a pro back in Ireland. He also is a respected teacher and coach of girls at Truman High School in the Bronx. The "white-on-white" Irishman is beloved by his minority community. Lastly, John's preadolescent son and my "horse" buddy, Patrick, is a great kid and a future star. He has the total game and is a "can't miss," even if he grows up to be a 6'9" or 6'10" runt.

The last Portledge player reference concerns an individual who, when he joined us, played in every one of our sites. Neither back-to-back days nor pain or soreness ever deterred him. Only his softball league and late-night doo-wop singing could keep him away. He is 6'5", bruising Larry Scott. The way he came to become a part of our "fraternity" was simply delightful. One morning after playing at Freeport, Mark "Glove" Rich was in a 7-Eleven store. Larry noticed this big guy clad in shorts and a tank top. Curiously, Larry asked him if he plays basketball. He said he was looking for a weekend game. Mark told him about the Freeport run, and Larry enthusiastically asked if he could join us. Mark then conferred with us and received our approval. Larry, originally from Springfield Gardens, the school that spawned Anthony Mason and was coached by Kenny Fieldler. The fitting conclusion to this story is from the moment that Larry walked into the gym, he became known as "Larry 7-Eleven." Today, Larry keeps in touch with us via e-mail. A job transfer has resulted in Larry's relocation to Dallas, Texas. He will always remain on our all-time good-guy team.

CHAPTER II

Blessings and Heartaches

IN FEBRUARY 1994 my school staff with the participation of the Division of Special Education honored me with a retirement party at the Fox Hollow Inn in Syosset, Long Island. It was a wonderful career culmination attended by my family, childhood friends, basketball buddies, and over 150 school and NYC Board of Education colleagues. It was truly a special a special and memorable evening, but it wasn't the termination of my involvement in education. I had a game plan that my good reputation enabled me to fulfill.

Initially, I worked two days a week as a special education consultant with the primary purpose of assisting untenured principals in their supervision of instruction. I also evaluated every Special Education School's safety plan and followed the process until approval was granted by the Department of Education. A few years later a unique situation developed that brought about a new assignment.

An outstanding principal, Robin Ward, had multiple sclerosis which began to affect her mobility. Her excellent special education school, PS 177 Queens, had no elevator, making it nearly impossible for Robin to get to the second floor. The district and the United Federation of Teachers agreed to permit me to help supervise and formally observe those teachers and paraprofessionals. Although I knew Robin very well, this formal association was the beginning of a continued close and personal professional relationship that existed until Robin's death. The school has appropriately been dedicated to her and renamed "The Robin Ward School." With the exception of my 177 affiliation, a late 1990s budgetary crisis resulted in the termination of my other activities.

I previously wrote about my many friends that teach at Nassau Community College. It was suggested that I explore opportunities to work in their remedial/tutorial programs. This appealed to me because I knew that many of their varsity athletes were academically deficient. They were unable to gain course credits until they passed through specific proficiency gates. The school's interest matched mine and I joined the Basic Education Program (BEP) as a tutor in upgrading writing and reading skills. In the two years that I worked there, I felt strongly that many were impacted by my assistance and informal counseling. Both basketball and football players that began in BEP improved dramatically and earned an associate's degree.

Best of all, in 2000, my friend Robin Ward asked me if I ever thought about teaching at St. John's University. My reply was "never." She had a good relationship with the St. John's School of Education as she accepted student teachers who were special education majors. I prepared a resume; she called the dean and arranged an interview. I was hired immediately as an Adjunct Instructor of courses for undergraduates preparing for certification as Teachers of Children with Disabilities. I began in fall 2000 and never looked back. Although I recently took time off due to a health concern, I'm still teaching on a part-time basis, and I love it.

An added pleasantry of my association with St. John's is that I really got to know just how terrific are four men synonymous with the glory days of St. John's basketball. They are Mel Davis, Ron Rutledge, Billy Schaefer and the Coach, Lou Carnesecca. After their playing and coaching careers ended, they remained employed by the university. I would stop in to see them, on campus, before or after classes. They are all classy people whose presence enriched the school and its mission.

My sons also had a specific focus and both exhibited determination and resilience that has resulted in success in work and most importantly, the enjoyment of their lives. My elder son, Jon, is an attorney, specializing in Environmental Law. After completing the University of Bridgeport Law School and serving his internship, he had obtained a job with the New York City Department of Environmental Protection. While working there, he met Nancy, a lovely outgoing woman, who has been his wife for more than a decade. Initially, they resided in Manhattan and then Brooklyn, before deciding to follow their dream to Vermont. Jon passed the Vermont Bar Exam and has advanced steadily up the ladder in the environmental area. He presently is part of the administration of the State of Vermont. His office is in our nation's smallest capital, Montpelier, and he makes home in the picturesque town of Marshfield.

Looking out of his huge kitchen windows, the high mountains seem close enough to touch, and a river flows directly behind their house. Jon's love of the outdoors and deep appreciation of nature's beauty was awakened in his summers spent in the Adirondacks at Raquette Lake Camp. Most interesting, his brother Seth has no such calling and wouldn't go pioneering without a luxury camper. Nancy, on the other hand, caught the bug from Jon and is a dedicated environmentalist.

With all the wonderful things accomplished by Jon and Nancy, for me, their crowning accomplishment is their thirteen-year-old son, and my grandson, Gabriel. He is a handsome, happy, bright child with a wisdom far beyond his age. He's a delight to be around. At this stage, he has just a passing interest in Grandpa's favorite sport; however, like a true Vermontier, he is a highly skilled skier. His fearlessness on the advanced slopes baffles me.

Their beautiful and lovable black lab, Bella, completes my New England family.

My Florida son, Seth, has had many twists and turns in his career as an educator, but always lands on his feet. He had meandered from special education classroom teacher, to crisis intervention teacher, to assistant athletic director, to long-term athletic director at Lake Worth High School and now to math coordinator teacher/trainer for Palm Beach County schools. Although he found the challenge of the AD position to be exciting, the extra evening and weekend hours with few financial benefits and unappreciative school administrators brought about burnout. His current job where he sees the fruits of his labor reflected in measurable math achievement is enjoyable and rewarding.

Who Seth is as a person is related to what he does to supplement his income. Now in his mid forties, Seth is a markedly fit and well-toned athlete. Like his father, basketball remains his major leisure activity and interest. He is the owner of a fashionable Delray Beach condo, the perfect bachelor pad for someone who is still single. Not that the still-youthful-looking stud hasn't had his opportunities, but he lacks that elusive soul mate. His summers since high school graduation have always included working in basketball camps. From his first counselor experience at Kutsher's Sports Academy in the Catskills, to owning his own camp in Florida, his hoops association is a labor of love. For several years before he set out on his own, he worked for the team of Barry Leibowitz, a tremendous college and pro point guard, and Marv Kessler, Seth's Maccabiah coach. When Barry and Marv dissolved their partnership, Seth went with Marv because his new operation was in Boca Raton, closer to home. For Marv, he was the coordinator, but found that his inability to delegate responsibility to others was unacceptable. Helped by good friend John Moran, who used his influence to obtain Rosarian School in Palm Beach, Seth established a basketball day camp which he calls "Future Stars."

Seth, the leisure basketball player, like so many others, became much better after college. Every aspect of his game dramatically improved. He relished playing point guard and remains remarkably fast for someone over forty. He is able to hold his own against younger and highly accomplished ex-collegians and professionals. His present home court is the lavish Lifetime Fitness Boca Raton Athletic Club. I so enjoy going with him to the gym to shoot around or compete in "horse." It may seem crazy, but on Saturdays, I'll play a bit of full court basketball and only if Seth is on my team. Objectively speaking, I rarely embarrass myself. I always feel flattered when the guys at the club compliment me for my shooting form or when they say that I must have been "something" in my day. Getting back to Seth, on every trip to Long Island, a highlight is playing against old friends at Lutheran and Portledge.

What I'm about to share is the most difficult part of telling my story. It pertains to the loss of many of my closest loved ones. I am not following strict chronological order, but all of it has occurred over the last ten years.

My mom lived in Brooklyn her entire life. Unlike my Dad who died in his early forties, she made it to the upper nineties. Right to the end, she was mentally sharp and independent, maintaining her apartment until her death in 2006. Her last years were so physically tough due to crippling arthritis causing the severe shrinking and distorting of her torso. Her fragile spinal column was replete with compression fractures, making it excruciatingly painful to get out of bed and move about. Yet she somehow did. Her first sign of bone weakness actually carries a humorous message about Mom. She was dancing with a friend at a Miami Beach hotel when she slipped and fell to the ground. She fractured her pelvis and was flown back to New York for the surgery. I was waiting for her at the airport along with the driver of the ambulette to take her to the hospital. Unbelievable, but she refused to go until she had her hair done. She had already made phone arrangements before leaving Florida. That certainly says volumes about her spirit and also her vanity.

In the late 1990s, my brother Howie was diagnosed with kidney cancer. Like most things, he approached his illness with cerebral determination. Brilliant and highly successful as a partner at Grant Thornton, a major accounting firm, he learned everything there was to know concerning prognosis, treatment, and the latest research for kidney cancer. Happily, he survived and enjoyed several years of retirement spent doting over his four grandchildren. Suddenly, in late 2010, he experienced continuous fatigue and shortness of breath. What he feared was unfortunately confirmed. Cancer had returned and with a vengeance. It spread to his liver and ravaged his body. Outwardly, he remained calm and even made jokes pertaining to his condition. However, in a serious moment a few weeks from the end, he confided to me that he felt his "life draining from my body," each succeeding day. By late summer 2011, Howie was gone. There was no one left in my immediate family. Two great losses and the strongest guiding influences in my life had disappeared. Although not the most important thing in the big picture, my mother and brother opened the door to give me the opportunity to realize my basketball dreams.

Many devotees of the past New York college basketball scene falsely remember that I and big Syd Levy played together at CCNY. In truth, we were teammates everywhere else, but not at our alma mater. My first year on varsity was the 1957–58 season where Syd's last year was 1956–57. We became the closest of friends after college. Our bond further strengthened when after marriage, we lived within walking distance off of Kings Highway in Brooklyn. Syd, his dynamic wife Elaine, and their three children were our family. They felt the same about me, Helene, and our two boys. In the late 1980s, the Levys with their children, all adults and established in the Northeast, moved to South Florida. Syd took advantage of a business offer in Boca Raton and settled in Del Ray Beach. We would still see each other regularly as by the late 1990s, we also purchased a condo in Boca. There is no doubt that at this stage of my life, Syd had become my best friend.

In the mid-2000s, Syd's wonderful productive life took a sudden, sad turn. The guy who gave so much to others, an imposing figure with a world-class sense of humor, was stricken with advanced lung cancer. He tried so hard to keep a stiff upper lip, but he kept sliding. Finally in late winter of 2006, this warm and gentle giant closed his eyes forever. His funeral was held in Manhattan the day after a monster snowstorm. Still, a few hundred mourners, including my son Seth, gathered together to celebrate a wonderful productive life. The service was highlighted by many poignant, sweet eulogies. Syd was indeed a treasure.

It was impossible not to notice Alan Seiden. He was so brash, so outspoken, and so blunt. He had the swagger, the confidence, and deep belief in himself. He was an acclaimed basketball player and a successful, if not overly ambitious, ticket broker. His relationships with women were monogamous in the sense that he was always exclusive with his latest love. However, he remained a bachelor because he felt it unfair to inflict his lifestyle upon someone else. He also had no desire to change or even compromise. As for his lifestyle, it was all about basketball, whether playing, spectating, discussing, or critiquing. His other favorite things were high-stakes poker and dining out and hanging with the boys. He sought endless fun and excitement while eating too much and sleeping too little. He easily spent more money on treating others than anyone I had ever met.

The huge fly in the ointment was Alan's refusal to be concerned about his physical condition and overall health. He never went to the doctor, nor took any of the diagnostic tests as precautions associated with aging. One Sunday at a party at Wally Szczerbiak's home, all the 6'5" and over guys, and 5'11" Alan had a guess who's the heaviest weigh-in competition. Alan's shocking 272 pounds was the top weight. About that time, while walking a moderate distance, a breathless Alan would put his arm on my shoulder to reduce the stress. It got to the point that his girlfriend, Ruth, would say, "If you don't do something to improve your health, I won't be there for you when you crash." Well, crash he did, because one day after Tony Jackson's funeral, Alan suffered a stroke. He was driving to work when he felt a loss of power to use his legs. He phoned his brother, Ron, who rushed to his side and brought him to North Shore Hospital in Manhasset, Long Island.

Within days after being stricken, it was clear that Alan didn't want to get better. He could stand, but not walk, and Alan wasn't paralyzed. His doctor told him that the damage was not irreversible and that with hard work, he should regain significant mobility. As days passed, he became increasingly bitter and pessimistic. As she had stated, Ruth visited a few times, and then discontinued her support and communication. He never said much about it, but in my opinion, this breakup destroyed his will to live. Alan, whose life was propelled by the quest for fun, excitement, and friends, simply gave up. He wouldn't rehab seriously, often refused medication and was belligerent and uncooperative with medical personnel. He lost significant weight, most of his muscle tone, and was visibly atrophying. Mental illness had definitely become a factor, adding to the complexity of his problems.

Alan's mom, Dora, his sister, Susan, and brother, Ron, were tremendously devoted to the desperate struggle to reverse his deterioration. An elevator was constructed at home to help transport Alan from basement to bedroom. They were constantly present, indulging him with his favorite foods, and cheering on the smallest signs of progress. As months passed, it became evident that their determined team would lose. Almost unthinkable, but even Alan's interest in basketball was waning. With the exception of a few people, he no longer wanted to have company. The group that visited him regularly consisted of me, Red and Mona Blumenreich, Richie "Buck" Mandor, and two true "mensches" (wonderful people from St. John's): Lou Carnesecca and Jerry Houston. Lou was the assistant coach under Joe Lapchick when Alan played and always held Alan in esteem. Their relationship was one of mutual affection. Jerry, the captain of the Lapchick's final NIT championship team, is several years younger than Alan and is just the warmest and most sincere person. Alan and Jerry played weekend ball together for many years and developed a strong emotional bond. Basketball aficionados may also remember that one of Jerry's fine children, son Kevin, was our nation's highest scorer at West Point.

Jerry Houston was the last of our friends to see Alan before he passed. Almost to the day of his seventy-first birthday, Alan departed. His funeral attended by hundreds was a celebration. It focused upon the good times, his triumphs, and his uniquely eccentric personality. I was honored to present one of the many on target eulogies. I ended by asking the congregation to stand and shout in unison "And one." This was Alan's signature message statement proclaiming that he scored and was fouled. Whenever our remaining crew gets together, we always take time to tell Alan stories. We will never run out of material.

My in-laws, Gussie and Ted Barish, relocated to Delray Beach in 1982. Gussie continued to work almost to age ninety and was Chase Bank's eldest teller. Ted basically remained retired and lacked the vitality of his very active wife. From the moment that I entered their Queens home over fifty years ago, they have treated me as a son. They were both loving and generous. Before Seth, Helene, and I established residence in Florida, we stayed with them whenever we visited. They thoroughly enjoyed the change to an ideal climate, had a new circle of friends, and loved going out to dinner with us. Seth became especially close to them and in their eyes, attained saintlike status. Bliss and contentment were disrupted by a horrible intruder. One of the Barish sons, Stuart, a Vietnam vet, was diagnosed with Lou Gherig's disease, lateral sclerosis. He was divorced with two children and successful in the jewelry business, and his decline was rapid and continuous. Stuart was an extroverted dynamo. His personality reminded me of Burt Lancaster in *Elmer Gantry* and Robert Preston as Harold Hill in *The Music Man*. The difference was that Stu was more ethical. He was certain that the disease was an effect of Agent Orange exposure in Vietnam and became prominent in the Veterans Rights Movement. The deterioration began first in his legs and then hampered dexterity in his hands and fingers. No doubt he was spared the worst when he prematurely choked to death in his sleep. In a way, it was a relief that he didn't suffer for many more years, but it took a terrible toll on the family, especially his aging parents. Sadly, more devastating heartaches would soon occur.

Ted's general health became quite poor, riddled with digestive problems and massive bone loss to his once sturdy frame. He became bedridden and gently slipped away in 2011. As for Gussie, she too had suffered greatly in recent years. Amazingly in 2014, she survived open heart surgery to replace a main heart valve. Now ninety-four, she still has the ability to smile and laugh especially when Seth takes her to the casino to play blackjack or poker.

As time and the Florida years rolled by, there wasn't much left of our marriage. Helene no longer wanted to spend time in New York. It was all Florida and nothing else. As for me, I wasn't willing to break my ties with productive activities, interests and family obligations in New York. I, therefore, settled into a pattern of frequent, very pleasant trips to Florida and stayed with her, first at our rental, and then at our condo in Boca Raton. I fulfilled my financial responsibilities and neither of us sought a legal separation

In reality, it was more than distance that kept us apart. The largest gulf in our increasingly tenuous relationship was our changing, differing lifestyles. Her existence was Spartan-like, governed by stringent nutrition, obsessive-compulsive exercising, and limited social involvement. Mine was easygoing, pleasure-seeking, and gluttonous (by comparison) eating habits. I maintained a vigorous social life with a wide circle of friends, both in New York and Florida.

Basketball also became a major sticking point, and she openly stated that it was always an impediment limiting the depth of my feelings toward her. She never expressed this viewpoint, except when Jon was an infant, and in fact, encouraged my playing, especially when it provided her with free time on the weekends. She now frequently expressed resentment that my career, and of course basketball, counted for much more than her happiness and her personal aspirations. How was it possible that throughout our courtship and marriage that this perceived hurt was rarely discussed? Equally as baffling, how could I, who consider myself to be an empathetic person, not have picked up on any distress symbols? For a reason to be revealed in the next few paragraphs, it was unfortunately too late to heal the wounds.

In the early fall of 2005, Helene developed a persistent cough. Initially, her internist diagnosed it as a stubborn case of bronchitis and prescribed traditional medications. As already mentioned, Helene was in excellent physical condition, obsessive about exercising, devoutly observant of research-based nutritional practices. It is an understatement to characterize her as a "health nut." Still, the cough worsened and began to affect her breathing. She became short-winded after participating in cardiovascular activities. On a few occasions, a bit of blood was coughed up following a vigorous workout.

Becoming increasingly frustrated, she sought expert opinions and underwent several intensive tests. Her anxiety was relieved as all were negative, especially those focusing upon the search for growths within her lungs. The recommendation was for rest and a temporary cessation of strenuous exercise. It was firmly stated that her daily routine of lengthy and fast-paced walking and stair climbing on cardio machines was the culprit, exacerbating her problem.

When weeks of rest did nothing to improve her condition, a gym friend recommended that she seek the opinion of Dr. Thomas Niederman, a respected South Florida oncologist. It was now February of 2006, and Helene desperately wanted an answer. It soon was revealed and hit like a sledgehammer. What Dr. Niederman suspected and discovered was both sad and shocking. Although there were no tumors, Helene was indeed suffering from lung cancer. It was a type known as non-small cell, and both lobes were invaded by countless runaway cancer cells. Even worse, the odds of beating it were overwhelmingly long as it was diagnosed at stage 4.

Despite the horrendous news, Helene vowed to fight on, stating that she would never surrender to the dreaded disease. True to her words, she battled ferociously. For three and a half years, she bravely faced every obstacle and setback, until finally succumbing on October 17, 2009. Through continuous chemo, steroids, incessant blood work necessitating a port placed in her chest, she never complained and always attempted to live as normal a life as possible. She raised our spirits by being optimistic, indomitable, and cheerful.

After she died, Dr. Niederman wrote our family a letter expressing his sadness while also stating that Helene was his most admired and loved patient. He called her the "muffin lady" as she brought an assortment of muffins, for all her "chemo friends" and the medical staff at each visit. He also graciously forgave the substantial remaining balance for her treatments.

None of the marital difficulties described here mattered in those last difficult, yet triumphant years. I was completely there for her, fully devoted to being a loving support in every possible way. She in turn embraced the bond that was absent for so long. I was awed by her strength, courage, and outwardly stoic attitude. Not for fear of dying or by hoping that God would show mercy if she displayed goodness in a time of such strife, Helene indeed fulfilled her potential as a person. Once again, she was more like the woman and loving teenager that I met in the Catskills so many years ago. She became a better mother, grandmother, daughter, and wife. She wrote notes of gratitude to loved ones and apologies to those from which she strayed or offended. Her deepest appreciation was demonstrated to her mom, who nurtured her in sickness as she did when Helene was a child, and to her son, Seth, who resides in Florida, and devoted a part of every day to uplift her spirits.

Helene requested to be cremated. At her funeral service held at Seth's Delray condo, and the nearby intercoastal waterway, the tone was one of celebration. At the conclusion of the emotional tribute, hundreds of balloons were released and flown over the water, a symbol that Helene's soul will endure.

A few months later, a memorial service was conducted in New York. Hundreds attended and again, a party atmosphere prevailed. Several of Helene's favorite songs were interspersed, along with the reflections of all members of our immediate family. At the conclusion of the service, Bocelli's rendition of the haunting "Time to Say Goodbye" was played at the recessional, leading to the buffet and warm reception. In retrospect, a highlight of the wonderful evening was the poignant musical message conveyed in the fabulous song "I Hope You Dance." It says that when things get tough, don't give up and "sit it out." As hard as it may be, just get up and "dance." As it applies to Helene, she certainly "danced" to the very end.

CHAPTER 12

Nostalgia and Tying It All Together

IN THESE FINAL pages, I'm going to reflect upon several basketball-related activities, events and occasions that keep the great game close to my heart. Much of it is nostalgic, illuminating the long, fascinating road that I have traveled. It is hard to imagine what my life would have been like without basketball. The pleasure that the sport has given me so outweighs any negatives that I have been both blessed and enriched by my intense involvement. Through all the injuries and pain and even the surgeries I have absolutely no regrets. If presented with the same opportunities, I would do it all over again. This time, however I'd attempt to work more on my right hand.

At about age fifty, my main physical education teacher at our St. Mary's adolescent program, and a good friend, Percy Watson made an interesting proposal to me. This has nothing to do with his plan, but Percy was a fleet running back at Elizabeth City College, one of the elite "Negro" schools, prior to true integration. He wanted to establish an end of the school year "Groveman

Award" to be given to the outstanding student foul shooter. A trophy would be presented to the school champion with the added incentive of a cash supplement, following the schoolwide competition. The unique point of this, which excited me, was that a face-off would occur between the champion and myself. We would each take twenty-five foul shots in segments of five.

If I were beaten, a $100 "scholarship" prize would be presented by me at the final sports awards program. I loved the idea, and the competition became a yearly highlight. Not to brag, but I never lost. It was great fun, and yes, the runner-up along with his trophy was given an envelope from me containing a $25 bonus.

The strength of friendships and the role of basketball in my Brooklyn childhood were beautifully illustrated in what became an annual Long Island reunion. Beginning in 1987, longtime friend "Cookie" Wolkoff, who in the adult world is known by most as Jerry, hosted a summer gathering of our Brownsville-East Flatbush gang. It was held at his exquisite and spacious home on the bay in Quogue, the gateway to the Hamptons. He and his terrific wife, Michelle, treated us to a fabulous day and evening of athletic and recreational activities, laughter, nostalgia, and food and drink sufficient in quantity and excellent in quality to satisfy a king and his court. It's wonderful that Cookie, who is hugely successful in business, has such deep feeling for his roots, and derives great pleasure from revisiting his modest beginning.

The following text of one of the memos sent by Cookie, to all the guys prior to the eagerly anticipated event, speaks for itself:

> TO: Oldtimers
> DATE: April 23, 1992
> SUBJECT: BASKETBALL OLDTIMER'S DAY
>
> Our sixth annual Oldtimer's Basketball Game is scheduled for June 27 (Saturday) at my basketball court on Long Island (Quogue, New York). June 28, (Sunday) is our rain date. To confirm a rainout, you can call on Saturday morning at ***-***-****.

You and your "wife" are invited to join the festivities at 11:30 a.m. The day's schedule also includes lunch, dinner, swimming, tennis, and boating.

We need to get a head-count, so call as soon as possible (but no later than June 1st).

A list of basketball players and directions for getting to Quogue are attached.

Remember to RSVP (my daytime, weekday phone number is ***-***-****)

Jerry Wolkoff

The usual attendees were many of the people from my Brooklyn childhood, who occupy a significant place in my life, and whom I have so fondly written about. These include Joel Tendler, Gerry Stuckelman, Harvey Richer, Lew Burke, and "Fuzzy" Kaplan. It was also so good to see numerous other neighborhood friends, who help to recall the schoolyard and BBC/BRC days, and the crazy times at Arky's Candy Store, and cruising the Brooklyn hangouts. The featured cast in this group were Sandy "Nifty" Jacobs, Al Schneider, Shelly Komorsky, Heshy Siansky, Jerry Stadler, Paul and Ronnie Feldman, Bert Seigel, Moish Goldzblatt, and the irrepressible Irwin "Miami Shami" Shane.

Our basketball actions at the reunions were often scary. The games were a hazard to the health of the guys that were no longer in shape to play basketball. Each time we played the intention was for it to be fun and noncompetitive. However, usually the seriousness and all out effort of brothers Paul and Ronnie Feldman brought out the beast in all of us. We have been lucky in that nothing worse than someone pulling a muscle brought the game to a welcome, premature conclusion.

The truly sad part of our early summer gatherings is that time has taken a disproportionate toll of our childhood crew. So many in our gang are gone, never even making it to enjoy old age. In what follows is a list of my departed friends from first to most recent passing. For each, my "free association" thoughts and the causes of death are written.

Moish Goldzblatt–Sports ticket scalper supreme. Threw parties at his apartment for most pay-per-view championship fights. A confirmed bachelor. *Cause of death*: Heart attack.

Irwin "Miami Shami" Shane–Most naturally comical person I've ever known. Just seeing him put you in a good mood. Devoted wife, Susan, dedicated a bench on the Long Beach, Long Island, boardwalk in his memory. *Cause of death:* Stomach cancer.

Big Gerry Stuckelman–My best friend from ages six through fourteen. Center on the great Thomas Jefferson 1954 City Championship Team. Gentle and good-natured. A most devoted father and grandfather. *Cause of death:* Diabetes.

"Battling" Lew Burke–Crazy to the very end. Successful boxer and dog trainer. A violent intellect, but sentimentally affectionate to his friends. An enigma. Has brilliant children, and Annie, a devoted wife, who was only seventeen when Lew married her. *Cause of death*: Everything. Totally dissipated.

Bert Seigel–Big guy with a huge heart. Debilitated by spinal and neural deterioration. Courageous. Struggled mightily to maintain independence to the end. *Cause of death:* Brain hemorrhage.

Ronnie Feldman–Died on New Year's Day 2014, a few hours after phoning me, worried about my health (bladder difficulties). Sudden death was most shocking. A picture of health and vitality. Exercised daily and coordinated physical activities for his residential community. Wonderful family man with terrific wife, Arlene. Fell in love at the BRC where Arlene was a cheerleader. *Cause of death:* Heart attack.

A second lavish annual gathering was also attributable to a person's generosity. In this instance, the host of the occasion was Al Schindler, a man of perpetual motion on the court, with infinite stamina. Al, originally a Queens friend of Alan Seiden, was one of the oldest guys in the workouts, yet rarely missed a run at Freeport or CW Post.

Each summer he invited most of his basketball playing friends, their significant others, and their children to his elegant

Melville, Long Island, home for a Sunday, after workout, brunch. The attractions were the magnificent kidney-shaped pool, the outdoor hot tub, flowing beverages, and delicious food. He and his then wife, Alice, matched Cookie and Michelle's graciousness out in Quogue. The parties were catered, highlighting by an ever-changing variety of delicacies, especially the pastries. Of course, Mr. Seiden dominated the conversation by reliving humorous basketball anecdotes and in-game "war stories." Wally Szczerbiak, first as a preteen right through his college days, was the leader of the pool antics. Al hung a hoop at the widest edge of the water and supplied it with small-sized basketballs. It was Wally who organized the pool games and got all the kids involved. True to his talents, he was also a prolific shooter in the water.

Super sports agent Gary Wichard only once made it to the Schindler extravaganza. His football star clients looked forward to the parties, but Gary, bigger than life in many ways, was somewhat reluctant to attend such events. I wrote earlier that Gary left the New York area and established his home and business in glamorous Malibu, California. I still spoke with him occasionally and would join him for dinner along with Alan Seiden, who of course picked up the check, whenever Gary came East.

It was disturbing when, in 2010, Gary looked so drawn and thin in a TV interview. Although at first his brother Neal downplayed it, unfortunately it soon became apparent that he was seriously ill. We learned just how bad it was, as it was revealed that Gary was suffering from pancreatic cancer. The worst of all the malignancies quickly took his life in 2011. There was a tremendous outpouring of sympathy and accolades. Most impressive, however, was the glowing praise expressed by so many of his player clients. They spoke of their loving friend Gary, not the shrewd businessman. In truth, our guys were always aware and were awed by how much he cared about them as people. A wonderful husband and father, Gary embraced his players as members of his family.

I'll end this segment with two vastly different anecdotes. Firstly, prolific writer Cameron Crowe said that Gary was his inspiration for his film hero Jerry Maguire. Secondly, this one is terribly unpleasant, and may have even hastened Gary's demise. Big Judd Rothman, Gary's accountant and the custodian of his clients and some relative's investments, was implicated, along with his son Eric, for embezzling funds. Judd, although never a social friend of mine, was an integral member of our workout crew. He was an articulate, warm, and likable person. Eric was also friendly, but over the years became increasingly flamboyant in his style and manner. He befriended my son Seth who already moved to Florida.

They, in fact, would get together when Eric would come to Florida on business. Seth noticed some negative changes; uppermost Eric's unreliability. Once the charges were brought against father and son, we never saw or spoke to either one of them again. Eric worked a plea deal and went to prison. Judd did not serve time, but reportedly paid back a huge sum of money. Perhaps most significantly, their deception had a devastating effect upon Gary. Neal, too, is still in the state of disbelief over what they did.

Alan Seiden could have easily been a character in a Damon Runyan story, but he was real. Mostly good, intermingled with a lot of shades of gray. I never met anyone like him. As might be expected, he was also the king of party givers. He threw them to commemorate past memorable St. John's games, to celebrate annual special sporting events, significant birthdays (his own fiftieth) to bid farewell to close friends (e.g., Darrel Ray, Jerry Holmes, and Sergio Luyk) and several to honor Wally Szczerbiak's achievements in college and in the pros.

His primary base of operation was his mother's home in Jamaica Estates, Queens. The secondary party place was the Peking House, Chinese restaurant, on Union Turnpike, close to St. John's. For some reason, he held the Wally festivities there. Getting back to the house on 188th Street, Alan the bachelor lived there as well as younger brother, Ron, whom he nicknamed "Jones," after a character in a classic novel. Sister Susan, the married Seiden, had a more traditional lifestyle, consisting of children and grandchildren. Alan was not a mamma's boy, although he loved his mother dearly. The home was his sanctuary, a place of peace and contentment, to rest his tired body and to enjoy home-cooked meals, whenever he returned from poker, girlfriends, games, etc. His wonderful mother, Dora, accepted all of his eccentricities, and had the red carpet out for him whenever he arrived. Not only did she accept Alan's penchant for holding the parties at the house, she thoroughly enjoyed the merrymaking, and was delighted to greet and mix with her son's large circle of friends. She never even seemed to mind the cleanup, nor expected Alan to help. Incidentally, Dora was widowed at a very young age. Her husband Mickey, a little guy, who was a prolific settlement-house basketball star, died many years ago. He passed on the athletic genes to Alan, and to Ron who played at Jacksonville University in the Artis Gillmore era.

My favorite among the many Seiden celebrations was the twenty-fifth anniversary of St. John's stirring, down to the wire 1959 Madison Square Garden victory over NYU. The seesaw game was won on a jumper by the marvelous Tony Jackson. For Alan, what made that game even more special was that it marked NYU coach Lou Rossini's strategy to have the 6'6" octopus-like Tom "Satch" Sanders defend him. It was an honor for little Alan to be guarded by a guy, who after college played for the Boston Celtics, and was to become one of the best defensive players in NBA history. Alan considered the ten points he scored in that game to be the hardest he ever earned.

At the cramped gathering, following the lavish buffet, the film of that "Garden" battle was shown to a "who's who" of assembled guests. The St. John's starting five consisting of guards Alan and Gus Alfieri, forwards Tony Jackson and Dick Engert, and center Lou Roethel, were present. Coach Joe Lapchick had unfortunately died but his assistant, the revered Lou Carnesecca, was there. Also there was NYU's coach, Lou Rossini, along with Satch, the great Cal Ramsey, and key substitutes Arty Loche and Joel Silver. Other past St. John's luminaries enjoying the special occasion were Hall of Famer Dick McGuire, retired Boston Celtic "Dutch" Garfinkel, and Jerry Houston. I was simply thrilled to be included. A comical outgrowth of that fabulous night was Lou Rossini's upset reaction after reliving that classic game. Ever the coach, he agonized over the flaws that he detected in his closing-minutes strategy.

A few years later, Gus Alfieri got hold of the tape of another monumental St. John's victory. This one was the 1959 NIT championship game against top-ranked Bradley University. Once again, the starting unit participated in the celebration. Alan and Tony were co-MVPs, although I still marvel at 6'4" TJ's final game performance. He scored in the mid-twenties while grabbing an astounding twenty-seven rebounds. How's that for flying?

In addition to those special guests who fit into this theme of the specific event, there was Alan's cadre of longtime friends who were always invited. All are, of course, basketball people. Of those that I have already written about, there were Stacey Arceneaux, who played for the St. Louis Hawks, a few years removed from high school. Irwin "Red" Blumenreich, by far the best in Yeshiva University history; Eddie Gard, excellent playmaker at LIU, implicated during the scandal but also unselfish mentor to Alan and so many other young talents; Les Yellin, one of my own childhood heroes and legendary set shot at St. Francis. Other important influences in Alan's life who were regular party attendees included Artie Benoit, Alan's backcourt mate and best friend in high school, a starter at Adelphi University; two Harlem greats, both all-city at Commerce and Benjamin Franklin respectively in Jack DeFares and Carl Green. They were also stars at Winston-Salem College in North Carolina, and Carl had a stint with the Globetrotters. Two venerable, somewhat older friends were the famed Howie Garfinkel, director of Five Star Basketball Camp, the first high-profile basketball showcase in the USA; and Larry "Scout" Pearlstein, the mysterious "maven" (Yiddish for expert), confidant and advisor to scores of top players and coaches.

For many years, Gus Alfieri was not on Alan's invite list. Although they were one of the best backcourts in St. John's history, they frequently clashed at practices and were not close away from the gym. It was therefore so heartwarming that their relationship blossomed during the last few decades of Alan's life. Brash Alan and introspective Gus kind of met in the middle and grew to appreciate each other and understood their differences. They both had excellent recall and were wonderful raconteurs, adding enjoyment and meaning to the gatherings. Gus was right there till the very end. Another thing of significance is that Gus is the author of *Lapchick* an outstanding book about the Hall of Fame coach. His tribute to his beloved coach doesn't end there as he and sportswriter Jimmy O'Connell have established the annual "Joe Lapchick Character Awards" presented mainly to former coaches. Lastly, they have raised funds to soon unveil a statue of Joe Lapchick at the entrance of the "Carnesecca Arena" on the St. John's campus.

The fun days at the Seiden home ended in 2006 when Alan suffered his stroke. Sadly he wasn't the only one of our merrymakers that were soon gone. Les Yellin, so full of life, had a fatal heart attack. He was on his way to Princeton to assist his good friend, Coach Pete Carril, when it occurred. Equally shocking and more recently, Red Bloomreich sat in his favorite chair early on a Sunday afternoon to read the paper and watch football. Unknown initially to Mona, he quietly shut his eyes and drifted away. We all believed he was recovering nicely from a heart bypass. Sweet, gentle "Red," except on the basketball court, will also be remembered as the king of crossword puzzles. Lastly, our surrogate mother, Dora Seiden, so warm and nurturing faded quickly, once Alan died. She always ignored her physical difficulties, but lost her will to fight. Overall, hers was a great life.

I was five years old when my family moved from Amboy Street in Brownsville to East Ninety-sixth Street and Linden Boulevard (just across from Beth-El Hospital). I had a great childhood in East Flatbush that became somewhat chaotic with the passing of my father in his early fortie. Growing up I've always considered my roots to be jointly East Flatbush and Brownsville. In East Flatbush I had many friends, went to good schools, had open-air and many endless fields to play on, and hung out on safe streets and the Remsen Avenue candy store. Brownsville was so different, ethnically mixed and with an ever-diminishing socioeconomic level. Yet for me, it was exciting and appealing. I was even strongly enchanted by "Murder Incorporated," the most notorious gang of Jewish mobsters. The real hook, however, was its rich basketball tradition. In the forties, fifties, and sixties, the neighborhood produced so many college and professional stars. Some of the best were Max Zaslofsky, Harry Boykoff, Hy Gotkin, Sid Tanenbaum, Jackie Goldsmith, Dutch Garfinkel, Boris Nachamkin, Elliot Press, Jerry Domerschick, Leroy Ellis, Tommy Hemans, Red Goldstein, Solly Walker, Sihugo Green, and Tony Jackson. I also revere those fantastic neighborhood teams; the Rimsters, the Viceroys, and the Rimsmen. Most importantly for me, it's where I became a player. It was the endless hours of practice and the high-level competition at the BBC/BRC that changed me from a high school scrub to a college high scorer. I never forgot any of what I've just written about, so whenever, in midlife until the present time an opportunity enabled me to reconnect with my Brownsville roots, I am eager to be there.

In the 1980s, I became aware of a fraternity of Afro-Americans athletes originally from Brownsville that held an annual dinner-dance and fund-raising gala. The organization "Brooklyn U.S.A. Athletic Association," composed of my contemporaries, most of whom were outstanding players of their day. In fact, many of them are people that I have written about in the pages of this book. In addition to sponsoring a championship caliber team in the National Oldtimers Tournament, the association does excellent non-profit work within the Central Brooklyn Community and is dedicated to improving the life for its youths. Of the group's many worthy involvements, two that stand out are its efforts in helping to establish the Jackie Robinson Center of Physical Culture and The Brooklyn U.S.A. Scholarship Program, which provides monetary awards to individuals who have demonstrated athletic and academic proficiency.

I attended for the first time with both Sid Levy and Zelda Spoelstra, of the NBA in 1985. Since then I tried to make it every year, and always am dazzled by their warmth, fellowship, and deep meaning. Zelda sat with us at the NBA sponsored table with several of my favorite players. I felt honored to be seated with my boyhood idol, Sherman White, and with two greats from CCNY's double championship team: Floyd Layne and Ed Warner. I finally got to meet a true legend, one of the pioneers leading to the growth and popularity of basketball. That man was John Issacs, a patriarch of black athletes throughout our country. John starred for Harlem's "New York Rens" (Renaissance), all black, and one of the best teams of the pre NBA era. He was already in his eighties when I got to know him, but he was still youthful in spirit and articulateness. He was working with young people at the Harlem YMCA contributing so much to the community. John, ageless in his grace and dignity, was in his late nineties when he died. His torch has been passed on to Floyd Layne, who out of respect and affection is called "The Chief."

A highlight of the special event is the annual induction of former players with a "Brooklyn" connection into the "Brooklyn USA Hall of Fame." The initial group into the ring of honor, dubbed "The First Five" were Tony Jackson, Floyd Layne, Solly Walker, Ed Warner, and Sherman White. Other ensuring inductees, all guys that I played against with the exception of the great Nate "Tiny" Archibald were Arnold Branch, John Crawford, Tommy Hemans, "Chink" Gaines, Connie Hawkins, Billy Burwell, Zeke Clements, Jake Jordan, Hank Whitney, and "2" Viceroy legends, Danny Culley and Gerry Harper, whom I grew up watching at Betsey Head Park. It was such a thrill to "schmooze" with them during the cocktail hour, and to get to know other formidable basketball names. One such group was the Philadelphia contingent headed by famed Temple coach John Chaney; another Temple and Eastern League star Jay Norman; Villanova and New York Knicks center Tom Hoover; and the charismatic Sonny Hill. In the fall of 2012, Brooklyn USA announced that Marv Kessler was to be added to the roaster of Hall of Fame members. How ironic was it that Marv's previously under-control malignancy had spread throughout his body. Of all the things that Marv accomplished as a player and coach, this was to be his proudest moment. He so loved playing for Boys High School and being a starter on one of NYC's greatest high school champions. Opinionated and dogmatic, Marv had both admirers and detractors, but had nothing but excellent relationships with his Boys High teammates, and did so much for the greater Afro-American community. Although he was hospitalized for an extended period of time, prior to the impending awards ceremony he spoke optimistically about being present for his Hall induction. He tried so hard, but didn't make it, dying a few days before the gala. However, on the Friday following his funeral, Marv's wife Irene, his two married daughters, and their families were at the El Caribe to accept his Hall of Fame plaque. What an emotional night it was.

Two other Brownsville occasions are truly memorable. The first one occurred shortly after I completed rehab following my knee operation. Don Goldstein and I participated in a Brownsville reunion game sponsored by Brooklyn USA. On a hot summer's day, the gymnasium at IS 275, just a few blocks from the Brownsville Recreational Center, was overflowing with a standing room only crowd. Other than two policemen, who were there for security reasons, Don and I were the only white people in the building. Yet we never felt more at home. The game and the festivities were fun, oozing with the spirit of wholesome competition and friendship. For the young spectators the presence of former NBA player, World B. Free and Greg Jackson, both products of Brownsville, added interest to the event. They gave a pregame clinic and doubled as referees. The special day brought us back to our childhood, and also served as a powerful reminder of the intangibles that basketball had provided. Don and I played well in our abbreviated time on the court, which helped to make the visit to our roots even sweeter.

Another Brownsville happening was, for me, personally meaningful and humbling. In the summer of 2000, CCNY brother Jerry Domershick and I received the honor of selection to the Brownsville Hall of Fame. The ceremony was held on a makeshift stage in the huge play yard adjoining the BRC. Thousands were on the scene, not for us, but because it was the culmination of Brownsville's "Oldtimer's Week." It was a festival of song, dance, flowing beverages, rich desserts, and endless amounts of "soul food." Once again we spent precious minutes with the remaining members of the Viceroys, the Jackson Brothers (Tony, Charlie, and Shelly) and that scintillating showman, Nurlin Tarrant. It was also a treat to chat with well-known Brownsville natives Sidney Green (UNLV and NBA), Phil Sellers (Rutgers and NBA), Curtis Redding (St. John's, Europe), "Fly" Williams (Austin Peey and ABA), Greg Jackson (Trenton State and NBA) and NFL football All-Star John Brockington (Green Bay Packers). The following is the inscription on the attractive plaque, which at its top, within a circle depicts two hands shaking in friendship:

> BROWNSVILLE
> HALL OF FAME
> Presented to
> MARTY GROVEMAN
> In recognition of your
> Contributions to
> The Brownsville Community
> Brownsville Oldtimers Week
> July 28, 2000

By 1990, my pal, Syd Levy, had settled in as a South Floridian. Around that time, he told me about an interesting article that appeared in a local newspaper. It concerned a group of retirees, mostly ex-NYers, who were former prominent basketball players. They called themselves "The Basketball Fraternity." They met weekly for breakfast and once each year celebrated during the December holidays with a dinner held at Fort Lauderdale country club. For us, the highlight of the story was quotes from two basketball friends with whom we lost touch when they left New York. I refer to tough-as-nails Jerry Fleishman and the silky-smooth Hy Gotkin.

Helene and I always vacationed in Florida when the holiday school break occurred. So Syd followed up on the information provided in the article and we made reservations to attend the function. Murray Alpert, who played for LIU in the Sherman White Era, came along with us. Murray was quite a few years older than us, but Syd and I, just over fifty, were kids compared to the Basketball Fraternity crowd. However, we had a ball. We were like babies in a candy store. We caught up with so many people from our past, and in the case of someone like Dolph Schayes, it was an opportunity to greet an admired legendary player. It was both refreshing and simultaneously nostalgic.

I have said it before, but there is a high degree of fate and destiny involved in the reappearance of basketball acquaintances at varied stages of life. There was an abundance of such significant individuals at the dinner. It was so wonderful to see Jerry and Hy again. Almost every moment I ran into someone who played a role in my life. There was Kenny Kern, my Union Temple teammate and coach; Abe Becker, the gentlemanly NYU star, who I admired from the Brighton Beach days; Sam Tolkoff, the Brown's Hotel ambassador of goodwill; and Norm Drucker, the esteemed NBA referee who, about thirty years ago, assigned me to my first Community Center job. It was also a pleasure to chat with early NBA standouts, and class acts Sonny Hertzberg and Ossie Schectman, and a blast to be in the company of my extended CCNY family who, in addition to Drucker and Hertzberg, included Irwin Damborot, Bernie Fliegel, Al Goldstein, Harold Judenfriend, Lou Lefcourt, Norm Mager, Bobby Sand, Arnie Smith, Mike Wiltin, Milt Trupin, and my coach, Dave Polansky. Jerry Domershick, Richie Garber, and Norm Goldhaber, all CCNY Beavers came later. For all the many wonderful things that can be said about the "Fraternity" gathering, it is indisputable that basketball is the singular passion and the magnet that brought us all together.

After attending once, The Basketball Fraternity annual event became a must for me. In the ensuing two decades, I missed just twice. I also brought so many ex-players/friends to the galas. My table generally consists of Don Goldstein, Steve Nisenson, Abe Kleinman my BRC coach now in his mid-eighties), Sy Gerstman and Sid Chicofsky (Brooklyn friends), Sy's son Michael (a Long Island player) and my son Seth who many of the octogenarians remember as a baby. The dinner has evolved into a buffet luncheon at the Polo Club and has grown tremendously in the number of guests and the program of prominent featured speakers (e.g., Dolf Schayes, Tal Brody, Rollie Massimino, Ira Winderman, Jeremy Schaap, and Barry Leibowitz). It's also a treat to see Manhattan Beach friends Hank Lam and Barry Goldsmith. Both have an appreciation for basketball history matched by very few.

Leadership has changed several times over the years, and is now in the hands of two non-NYers who do a tremendous job and are most responsible for the continuous growth of the organization. These dedicated gentlemen are David Weissman from Massachusetts and Stan Diamond, a Maryland Terrapin. Both work tirelessly and unselfishly without pay, but with much love for the unique show of camaraderie. David, in fact, in a truly humane gesture, flew to NY to be present at the posthumous induction of Marv Kessler into the Brooklyn USA Hall of Fame. As we, in the fraternity, are primarily a population of retirees, death has taken many of our best. To mention just a few that are so important to me, I have said goodbye to Jerry Fleishman, Hy Gotkin, Marv Kessler, the brothers Abe and Sid Gerchick, Sid Roth, Tom Galezzi, Sonny Hertzberg, Ozzie Schectman, Bernie Kirsner, Murray Alpert, and Syd Levy. Leave it to wonderful Syd to have injected a bit of sardonic humor regarding the tradition of reading the names of those who have passed between occasions. In one year of heavy losses, Syd raised his hand and offered the following: "I suggest that we hold these dinners semiannually."

My latest basketball haven is one called Sport's Club L.A. For many years that same Manhattan structure was the exclusive Vertical Club. It's on East Sixty-first Street between First and Second Avenues, where those working out can be seen while driving into Manhattan on the Fifty-ninth Street Bridge. The person who introduced me to the Sport's Club is a magnetic, gregarious, and prosocial individual named Archie Sinuk. I first met this physically imposing (6'5") guy in the nineties through his friendship with Alan Seiden. He was one of Alan's fellow high-stakes poker players and perhaps the only one that the enigmatic former St. John's great embraced as a friend. They clicked beyond poker, and Alan started to bring him to our workouts and fun-filled eating experiences. Everyone likes Archie. He is affable and a wonderful joke and storyteller. He also has the uncanny ability to approach people that he does not know, and instantly put them at ease.

At the club's seventh-floor gym, I reunited with basketball "junkies" from the past. The main one is Herbie Wein, one of my top Brownsville basketball influences, who at Seattle U was tough one-on-one competition for the great Elgin Baylor. Steve Resnick, nicknamed "Stevie Long Shot" by Alan Seiden retained his basketball fervor. I also caught up with two outstanding shooters, Steve Scheinblum, from Brooklyn College (who I will shortly write about in greater detail), and Peter Rosenblatt, in his seventies, but one of the country's most accurate foul shooters. Peter played at the University of Miami in the Rick Barry era. All but Peter and me can still hit from way past the three point line. We are the midrange kings and are deadly in "horse." The others compete in shooting games where the shortest distance is nineteen feet. Herbie over eighty, is ridiculously accurate from ten feet beyond the NBA three point line and Archie is not far behind! Another friend, Jay Cummings, is our comic relief and makes mind boggling shots from behind his back, over his head with his back to the basket, and deep-deep running hook shots. Jim Signorile, the only one of us who works full-time, joins us when he can and amazes us with his world class hook shot. Needless to say, we have a blast in the gym.

An acquaintanceship from more than forty years ago became a close friendship at the club. Steve Scheinblum was one of Brooklyn College's best players in the sixties. I didn't know, however, that he was such a special person. Firstly, in terms of athleticism and physical condition, I believed that he was as fit as any seventy-year-old that I've ever seen. He exercised several hours daily, had almost no fat on his trim, muscular body, and possessed the stamina of a young man. Secondly, regarding basketball, I already mentioned that he was one of our long-range bombers and, in fact, was the most consistent in the group. This he accomplished despite violating some major principles of shooting form. He would hold the ball behind his right ear and catapult it upon its release. On the way to the basket, the ball rotated sideways, and astonishingly tickled the net at a very high percentage. Steve preferred playing to simply shooting, but he had to give it up as his knees became increasingly arthritic.

My third description of Steve, and the most important one, was his essence as a human being. He exuded warmth, friendliness, sincerity, and compassion. The word *compassion* cannot be overemphasized because time and time again he demonstrated extraordinary concern for friends who weren't well. Two vivid examples were the devotion he showed to blustery Norm Ostrin and beloved Nick Gaetani when they were battling irreversible health problems. He took them out, drove them to appointments, and remained instantly available through their final days. In phone conversations with Norm, Nick and even relatively healthy me, he would always end with "I love you, buddy." And he truly meant it.

A few paragraphs back I wrote that "I believed that he was as fit as any seventy-year-old." The key word is *believed* because his outward appearance belied what was happening internally. Incredibly, while riding his bicycle in Manhattan, in May of 2014, he suffered a fatal heart attack. His death is something that I and the guys cannot fully comprehend. Factors have since been revealed which signified warnings, yet he was always so upbeat and full of vigor that the finality, instead of some serious treatable illness, is so unfair. I wake up some mornings and immediately think of Steve, hoping that it was just a bad dream. Unfortunately, it is all too true.

The passing of Steve disturbingly wasn't the end of Sports Club L.A.–related tragedies. In one of my club visits a few years ago, I was delighted to see two people whom I had long admired, working together with a few NBA hopefuls. These individuals were Jerry Ingenito and Tom Emma. Jerry, a fabulous coach and basketball skill developer, had a world of success at Queens College and Christ the King High School. He has also been an expert at recognizing raw talent and turning their natural resources into finished products. Some of his one-time trainees are Derrick Phelps and Brian Reese from North Carolina, Khalid Reeves of Arizona and Division II All-Americans Brad Wysczbiki and John Sindrich. Tom Emma from Manhasset Long Island was one of the highest-scoring high school players in New York State history. He then went on, in the early eighties, to start at Duke. For a while after college he entered the business world, but soon realized that his future necessitated a return to the basketball scene. Tom, like Jerry, was a specialist at training individuals and teams. His approach, however, was a scientific one, focusing upon the simultaneous upgrading of conditioning, athleticism, and basketball efficiency. He worked with several NBA teams and top colleges.

Jerry, a severe diabetic, was so brave. Through his adult years, he lost several fingers and toes due to the failure of sores and infections to heal. There were times when he was temporarily wheelchair bound, yet his spirit was never broken. I literally never was in his presence when he had a gloomy demeanor, nor did he ever express pessimism. In early 2013 in order to avoid a future amputation, he opted for a surgical procedure that seemed initially to have gone well, however suddenly his breathing became increasingly labored. Within a few hours, he went into heart failure and perished. At Jerry's wake and funeral, hundreds of Jerry's shocked friends and others who were touched by his goodness attended. There was a tremendous outpouring of expressions of affection and respect. As one illustration of the tributes in Jerry's memory, George Bruns, at his basketball camp, established the "Inge" (Ingenito) Award to be presented to the player who best epitomized Jerry's values.

Jerry's good friend and kindred basketball innovator, Tom Emma, was about a half dozen years younger and seemingly in excellent shape. My experience with Tom as was the case of most people who knew him, was that he was always personable and showed genuine interest in what was occurring in their lives. Sadly, the pain he was suffering internally contradicted the outward contented appearance. On one late morning in 2012 at the New York Athletic Club where Tom did much of his skill training, he left the gym after indicating he would return shortly. This never occurred. Unbelievably, he went out to the roof of the athletic club and leaped to his death. It was incomprehensible. How could such things happen to a person of such worth and accomplishment? One of Tom's closest friends and most fervent admirers, Bobby Anastasia, the heart and soul of Manhasset basketball, walked in a daze for about a month. We learned that Tom was disturbed about persistent abdominal difficulties and believed that he had advanced stomach cancer. This hasn't been verified and even if there was some substance to the speculation, it isn't a sufficient answer for the emotional pathology responsible for his despair.

My final Sports Club L.A. topic is a welcome relief from the sharing of sad facts of three good human beings who deserved so much better. A mood changer is overdue. All manner of college, European League, and NBA players worked out at the club. Archie was on friendly terms with most of them. NBAers primarily were there to keep in shape during the off-season. College seniors and the European players were showcasing their skills, hoping to be drafted or given an opportunity to sign as a free agent. Through Archie, I was introduced to many in all categories.

The three NBA veterans that most impressed me are Emeka Okafor, Mike Dunleavy, and Troy Murphy. Okafor, a great defender and shot blocker, is bright, articulate, and pleasant to talk with. Mike Dunleavy, whose dad I played against in the schoolyard across from Nazareth High School in Brooklyn, is simply a gentleman and a class act. On the court, his best assets are his deadly long-range shooting and superior basketball IQ. Archie and Mike have become close friends. We joke that Troy Murphy values Archie's street smarts so greatly that Archie has become his "life coach." Troy, quick-witted and always interesting, is fun to be around. I have spent considerable time in his presence and have developed a warm relationship with the former first team All-American from Notre Dame. It is worthy to note that for much of his NBA career, he had been one of the league's leading defensive rebounders. Troy is now retired. He could have continued, but was frustrated by reoccurring nagging injuries. I firmly believe that at 6'10" with excellent three-point shooting ability, he could have easily been a Greg Novat–type specialist. In the gym when Troy and Mike were practicing, Archie's constant advice is to "bend the knees and extend the arms." When Troy was playing for the Indiana Pacers, he commented to Team President Larry Bird that the "bend and extend" mantra of his shooting coach, Archie Sinuk, has improved his efficiency. Bird said it seemed that it was good advice, concluding with "Funny, but I've never heard of this guy." One last and most admirable thing about Troy: he never graduated from Notre Dame as he entered the draft following his junior year. Now that he has retired, he has returned to college to earn his degree. He began classes at Columbia University in the spring of 2014 and has now earned his degree. What a great job!

The culmination of meaningful occasions was one that gripped me with joyful anticipation of a child awakening on Christmas morning. It was an invitation from Allen Schiffman, a childhood friend, to attend a summer barbecue at his home in the Hampton Bays, Long Island. The guest of honor was my first coach and inspirational mentor, Venty Lieb. It was to be the last time that I'd ever see him as he died a short time afterward. All of those present were graduates of PS 233, where he taught and coached over fifty years ago. A few, such as Norm Nebel, flew in from distant places. Norm, although completely hairless, looked very much like the spindly plastic man with the velvet shooting touch and sharp breaking curve ball.

I hadn't seen Venty for at least thirty years. When he retired from teaching and sold his camp, he relocated to Florida. Seeing him was wonderful, but strange. It wasn't that he had grown old. It was more that he suddenly appeared to be so frail and small. Yet that devilish twinkle was still dancing in his eyes and I was thrilled to be in his presence.

During the course if that day I had an opportunity to spend some private moments with Venty. Nervously, I told him that he was my basketball inspiration, and that he greatly influenced my life's direction. It wasn't easy for me to get the words out to someone whom I looked upon with such awe. Once I did, however, it felt good to tell him things that for so long I wanted to say. He shocked and delighted me, by what he stated in return. He asked me if I remembered an evening, a year or two after graduation from high school, when he invited a bunch of us to play against his team at the Brooklyn Kingsway Jewish Center, where he was the recreation director. His bringing it up brought it back into my consciousness. Venty went on to say that he saw a spark in my performance that signaled to him that I was on my way as a basketball player. I didn't recall it, but he said that he told me not to give up. That was the spring before I tried out for the CCNY team. Once I began my career at the college, Venty said he became my biggest fan. He searched for game summaries and box scores in the newspapers, and looked on at my basketball development in proud silence. His words and emotional tone touched me very deeply. I was both flattered and appreciative to hear such praise from Venty. Its impact will remain with me forever.

At some point in the afternoon the guys drifted over to the basketball court. We didn't play a real game but engaged in a "horse" contest. For one more time I wanted to impress Venty. I wanted to demonstrate that his faith in me was justified. Actually, this mind-set indicated considerable middle-age immaturity. Nevertheless, I was ecstatic when I won. Venty and I exchanged smiles. My unverbalized thought was "That one was for you, coach."

I believe that I've written just about all the things that I wanted to express here. I also realize considerable space has been devoted to friends, relatives and associates who have died. Going back over the pages I stopped counting when I got to forty. I hope that this won't turn off the reader, or diminish interest in what I have attempted to do. I purposely wrote extensively of the departed because I want them and those they left behind to know they are remembered and occupied an important place in my life. As I detailed what happened to each person, a persistent thought kept flashing into consciousness. It is the poignant tradition in the Jewish religion of placing a stone at the grave site of a loved one when visiting the cemetery. The stone represents remembrance and respect. My words about those individuals, who are greatly missed, are my stones.

References to people far greater in number than those who passed away are those that I played with or against. Why would I mention so many, regardless of ability, known only to friends and family? Why not limit player comments to those with established names having a resume of accomplishments? Well once again I feel strongly that it is important for me to acknowledge the role of the ordinary guys in my basketball journey and to inform them that they mattered to me. They also deserve mention because we share a lasting love for the game.

The final meeting with Venty, the Seiden, Schindler and Wolkoff parties, the Basketball Fraternity and Brooklyn U.S.A. dinners, and the shootarounds at Sports Club L.A., all speak volumes about who I am. Even when I'm not actively playing, basketball is so totally ingrained in my essence that its aura and influence are ever present. At times, my basketball passion has distracted me from other, more serious concerns. Like all people, I have made mistakes, but overall believe that I have done my best to embrace the responsibilities of being a husband, a father, a son, a brother, and a friend. In my career as an educator, I have been guided by the principles of communicating with and behaving to others in the manner that I would like to be treated. In particular, my relationships with African-Americans were forged on the courts of Brownsville. This applied both to adults and especially the children entrusted to me. I am convinced that my intense and continued involvement in basketball has taught innumerable lessons which I have applied in work and in my personal life. I didn't play the game to become a better person, yet I think that this is what has happened to me. I know that I would be greatly diminished without basketball.

Profound effects of basketball aside, it has provided me with a lifetime of diverse and wonderful treasures. Uppermost are the thrills of competition, the stars that I saw, played with and competed against. Equally satisfying are the hundreds of people that I met through basketball, many of whom became friends and/or impacted significantly upon me. In telling my story, I've recounted a bushelful of exciting, humorous, and just plain wacky incidents. I've also shared much sadness. The scale, however, tilts strongly to the side of happiness and fulfillment. Scanning the big picture, I feel that I have led a most interesting and productive life. In another context, I look back fondly at the numerous places in which I have played, each with a distinct character and flavor that crafted imprints of blissful memories. Lastly, I love the game's pure and simple pleasures. For me, an overachieving lefty, of average size and modest talents, threading the needle with a pass which leads to a basket, or hitting Seth backdoor for a layup, or rippling the net with a jumper is as good as it gets.

Our terrific 1955 Tilden High School Team that challenged for a NYC championship: Tendler (top left) Berlin (top, third left), and Mandel (bottom for right) were outstanding. Tendler would play baseball and basketball at LIU. Berlin excelled at Gonzaga. "Snake" Mandel, our free spirit, went to college for about a week.

In Don "Red" Goldstein (bottom middle) we had a unanimous first team all-city. He then became an All-American at Louisville and won a Pan-American Gold Medal starting along with Oscar Robertson and Jerry West.

I (bottom far left) had not yet discovered my jump shot and was simply an appendage.

From the left, front row, are City College Coach Dave Polansky and Marty Groveman, Joe Bennardo, and Stan Friedman. Back row, from left: Joel Ascher, Bob Silver, Julio Delatorre, Len Walitt, and Hector Lewis. Coach uses magnetic figures to show a play.

It was 1957–58, my sophomore year and by far the best team at CCNY in my three seasons. I'm bottom left next to Coach Polansky. Our three big men, Ascher, Silver, and Lewis were all over 6'5", and Joe Bennardo was a high-level, mistake-free guard.

Brooklyn College = 1957–58

My sophomore season at CCNY. Shooting a jumper off the backboard against one of Brooklyn College's finest teams. Not my usual form, but I was fouled by the unseen player. And the basket was good. Two good friends, No. 13, Lenny Schroeder, and No. 5, the best ever at BC, Nick Gaetani, are under the basket.

Two-pointer: Sophomore Marty Groveman drives in for a layup in City's game against St. John's University last Saturday.

Certainly *not* a layup. Like many lefties, I shot a running hook off the backboard. St. John's No. 34 is Lou Roethel who is attempting to block my shot. Years after graduating, we became good friends and played together in several leagues.

CCNY vs. Wagner. I'm trying to beat Milfred Fierce (from Boys High) off the dribble.

Silver-haired legendary coach Nat Holman is always teaching, and that's what he's doing in this 1959 picture (his last season).

The players are (bottom) Teddy Hurwitz (little guy, big heart); Marty Groveman (third year as high scorer) Guy Marcot (terrific handle); (middle) Herb Waller (ex-marine, high energy), Julio Delatorre (dynamic but streaky), Barry Klansky (smooth, always injured); (top) Hal Bauman (rugged, good defender), Hector Lewis (amazing athlete, leaper; never fulfilled potential).

Never played on a better team. It was 1960 in the army at Fort Dix, New Jersey. Our team represented the NCO's living in Browns Mills, a town just off the post. We featured Cal Ramsy, NYU All-American, and Lonnie West, Wagner and Boys High star. Relatively Little me is at the bottom, second from left.

Browns Mills Squad: Currently leading the Mill Dam Park Summer Basketball League is this smooth-working Browns Mills team with a 12–0 record. On the squad are Cal Ramsey, Lonnie West, Bill Gray, Archie Mc Cord, Marty Grovenan, Joe McAndrew, Ron Manwarren Ivory Collins "Pappy" Baldwin, and Bill Volk.

Three of my favorite CCNY guys: ferocious rebounder Bob Silver, one of my best friends, 6'10" Syd Levy, and coach and mentor Dave Polansky. Great people.

In the Hamptons, early seventies, when we were all a lot younger.

My son Seth and the USA Open Maccabiah Team. It was a repeat of the USA Olympic Fiasco, but this "robbery" occurred in Venezuela. They were silver medalists. Seth is at bottom, second from left.

Unforgettable character and St. John's great, Alan Seiden, at his Queens home with Wally Szczerbiak about the time he was beginning college at Miami of Ohio. The full-sized Michael Jordan cardboard figure was placed in his kitchen window, to scare away potential thieves. Only Alan would do this.

Ronnie F.
Deceased

Moishe G.
Deceased

Harvey R.

Cookie

Slats

Miami Shami
Deceased

Joel T

"Big Stuck"
Deceased

My childhood Brooklyn friends at one of Jerry "Cookie" Wolkoff's Saturday all-day/night bashes at his home in Quogue LT. Several are no longer with us.

Our Tilden Team of 1955 reunited in 1997. From left to right: Jerry Bloomberg (Lousville Frosh), Joel Tendler (LIU), Don "Red" Goldstein (Louisville), Marty Groveman (CCNY), and Joel "Snake" Mandel (could have played almost everywhere).

Our immediate family in Florida. One of the last healthy pictures of Helene, prior to the diagnosis of stage 4 lung cancer. The Vermont pioneer Jon is at the top. Adopted Floridian Seth is at the bottom.

Our Diminishing Group of Lifetime Friends

Spring 2016 get-together at Tony's Dinapoli on Manhattan's Upper East Side.

Seated left to right: Herb Wein, best long-distance over 80 shooter anywhere; Cookie Wolkoff, another great set shooter and renowned developer; Sandy Jacobs, prototypical point guard before the term was used, best known as a Broadway show producer–and for Hamilton too; Marty Groveman, author of this book, career special educator and lefty jump shot. Standing from left: Joel Mandel, amazing athlete, CEO of Key Foods; Harvey Richer, defensive ace and commercial real estate dynamo.

What a sextet!
Summer 2016 at the Bruns Basketball Camp

Marty Rigger, esteemed coach and director of NY Knicks Summer Camp; Wally Szczerbiak, former NBA star, broadcaster/analyst for MSG and CBS College Basketball; Jack "Black Jack" Ryan, basketball skills showman, Harlem Wizard and three-point-shooting champion; George Bruns, "all everything" tremendous player, coach, and owner, and director of highly regarded Basketball Camp;

In back: Walt Szczerbiak, all-time European Pro "Real Madrid" and Wally's dad.

Right front: me, the author, Bruns Camp coordinator, stuck in "catch and shoot" pose.

CPSIA information can be obtained
at www.ICGtesting.com
Printed in the USA
BVHW031454021019
560012BV00002B/56/P